From Clogs
to Shiny Shoes
A Windermere Lad's Memories
of South Lakeland

Miles R. M. Bolton (Mike)

HAYLOFT

First published 2002

Hayloft Publishing, Kirkby Stephen,
Cumbria, CA17 4EU.

tel: (017683) 42300
fax. (017683) 41568
e-mail: dawn@hayloft.org.uk
web: www.hayloft.org.uk

© 2002 Miles R. M. Bolton

ISBN 1 904524 02 8

A catalogue record for this book is available
from the British Library

Apart from any fair dealing for the purposes of research or private study, or criticism or review, as
permitted under the Copyright, Designs & Patents Act, 1988, this publication may only be
reproduced, stored or transmitted, in any form or by any means, with the prior permission in
writing of the publishers, or in the case of reprographic reproduction in accordance with the terms
of the licenses issued by the Copyright Licensing Agency.

Cover illustration Windermere from Kirkstone Pass, Peter Koronka.

Produced in Great Britain
Printed and bound in Great Britain

CONTENTS

ACKNOWLEDGEMENTS

My thanks firstly to my wife Wendy for putting up with me over the last 40 years. Thanks too to my uncle George L. Bolton of Leyland, himself an author of several books of historical interest, for the encouragement he has given me to write this book.

Also special thanks to Peter Silvester, chairman and Jean Chatterley treasurer of the North Lancs. Branch of the Motor Neurone Disease Association for their help in bringing this book to print.

Mike Bolton

INTRODUCTION

During the process of writing this book the thought has occured to me that the reader could well come to the conclusion that I was a bit of a 'clever sod.' The considerable number of jobs and different involvements with which I have been involved could suggest this. However this is not the perception that I would wish to leave and I trust that you will understand the reasons and motives for my moves.

Along the way I have met many wonderful people and made many friends. Practically everything I have done has involved the use of my initial experiences working with animals in this wonderful Lakeland landscape. For over 50 years I have been saddened to watch successive governments trivialise the role the land has in our lives.

I hope you will find some of my accounts amusing and some very much less so. All the details are, as far as my memory allows, absolutely true.

The story I have told does not end in the way which I would have chosen, had I any say in the matter, but then none of us have the last word in our own destiny. I hope that my ramblings give you with a few hours entertainment. By buying this book you have helped a very worthwhile cause as all royalties will go to the Motor Neurone Disease Association to help fund research into this nasty disease.

Mike Bolton,
December 2002

4

MY EARLIEST MEMORIES

I was born on 28 February 1936, which was a Friday. I didn't enter this world entirely on my own, but was followed some three hours later by my twin sister, Margaret, or was she truly my twin? Mother insisted that I was actually conceived two months after Margaret, a 'phenomenon' that is not unknown. I was a weakly sort of infant, my sister being almost half as heavy again as me. As was the case in the majority of births in those days, my twin and I were born at home, delivered by a travelling midwife. Home in our case was the house of my grandparents on mother's side.

The house in question was No. 10 College Road, in the village of Windermere, in the county of the then Westmorland, later to form part of the much larger county of Cumbria. To the best of my knowledge, the house had never had a private name, just a number and was always simply referred to with great affection as 'Number Ten.'

The building itself was of some considerable size. It was built in the early 1900s in the Edwardian style, with blue-grey slate from the nearby Applethwaite Slate Quarry. A not particularly imposing front door was actually on the side of the house, while stone steps at the back of the building led down to a below ground-level cellar which was used as a kitchen. This room, lit only by a solitary light bulb, which dangled unshaded from the low ceiling, included an old fashioned black lead fireplace and an old cast iron gas cooker. The only natural light came from a window above the stone sink, from which you could see the lower half of any person about to descend the cellar's stone steps.

At the back of the kitchen was a narrow passage which led to an even darker room used mainly for storage. These two rooms seemed to me to be in the very bowels of the earth. Huge blue stone flags added to the almost cave-like atmosphere which always prevailed. The rest of the house consisted of two large rooms at ground level. One of the rooms, a dining room, was accessed from an internal staircase from the cellar, while the other room, a sitting room had a pleasant outlook to the road. There were several bedrooms on two further levels. My twin sister and I first saw the light of day in a first floor bedroom looking on to College Road.

I probably got one of my names from my grandfather, Miles Stanley Turner. I never have been certain as my grandfather on my dad's side

*The author's
parents, Harry and
Helen Turner, around the
time of their marriage.*

was also Miles. Grandad Miles Stanley and my grandma Alice Jane Turner, owned and lived in No. 10. The house was run as a guest house and my parents lived with them so that my mother, when she wasn't tending to the needs of her own family, could assist Nanna more or less full time with the bed and breakfast business.

My family consisted of my dad, Harry, my mother, Helena Mary (Mollie), my elder sister Marcia Yvonne, myself, Miles Robert Michael, and of course, my twin, Helena Margaret. A later addition to the family was my younger sister Florence Alice Marion. All our first names started with 'M', except my dad's. Dad was employed as a road scout by the Royal Automobile Club (RAC), but more about that later.

The Turners historically, had been the owners of the estate known as 'The Row,' situated in the Lyth Valley, now famous for its uniquely flavoured damsons. The Row was an estate of some 126 acres on which several small cottages and one main farm had evolved over the years. There are records dating back to the early 17th century showing the Turner family as incumbents. No doubt in earlier days the Turner family was considered well off. However in 1873, at the age of 30, Robert Turner, Miles' father and my great-grandfather, sold off The Row estate to a Frank Atkinson Argles.

My grandfather, Miles Stanley, had, as a young man, gone over to the USA to Tom Green County in Texas, where some of his kinsfolk were already established. Miles had a ranching enterprise in the Carlsbad area. On one of Miles' visits back to England, he met Alice Jane Bonney. Miles, at that time in his early 30s and single, must have seemed quite an exciting chap to the beautiful 21-year-old Alice. She was twelve years his junior but was no doubt captivated by his exciting tales of the Wild West. Miles must have made a considerable impression because in September 1901 the two were married. Soon into the marriage, Alice Jane became pregnant, (they were to have seven children). Grandfather wanted to return to Texas but grandmother would have none of it. She refused point blank to go back ranching with him - I will never know the exact details!

Grandad must have finally agreed to stay and disposed of his interests abroad. He never did return to Texas, but instead joined his in-laws in their family business, Bonney's Plumbers, Painters and Glaziers. He spent the rest of his life bringing up his family in Windermere.

Despite being a square peg in a round hole, grandad worked at the plumbing business to the best of his ability. He was a very clever, inventive chap. I was told by one of his sons, my uncle, that it was grandad who invented the immersion heater, but grandad, living up to his by then nick name 'Alfie' had not bothered to patent the idea. In his spare time, grandad put a great deal of energy into promoting local sports and athletics. He was particularly keen on water sports and was a very strong swimmer. He was of the belief that all children should be taught to swim at an early age. He was on the committee of the local council which brought about the fencing off of part of Windermere Lake to form the well know Miller Ground Swimming Pool. Needless to say, all the Turners swam like fish!

By the early 1920s, possibly because his heart was still in Texas, grandad had gradually given up the work aspect and spent more and more of his time getting involved in activities which were possibly of greater use to the community in general rather than his family's economy and welfare. Grandad's diminished contribution was, in all probability, the reason for my grandma to establish a guest house business, the income from which no doubt ensured the smooth running of the household; hence my mother's involvement at No. 10.

Grandad, now being somewhat surplus to requirements, was more or less banished to the Coach House at the top of the garden, to keep out of the way. The Coach House was a solidly built structure, again built with Applethwaite slate stone. There were two levels - on the ground floor a room where in earlier days a coach or pony trap would have been kept and next to this a stable for the horse. Above these two rooms was an old hay loft. It was accessed by a vertical plank with horse shoe shaped cut outs, nailed to the wall and acting as a ladder. You climbed through a hinged hatch and into a large loft. I do believe grandad slept up in the loft, at least in the warmer months.

One of my early memories is being at the top of the garden by the Coach House and watching my Dad changing the side cars on his motorcycle combination. During the week he would have in place his RAC box, bright blue in colour and about five feet long. This was attached to the sidecar chassis which in turn was attached to his motorbike. In this box he would have, neatly packed, all the tools and equipment which he might require to repair a broken down car, the owners of which had had the misfortune to be stranded, usually out in the countryside where they

Miles Stanley Turner

would be unlikely to find a garage. It was a road scout's job to try to affect a repair, or at least fix the problem long enough to get the car and owner to where the fault could be repaired permanently.

At weekends, as the bike was Dad's own, and only hired to the RAC, off would come the bright blue box, and in its place he would fix a double adult sidecar in which there were two full sized seats sufficient to accommodate my mother, my older sister Marcia, now nearly eight-years-old, my twin Margaret and myself. Sometimes mother would ride behind Dad on the pillion seat, but this depended very much on the weather conditions.

Dad was well used to riding the bike in all weathers. When he first started working for the RAC he was given a push bike, progressing from there to his own AJS solo bike, then his 600cc Ariel Square Four, which was a super bike of its day. The last bike which Dad owned and used for this dual-purpose role of work and pleasure, was the daddy of all motor cycles of that era and considered the absolute Rolls Royce of bikes. It was a Brough Superior SS 90. Dad bought this bike new from George Brough's factory in Nottingham in the June of 1938.

All RAC scouts were given a base camp from which to start from. In Dad's case he had two base camps some seven miles apart. One was just

9

outside Windermere village, on the northern side, at the Cook's House crossroads, where one of the familiar blue and white cabins was sited. These boxes, as they were usually referred to, were little different in size to a telephone box, in fact, a phone box is exactly what they were. Motorists who were signed up to be members of the RAC held a key which opened these curious little huts. Inside members would have access to maps, first aid and, of course, a phone. Similar boxes were sited all round the country at appropriate locations.

Harry Bolton outside the Kirkstone Inn with his Brough Superior and RAC box.

Looking north from Cook's House, with Windermere village behind you, is the road which follows Windermere Lake to its head at Waterhead, Ambleside. Nearby is Rydal village, famous for its connection with William Wordsworth who lived the last 30 years of his life at Rydal Mount. Travelling yet further on the same road would take you past Grasmere Lake and village, and over the steep ascent of Dunmail Raise to Thirlmere, Manchester's reservoir, and on to Keswick. The north-easterly road from Cook's House climbs the seven mile route to the top of the Kirkstone Pass at about 1500 feet above sea level where you find the Kirkstone Pass Inn. Just a few yards before this inn, on the right hand side of the road, stood the second of Dad's little blue boxes.

The road between Cook's House and the Kirkstone Inn constituted the main part of Dad's daily travel. He would look for distressed motorists and there were plenty with over-heated engines after constantly climbing the pass, especially from the other side, the Patterdale side, as it climbed in only two miles to the same height above sea level which had taken seven miles from the Windermere side. Some of his clients would already be members of the RAC. Whether or not, it made no difference. If not already members, hopefully they could be persuaded to enroll. The basic wage for a road scout in the late 30s was around three pounds a week. This could be increased by about fifteen shillings if a new member was signed up.

I guess my father would consider himself to be extremely fortunate. It could be said that his was possibly the most scenic 'workplace' in the whole of the British Isles. The scenery on both sides of the road as you climb up the Troutbeck Valley from Windermere is unbelievably beautiful. From any angle it would be possible to take 'picture postcard' photographs. On arrival outside the inn, standing with your back to the building, you would be looking at the scree beds of Red Screes where millions of tons of loose rock are tumbling away from the mountain side from another 1000 feet above you.

It would not be right to continue on over the pass without first looking back towards Windermere Lake. On a clear day the fells above Coniston village, made famous by the water speed ace Donald Campbell, can be seen in the distance with Morecambe Bay and the Irish Sea beyond them. Whatever the weather, dry days or cold wet days, Dad would patrol the route in the execution of his job.

As a boy Dad had been educated at Balshaw Lane Grammar School in

Leyland, Lancashire. His childhood interests included horse riding and playing the violin, both of which would play a part in his early manhood. After leaving school he had a spell working in Baxter's Rubber Works as an apprentice, where his father, Miles Bolton, was works manager. I do not know why he gave up the rubber trade but, in his early 20s he joined the army, the Duke of Lancaster's Own Cavalry Division, which was part of the Territorial Yeomanry. In the five years he served, from 1921 to 1926, he attained the rank of Lance Sergeant.

The Wheatsheaf Hotel.

Southampton.

Feb 6 th. 1926.

To Whome it may concern.

I have pleasure in stating that Mr Harry Bolton has filled the position of First Violin in the band engaged at the above hotel for the last four months

He has proved himself avery capable and accomplished musician,he has a striking stile of showmanship,is always pleased to oblige with those few extra numbers that are often requested by his audience,a good tempered companion,and at all times a thorough gentleman.

He leaves me entirely at his own request,as he wishes to go to Sea.

I wish Mr Bolton all the success he deserves,and would congratulate anyone securing his services.

Faithfully Yours.

MANAGER.

From being a boy, Dad had been encouraged to play the violin and had become quite an accomplished musician. On leaving the Army he joined a small dance band playing in hotels and dance halls. In 1926 he enlisted in the Merchant Navy as a bandsman and joined the *Lanovery Castle*, a cruise ship, to play first violin in the ship's orchestra. His next ship was to be the *Kildonan Castle* which took in exotic places such as Cape Town where no doubt the musicians would have plenty of time to explore.

It was in a break between ships that Dad met up with a childhood friend and fellow musician, a pianist called Arnold Baron, who was also from the Leyland area. Together they took on temporary jobs, one of which was playing at the Wheatsheaf Hotel in Southampton. There must have been a spell when no ship was requiring either a violinist or a pianist because Dad and Arnold Baron found themselves in Bowness-on-Windermere playing for the silent movies at the Royalty Cinema. This assignment was to change the lives of both men!

My mother was the second of seven children born to Miles Stanley and Alice Jane Turner. She had grown up in the sporting swimming environment of the Turner family. Mother had, in her

FORMER TEXAS RANCHER

Man Who Inspired Lake Swimming Club

LATE MR. M. S. TURNER, WINDERMERE

After three weeks' illness, the result of a fall. Mr. Miles Stanley Turner, College Road, Windermere died on Tuesday at the age of 72 years.

A native of Windermere, in his younger days, he went out to Texas, where he had a sheep ranch which he ran with success until he was 32 years of age, and then returned to his native village, where he carried on business as a master plumber and painter until he retired. He was a man of no ordinary intelligence, a great reader, and unusually well-informed on most subjects. Horticulture was one of his hobbies and he was a skilful gardener. He was also interested in geology, a science to which he had devoted some study.

Mr. Turner was a good athlete in his younger days, and an accomplished swimmer, and taught great numbers of children. It was largely through his efforts and inspiration that the Lake Windermere Swimming Club was formed. All his family are fine swimmers, cross lake swimmers with good records. When surf-riding was included in the programmes, Mr. Turner's sons were amongst the most expert in the art. They were also clever motor-cyclists. In politics, Mr. Turner was a keen upholder of the Labour Party. He was also, for some years, a member of the Windermere Urban Council, frank and outspoken, but practical and experienced. He is survived by his widow, three daughters and two sons.

The funeral took place at Bowness Cemetery, yesterday (Thursday) morning.

Miles Stanley Turner's obituary which appeared in "The Gazette" on 17 June 1939.

13

youth, won a ladies swimming race across the mile wide stretch of Windermere Lake from Miller Ground to the Bark House, on the western shore of the lake. My uncles invariably took the men's title.

Mother was quite a tall person, about five feet nine, well built and considered by many people to be rather beautiful, and indeed won a number of prizes for her looks. One of the competitions she won, was with a photograph submitted to the *Sunday News,* for which she was awarded £24, quite a nice sum of money in those days! As well as being quite a beauty, mother was also a fair singer and a pianist. She sang at the Mary Wakefield Music Festival, which takes place bi-annually. For this she received a medal.

As mother was musical, Dad had arranged for her to take lessons, not for the piano, but for the drums. Mother was a good learner and, together with a couple of musicians, they formed a dance band, with Dad on the violin, mother the drums, a trumpet player and a pianist. They were soon popular in local dance halls and were able to supplement the family income.

My mother told me that at the time she had met Dad she had been walking from Windermere to Bowness exercising the family's St Bernard dog. Dad had used the dog as an excuse to speak to her, but in all fairness Dad was very much a dog lover, so I guess it was fifty fifty. At that time mother, who was a trained nurse, was working at the Ethel Hedley hospital at Calgarth where they treated children with TB.

It was late summer when my Dad asked Miles Stanley if he could have his daughter's hand in marriage, to which his prospective father-in-law had replied with the question: "Is there any insanity in your family?" Father had replied: "Not to the best of my knowledge." Dad's reply must have been satisfactory, as they were married at Kendal Registry Office on 7 October 1930. Grandad's question about sanity was not forgotten. As history would prove, it was Miles Stanley whose sanity would be doubted, as he was by far the most eccentric member of the Turners. Regrettably on 13 June 1939 he died - he had reached the age of 72. On grandad's death certificate the cause of death was recorded as cerebral haemorrhage and senile decay. I have always regretted the fact that I never got to know him. I feel that we would have been great pals.

BISKEY HOWE TERRACE AND STARTING SCHOOL

Margaret and I had not yet turned five when our parents moved us to Biskey Howe Terrace in Bowness village, leaving Grandma Turner at her beloved No. 10. We moved into the top half of a four storey house which was next door but one and in the same terraced block as my great grandmother Bonney. She was, of course, the mother of my grandma Turner. Although she was of a great age she was still very much alive and was looked after by my great aunt Florence, spinster sister of grandma Turner.

I have some memories of great grandma Bonney sitting serenely in the corner of her ground floor living room. She had a great love for us children, although I have learned since that she was rather difficult at times. Her daughter Florence had quite a hard life keeping her happy. My great aunt Florence was a tall slender lady of the most upright bearing. She never sat in a soft chair, preferring to sit bolt upright on a hard wooden one. Poor aunt Florence had always been in the shadow of her older sister, Alice Jane, who no doubt was more outgoing and flirtatious. Florence was made to take on more of the responsibilities in assisting great grandma Bonney in the running of the household. Both sisters had been taught needlework to a very high level and aunt Florence spent many of her middle and later years teaching the subject.

During the Great War, 1914-18, aunt Florence had been head forewoman in the Howitzer Department of Messrs. Vickers Ltd, Barrow-in-Furness. On 13 December 1918, she was presented with a writing case and a testimonial from all the women who worked under her. Some of the wording was as follows: "We all trust that you may live long to use this case, and that on each such occasion it may recall the many happy hours spent in providing the boys of the 'little contemptible army' with the necessary munitions of war to destroy the barbarity and inhumanity of the Hun." The names of most of her charges were then listed in gratitude.

It was whilst living at Biskey Howe Terrace that two major events took place within our family. In February 1940 my baby sister was born. She was named Florence Alice Marion - Florence obviously after great aunt Florence, Alice after my grandma and Marion after my Dad's sister. I don't really know if it was intended, but now we had five out of the six members of our family with names beginning with 'M'. It was suggested that Dad should change his name from Harry to Moses!

The second 'happening' was that, to aid the war effort, Dad was drafted from the RAC into the police force as a Special Constable, serving locally. He was by then of course, too old to be called up for the Forces. At first Dad's duties were patrolling premises checking security. He also did point duty, a job that he was used to as doing traffic control was one of his jobs for the RAC. Nowadays, with many times more cars, it would be a brave person who would stand in the middle of the road at a busy junction. Policemen on point duty have been replaced with either 'sleeping policemen' or traffic lights.

By now Margaret and I were turned five. We hadn't had any playschool lead up to school, but were simply taken on an appointed day and left for the first time with people we had never seen before. It was in itself a shock, but that was the way it was done in those days.

My memory was of being left in a dark room with lots of rails and coat hooks. All around me seemed to be a sea of activity. It was the first time I had been in amongst so many children, most of them a lot older than myself. One or two grown-ups were attempting to sort out the chaos with shouted orders. Myself, my sister, and several other small children, both boys and girls, were ushered into what seemed a huge room which had a flat area at the front, then climbed up a terraced rise to the back of the room. Tall narrow glass windows reached for the high ceiling, making the room seem rather church like.

My first teacher was a stout red-faced lady called Mrs Marshall. She seemed to me, possibly because of her glowing red face, to be a rather happy person and that gave me some reassurance. Rows of tiny desks with seats attached gradually climbed to the back of the room. I was allocated one somewhere about the middle, whilst my sister was placed at the back of the class. We were all handed a grey stone slate which was encased in a narrow wooden frame. With each slate came a scratching tool which, when dragged across the surface of the slate, made a chalky white mark. These were the only 'writing tools' we would receive in our first year. To help us learn to count we were given a handful of sea shells - ten sea shells, take away five you are left with five and so on.

It was when I tried to copy letters drawn on the blackboard that it was realised that my eyesight was particularly bad. Up until then it had not been thought necessary for me to wear glasses but it became apparent that I would not be able to progress until I had some.

Mrs Marshall's persona as a cheerful cuddly lady had survived up to this point, but on one occasion, which I remember to this day, my opinion was sorely tested. One of my fellow pupils, a girl called Leslie, had picked up on a very rude rhyme which related to a teachers behind. Leslie asked me to repeat the words after her which I naively did, whereupon Leslie went straight to Mrs Marshall telling her that I had told her this rude rhyme. I think it would be the first time in my life that I saw real anger in anyone's eyes. My teacher's face changed from her usual happy expression to that of someone who had just suffered the worst insult in her teaching career. She reached for a long bamboo cane, but not to use for her normal purpose of pointing at the blackboard.

"Stand out here in front of the class," she demanded of me. In my short life I had never suffered anything more than a smack across the back of my bare legs when being naughty. This was going to be something different I sensed. "Hold out your hand," she demanded. I did so hesitatingly. "Right out!" she pulled my arm up and twisted my hand into a receptive position. I can still remember the pain of the cane landing on my tender five-year-old hand. I dropped my arm and

This picture was taken in 1938 on the front door step of 10 College Road, Windermere. It shows Marcia and twins Miles and Helena Bolton.

grasped the burning hand with the other.

"Again!" she rasped, "Hold it up again." I obliged with tears running down my cheeks. Swish, down came the cane for the second time, my hand was on fire for quite some while. I learned a lesson that day, but not the lesson Mrs Marshall would have me learn. I learned that the truth does not necessarily always prevail and to keep my head down and avoid trouble.

After two years at the infants' school, which of course was mixed, I moved just up the steep hill to the 'big boys,' as it was called by the local children. The school's proper name was Bowness Endowed Boys School. The big boys' school immediately overlooked the infants' school and from its main entrance could be seen a view the likes of which I have never seen better some sixty years on. Immediately below lies the village of Bowness and beyond, Windermere Lake surrounded by a distant 180 degree arc of mountains that include Scafell, England's highest mountain and the Langdale Pikes, which stand out looking like the two, humps of a camel's back.

The school had a staff of two - headmaster, Mr Sydney Hare and Miss Holliday. Mr Hare was a tall square-built man with an upright bearing. He was lantern jawed and wore thick lensed heavy framed glasses. For the first two years I was in Miss Holiday's class. She was a rather prim and slender lady with rosy cheeks. All the ladies I came across at that time seemed to have rosy cheeks - it must have been the clear fresh air in that part of Lakeland. Life under Miss Holiday's care was, I remember, quite acceptable to a seven-year-old. She was a little highly strung but really quite kind. I suppose she had to justify her role to her superior who I had already realised was quite a different kettle of fish.

On turning eight, I automatically moved up into Mr Hare's class and would be there until I took my eleven-plus exam. He was, of course, my fist male teacher. I was already in awe of this man and very fearful at having to please him. From my memory, I see him always immaculately dressed in a brown pin-striped suit together with the obligatory stiff collar and tie. His square jaw could have been welded nearly shut as he always spoke through semi-clenched teeth.

Learning now became deadly serious. Mr Hare was able to command every second's concentration which I and my fellow students could muster, but even this didn't satisfy him. Other than my one brush with

Mrs Marshall at the infants' school, I hadn't ever before experienced this state of constant nervousness. I guess I was what might be described as a rather timid sort of a child.

There was one occasion that illustrates the general everyday occurrences that my fellow pupils and I might expect. I was called out to the front of the room over some supposed problem with my schoolwork. Mr Hare for a minute or so 'read the riot act' and in so doing worked himself up into a rage, culminating in him finally giving way to his feelings and taking a swing with the flat of his hand at my head. I must have seen the blow coming and instinctively moved my head sideways. In that split second his hand passed my face missing me, but his fingers caught the edge of my glasses sending them flying across the room. Mr Hare didn't follow up with another attempt but snarled at me: "Go and pick them up and then sit down." I guess that even he had realised that such treatment was not justified.

That evening when I had related the day's happening to my parents, my Dad had been, I guess, extremely annoyed. As well as the fact that Mr Hare had struck at me, the truth was that my glasses could have been broken which would have brought the unnecessary expense of repairing them. Dad must have been pretty angry because he put on his coat and marched up to the home of the offending gentleman who, when confronted with his alleged indiscretion, denied the attempted blow and instead insisted that he had only put his hand round the back of my head with the intention of guiding me to another room. I had unfortunately moved my head and the glasses had dropped off!

I have no idea what Dad had said in reply but, when he told me where he had been, I was somewhat apprehensive about going to school the next day and having to face my tormentor. I need not have worried because nothing further was said about the matter. For a short while Mr Hare seemed slightly more kindly disposed to me - well I suppose he would be wouldn't he, my Dad being a policeman? Besides the usual lessons, the three Rs etc., we students had certain duties which we did on a rota basis. One particular task, because of the potential danger, would have the education authorities of today in the High Court if they even thought about allowing this practice.

Our school had around its inner walls, a number of huge cast-iron radiators that were served by a coke-fired furnace, which was situated in an outbuilding in the school playground. The furnace itself was a huge cast iron affair with a heavy iron door swinging from cast hinges. Presumably because hot water rises, the furnace was down below ground level in a square concrete pit, accessed by a steel ladder fastened to the wall. The whole thing was known as the stoke hole.

The pupils from Mr Hare's class were responsible during the day for keeping the fire going. This of course only applied in the winter months. Children as young as eight would, unaccompanied by an adult or another child, climb down the steel ladder, open the furnace door, and with the huge coke shovel provided, throw coke which was left in a heap on the bottom of the pit into the roaring flames. I was shown the procedure once by one of the older boys and from then on took my turn. The part-time school caretaker would service the thing early in the morning and shut it down for the night.

There being a war on, we all had to have close at hand one of the gas masks supplied by the government. At regular intervals we would all be marched out into the covered concrete veranda at the back of the school near the outside toilets. We would all be made to squat down sitting on our heels and put on these masks. This would have to be done in a hurry in the event of an attack from German aeroplanes. Fortunately I never experienced the real thing first hand.

Very occasionally we were all asked to bring to school an empty glass jam jar. The good people of America sometimes sent food parcels amongst which would be large tins of drinking chocolate. This would be ladled into our jar to be taken home. On one occasion my jar only got as far as the Royalty Cinema, where the string provided to fasten and carry it slipped off causing my jar to hit the pavement and smash, leaving my chocolate unusable mixed as it was with fragments of broken glass.

Sweets were rationed to, if I remember correctly, about four ounces per person, per month. To buy them you had to use sweet coupons - that was if you could afford them. I would be about seven or eight when I saw my first banana, as they had to be imported and were classed as a luxury. They were low priority in war time and weren't seen in the shops. The banana I saw belonged to a boy called Tom Kennedy, whose brother was on leave from the Navy. He had picked up a few whilst overseas and had given some to Tom. He very kindly gave a small piece to a few of us. The thought was nice and at least we got a taste.

THE FAMILY MOVE TO PRINCE'S ROAD

In 1944 my parents moved our family to a house called Eller Howe on Prince's Road. It was situated about half way between the villages of Windermere and Bowness, and was just off the main road. The house was the end house on a block of three storey buildings, most of them owned by Pattinsons, a family who between them were the biggest property owners in the area. Dad was able to rent the house for a reasonable rent. Probably the fact that he was a policeman, and the Boltons and the Turners were well known and respected in the village, helped. Decent properties weren't easy to find just at that time.

Being now in the police force, Dad's work vehicle, a sidecar outfit was replaced by a solo police bike. He seemed to have a variety of these. One which comes to mind was an Indian. It had a foot clutch and running board foot rests. It seemed half as long again as any other bike I had seen. Dad would come home sometimes in winter just about rigid with cold. Another bike was a Norton. This was a beast of a bike which used to kick back when attempts were made to start it. This bike kicked back once too often and Dad finished up with a Pott's fracture of his ankle which put him out of action for a while. It later turned out that the engine had been wrongly timed causing the engine to fire prematurely.

My happiest times were the school holidays. I used to go up to a nearby farm called Lickbarrow, which sadly no longer exists as a working farm. Most of the land has been taken over by neighbouring farms, and some of the land has been built on while all the farm buildings have been converted into dwellings. In those days the farm had its dairy herd, pigs, poultry and four beautiful Clydesdale heavy horses - Jewel, a sturdy dark brown mare and Prince, Duke and Royal, all geldings. Royal was the youngest and was probably three or four years old. A stag is the name given to a young only part-broken novice. All stags have to be watched carefully as they are unpredictable and are liable to take flight. As you can imagine, the best part of a ton of horse flesh can take some controlling if they decide to do something different from what was planned!

Lickbarrow Farm was owned at that time by a chap called Bob Raw, but managed by Bill Patterson. He was a rather callous sort of a chap who took delight in playing tricks. On one occasion and despite my protests, he lifted me on to the back of Royal, the young stag, who at the time was being let out to drink at the water trough at the end of the yard.

Here I was, only a small boy perched on the bare back of an excitable horse with only his mane to hold onto. When Bill struck the animal across the haunches with the flat side of a muck fork Royal jumped forward and set off at a gallop across the yard. Fortunately the gates had been shut and my mount was not able to get into the adjoining field, otherwise I might have been galloping for miles.

Another trick of Bill's was at milking time. He would be sitting beside a cow on a three legged milking coppy or stool and, if you were in range, he would direct a jet of warm sticky milk which would usually hit you in the face. In my case I would be left trying to clear the white sticky substance from off my glasses. If Bill had been the only man on the farm I would eventually have been put off farming possibly forever, but the farm also employed a hired man who I only remember as Joe. His second name escapes me. Joe was a quiet kindly chap who probably disliked the callous ways of his superior but was powerless to do anything about it. By today's standards Bill Patterson's disregard for safety would get him into trouble, but these two incidents and numerous others failed to discourage me from farming as later events will testify.

During the war, children were encouraged to help with the war effort. One of the ways of helping was to collect waste paper and rubber, such as inner tubes, burst hot water bottles etc. for which, in return, they would be given a free ticket to the cinema, provided they had collected enough to qualify. On a piece of waste land just along the road from our house was erected a wooden hut, the doors of which were like those of a stable - the top half could be left open whilst the bottom half remained closed. People would bring waste paper and throw it over the closed lower door. When the cabin was so full that no more waste would go in, the authorities would send a truck and remove it all. We kids would spend hours up to our necks in paper, searching for clear sheets which we would take home and draw on, later bringing them back used with our waste.

Not all my holidays and breaks were taken up helping on the farm at Lickbarrow. I had a lot of friends most of whom lived close by. There were the Hadwin twins, Peter and Robin, whose father drove the laundry delivery van. Another friend was Tony Robinson whose father was on crutches and worked on the rowing boats in the summer. He would stand on the promenade down by the lake and try to persuade passers by to take out a rowing boat or take a trip in a motor launch. Donald Tatterson was another in our gang. His Dad was in charge of the coal yard at the railway station. Finally there was John Gibson, whose father was in the Air Force.

As a gang we would roam the woods playing games, such as building dams in the stream which ran through Sheriff's Wood, which was one our favourite haunts, or making rafts from oil drums and lumps of wood which were lying about. One mischievous game we would play was to gather bunches of a rather obnoxious smelling plant that had an onioney, sagey smell. This plant was always found in shady, boggy parts of the wood. We would then build a fire and place this plant in an open topped drum and boil it on the fire until it produced a black evil smelling juice which we would strain and pour into lemonade bottles or similar. The real fun came when we poured this potion, which we nicknamed 'Pongasthetic' on the floors of places where a number of people might be. It was, to our immature sense of humour, hilarious to see grown ups looking about themselves and sniffing the air wondering where the terrible smell was coming from.

Even during school term time we, as small children, managed to find time for recreational activities - one of my favourites was fishing. On the way home from school, some of us would slip down to the lake which was less than a quarter of a mile from the route home. We all had hiding places where we kept a bit of fishing line and a few hooks and knew where to locate a few worms. On the side cladding of the largest pier, the pier which had been built to accommodate the huge steamers which, due to the war were only used occasionally, were large heavy planks. We discovered that one of these heavy planks could be slid aside sufficiently to allow a small boy to gain access to the underside of the main structure. Underneath long wide wooden boards ran the full length of the pier and it was possible to crawl on hands and knees to the end. It was like crawling along a wooden tunnel.

The deck of the pier, now above your head, acted like a canopy, which excluded a lot of the daylight. This enabled us to look into the ever-deepening water as we crawled toward the end of the pier. The effect was marvellous. The water appeared to be a most vivid green. It was like crawling across the top of a giant aquarium. Often there would be perch swimming below, the dark stripes on their bodies accented by the fluorescent glow of the green water. Sometimes we would see eels wriggling along the bed of the lake like snakes. If we were lucky, we might even see a pike, a ferocious looking fish with its elongated bottom jaw and mouth full of razor sharp teeth.

The object of the exercise, of course, was to catch fish. Quite often a perch would seize a wriggling worm and would immediately be hauled to the surface. Very occasionally one of us would catch an eel although I wasn't keen as they soon had your line in a tangle before you could get the hook from their mouth. I don't ever remember a pike being caught by this method. Mr Pike was far too smart!

My mother having been brought up to use the lake as a playground, was very keen on fishing. It was she who would persuade my Dad to hire a boat about twice a year and take the whole family out on the lake fishing for a full day. The family, plus any uncle or aunt who happened to be staying at No. 10 with my grandma, would pile into the biggest rowing boat available, first making sure we had enough rods, tackle and worms to last for the day, not forgetting the most important piece of equipment, the anchor. We would set off about 10 am and row out to our favourite fishing spot, usually where there was about fifteen feet of water. We would then drop anchor, not making the mistake that so many people have made of not first tying the end of the anchor rope to a seat. Many anchors have been lost by not observing this procedure!

A good indicator of where shoals of perch could be found was where there was a 'meakin bed.' These are a plant rather like a cabbage on a long stem which grow on the bed of the lake and reach almost to the surface. Perch seem to like to congregate round these plants. We would fish all day, sometimes taking a break on one of the islands. We always had plenty of sandwiches and lemonade, packed that morning by my mother. By the end of the afternoon all of us children would be tired, as the excitement and the fresh air took its toll, but we were never too tired to thread all the fish, usually around a couple of hundred of them, onto strings which we passed through the gills and out of the mouth, in bundles of 50 or so. We children would carry them proudly on our backs through the crowds of visitors as we made our way home through the village.

Dad, still in his war time roll as a Special Constable was by now, together with a colleague, patrolling the area in a police car. One route to which he was directed was the A6 which climbs north out of Kendal and up the infamous Shap Fell. This road was notorious for bad weather conditions, and was recognised as one of the worst roads in the country to travel, particularly with the heavy trucks of that era. The lorries were likely to overheat going up the terrible inclines and quite often would overheat their brakes coming down, often with dire consequences. A task which fell to the police on many occasions, was to check out the considerable number of vagrants who travelled over Shap. The A6 was the main link road between England and Scotland and most of these people had been displaced by the war. There were times when the police had to work together with the military and occasionally they were warned to look out for deserters. There were law breakers and some who were just habitual wanderers, who were normally referred to as tramps - they were all to be checked.

Dad stayed in the police until just after the war ended. He had been drafted into the force mainly because he was too old to serve in the Army. Although I am sure he would have done everything that was expected of him to the letter, I don't believe that he was a policeman at heart. He was much too gentle a person, not to be confused with being soft, far from it, just that I know he would much prefer to help someone rather than to take them to task.

The police duty behind him, Dad again joined up as an RAC scout, a job which he really enjoyed and was very good at. My sisters and I would wait at the bottom of Prince's Road when he was due back from work. He now had a nice new Norton bike and side car box, which was bright blue and was provided by the RAC. We would listen for its easily recognisable thud, thud, thud, just before Dad would round the bend and see us waiting. We would then climb on the box and hang on. I always claimed the front where I could wedge my feet behind the large RAC badge which adorned the front. At that time we had not yet acquired the family's first car and so any sort of a ride was a treat.

On one occasion Dad was to travel to Grasmere to assist with the car parking at the famous annual Grasmere Sports which had been suspended during the war and were again taking place. It would be unheard of today but I was allowed, still in short trousers, to ride with him all the way from Windermere to Grasmere, a distance of about fifteen miles or so. I guess doing the same today would be illegal, but at that time I don't suppose anybody raised an eyebrow.

GRAMMAR SCHOOL AND DAD'S NEW JOB

The year was 1947. Margaret and I were now turned eleven-years-old, and it was now time to sit the exam known as the "eleven plus". Margaret was probably the cleverer of the two of us. She seemed blessed with an exceptionally good memory. She could listen to a song on the radio once and then sing it word for word whereas I still don't know a song all the way through. However we both passed the exam which meant that I would go to Windermere Grammar School and Margaret would go to Kelsik Grammar School in Ambleside. My new school was boys only while hers was mixed.

Ambleside geographically is about six miles from Windermere and Margaret's school was situated half a mile up an extremely steep hill above the village. Windermere pupils attending Kelsik had firstly to take a long bus ride followed by the laborious trek up the hill. Fate had it that I was in exactly the opposite position. I lived virtually on the other side of the road from the main gates of my school. In fact I actually lived nearer to the main part of the school than the twenty or so boarders who lived in the huge school house occupied also by the headmaster Mr. Lewis. I remember Mr. Lewis as having the rather unusual habit of constantly looking skyward as he talked to us.

I started school at the beginning of the summer term. The war had been over for about two years and the country was starting to get back to some degree of normality. The school was divided into three groups which were referred to as houses. Each house was named after a prominent local mountain (or fell) - Fairfield, Scafell and Wetherlam. I was directed to the latter. All school activities whether academic or social were subject to a point scoring system for one's house. The school was divided into two streams, namely the As which on the whole were the classes for children with academic potential, and the Alphas, who were considered at the time of placement to be more 'hands on.'

On the day I joined Windermere Grammar School I was placed in class 1A. I was to be taught, amongst other subjects, Latin, French, English, Maths, Geography, History, Science and Physics, plus non-academic subjects such as art and woodwork. There was something of an irony in that the Alpha classes didn't take languages, instead they were taught gardening and even kept hens. I was not to know it, but time would prove that I was in all probability wrongly placed. I have never knowingly benefited from either Latin or French, but I have certainly kept hens.

Amongst the masters, all of whom bar one were male, was one who I shall not mention by name. Suffice to say that he had earned himself the nickname of 'killer,' although I never knew of anyone brave enough to address him as such. The name killer was well earned. I have seen boys stand rigid with fear when he shouted out their name. I would not normally dwell on the infamy of a teacher but, in his case especially, I feel strongly that his technique of teaching should not go unmentioned if only as a record of the extreme unhappiness he caused to myself and many others.

Killer's favourite teaching aid was a billiard cue, which he referred to as 'his memory tickler.' He would approach a pupil sitting at his desk who, on the insistence of the master, would have his arms folded across his chest and be straight backed. Killer would place the pointed end of the cue against the chest of the pupil before him. What happened next depended on the ability of the lad to answer the question put to him with an appropriate answer. Should the unfortunate lad give any indication that he was unable to respond, Killer, by now his eyes starting to bulge from their sockets, would start tapping on the blunt end of the cue. "Can you remember?" he would snarl, the thin end of the memory tickler starting to hurt as it was being jabbed into the chest.

By now the unfortunate pupil's mind was spinning in a desperate search for the answer that would prevent the all but inevitable. "Can you remember? Can you remember?" Killer by now would have worked himself into a near frenzy and would tap even harder. The natural reaction of anybody being jabbed in a rather tender part of the anatomy is to try to remove the cause of the pain. The pupil would start to unfold his arms, but this was just what the irate master was waiting for and his right hand would travel at high speed in a sweeping curve and connect with the lad's head. It would be quite often the case that the recipient would be sent crashing out of his seat and would finish up in a heap on the floor.

The account to which I have just related was not about one specific incident and not one fabricated from an over zealous imagination, but a typical example of the everyday behaviour of one master who was not unique in his method of teaching in and before those days. Oh and yes, I was on the receiving end of such treatment from that very same master on more than one occasion!

There were one or two civilised teachers, to whom I am eternally grateful. They were teachers who did not need fear to command respect. One such master was an English teacher called Mr Saxton or Tommy, which was probably a nickname. Tommy was a square shouldered straight-backed chap with a neat head of red hair that he constantly combed. To go with his red hair Tommy had reddish bushy eyebrows that he regularly tweaked into quite a pronounced point giving him a rather sharpish **?** look. I never remember the dear man ever striking a boy, although I have seen him throw a blackboard eraser to the back of the room, possibly to get more attention. Although sometimes quite caustic in his remarks, Tommy had a natural ability to inspire his pupils to want to do their best. This in my case was achieved very much because the fear of punishment was removed.

Nowadays school bullying is often in the news and is banned by law, the irony being that in my days at school it was not aggressive pupils who were the main perpetrators, but a few of the masters. A queer world isn't it? Living as near the school as I did, I soon realised that if I set off late in a morning, it was impossible to make up time, whereas my twin sister could always run to catch her bus. I made sure therefore that I set off in good time. The consequences of arriving late were detention and, as I lived so close, I would get no leniency.

I guess my mother must have had an eye for business because she saw an opening to help the family's finances and started a small shop in the hallway of our house. She contacted a firm called Marsh's Soft Drinks from Barrow-in-Furness, who delivered into the area. One particular soft drink the firm was famous for was their Sarsaparilla, a brown, sticky, fizzy, sweet-tasting drink. Mother let it be known that she had for sale this 'Sass', dandelion and burdock cream soda and a further selection, together with Smith's potato crisps and a few toffee bars. The result was that our house during the day quickly became a school tuck shop.

In addition to selling pop at the front door, mother took in bed and breakfast guests. Most of them were cyclists who had come to the lakes for a few days touring. Sometimes we would have six or eight, always men it seemed, who would in all probability be from the same cycling club. I sometimes wonder where mother put them all, as we only had four bedrooms in the house. It was my job to see that all the bikes, which were left in our enclosed back yard, were covered up with pieces of tarpaulin sheet that we kept for that purpose (plastic sheeting was unheard of in those days).

Thinking back, mother must have worked extremely hard as, in those days, there were no electric dishwashers or clothes washing machines. She used a copper boiler for washing. It was a brick-built box about four feet square and two feet six high and was the washer of the day. This contraption was built in the corner of the kitchen. It had a cast-iron bowl in the middle that probably held about ten gallons of water, into which she would place all the family's dirty washing. Underneath the bowl was a small furnace that was accessed to feed the fire by a small cast iron door. When I was available, I would help by keeping the flames roaring up the cast iron chimney. You could always tell from outside the house that it was washing day by the plumes of black smoke. Unlike a present day washing machine, the clothes had to be agitated by hand with a dolly three legs, which was a three legged stool with a handle which had to be twisted left then right, up and down - it soon made your arms ache!

The next step was to put the clothes into a galvanised tub where they were 'possied'. A 'posser' was a round copper thing which resembled an upturned porridge bowl with a broom shaft sticking out. The 'posser' had holes right through what would be the tip of the bowl. By pushing the thing very hard down onto the submerged washing, it would force air and water through the material, thereby forcing out the dirt. The clothes were then put through a hand-turned 'mangle' or 'wringer' which would force them between either wooden or hard rubber rollers, thus squeezing out all the water. Sometimes the whole process would be repeated, depending on how dirty the clothes had been in the first place. This procedure was hard enough during the cold winter months, but in summer I have seen my poor mother absolutely wet through with perspiration mainly due to the heat from the furnace.

Some of the things we used in the old days are not long gone. Fridges have replaced 'meat safes' that were built rather like a rabbit hutch with a fine metal mesh screen all the way round which allowed air to circulate but kept out flies and blue bottles. Meat safes normally had a sloping tarred and felted roof. Although they were called meat safes, milk, cheese and any other perishable foods were also kept fresh in them. A safe was always outside the house, never inside, and was usually in the shade where possible. These safes worked well except in very hot or thundery weather when milk would go off.

In the house, most of the hot water was drawn from a tap from the boiler on the side of the black leaded iron fireplace. To fill the boiler, a lid or 'plug' on the top of it was lifted using a specially shaped iron tool which was inserted in a hole in the plug. Next a bucket of cold water was poured in and the plug replaced. How long you waited for the water to boil depended on how big a fire was kept. At the back of the fire was a back-boiler which forced hot water up pipes running up the chimney breast and into the bathroom where it could be run off into the large, white cast iron bath. When the water reached near boiling point, it would cause the pipes to vibrate terribly. There was such a terrible clattering and banging we children used to say that rats were dancing on the roof!

At school, like other children, I had subjects that I had grown to hate and others that I enjoyed intensely. Not surprisingly, perhaps, English, art, woodwork and music, came into the latter category. Also, perhaps not surprisingly, the least appealing of the subjects were usually taught by the least understanding of the teachers. My father helped me decide to take up the violin. After all he had, just the same as me, started as a young boy and had succeeded in becoming a first class player. Mother would play the rather nice piano that we had in our front room. Dad would allow me to play the melodies and he would play an accompaniment. I was starting to play quite well but, surprisingly after leaving school, I would never again pick up a violin but would opt in favour of other instruments.

Another facet of living in the 1940s was that horses were finally giving way to motorised vehicles as a means of transportation on the road. A few 'diehards' remained, one of whom was our milkman who was called Alan Park. Mr. Park also farmed at Broadgate Farm, Ings, which lay about three miles east of Windermere village. Each morning Mr. Park would come along Prince's Road with his horse and trap. His horse knew where to stop for each customer. The back of the trap was open which allowed access to a shiny brass tap attached to a tall conical milk kit, that was wide at the base tapering to the lid. On board the trap were carried a number of measuring tankards - the smallest was half a pint and the largest a gallon - from which beautifully fresh milk would be dispensed, still frothing, into the customer's own jug.

Where there are horses there will always be horse droppings. We, as kids, were expected to run and get a bucket and shovel it up, if any was dropped in the road in the vicinity of our house, that was unless somebody else beat you to it. The reason for this task was that, like many of the households, we had a small garden in which we grew a patch of rhubarb and a mint bed, both of which responded quite dramatically to a treat of horse manure.

Dad had been quite happy to return to the RAC. It was a great job during the summer months but a punishing job in the depths of winter, with snow, driving rain and freezing cold. The fact that outdoor clothing was still barely waterproof and that Dad was not getting any younger both took their toll. Had the RAC replaced their motorbike and side cars earlier with vans he would probably have stayed indefinitely. Unfortunately a windshield and a pair of leg guards offered little protection from the elements.

To add to the problem Dad was again playing in a dance band several nights a week. He had joined up again with his old friend, Arnold Baron, who had formed his own band which went under the name of Arnold Baron's Dance Band. Hunt balls were very popular. The idea behind these was that the organisers of the several packs of foxhounds dotted about the district would organise a dance, the proceeds from which would help to finance the upkeep of their particular pack of hounds. The hunt balls that Arnold Baron's Band would play for were generally held in village halls within about a twenty mile radius and were mainly supported by the farming community.

Whether it was the constant wettings or the fact that Dad would be more or less his own boss, he decided to leave the RAC in 1949 and take on a job as an oil company representative. The name of the company was Sternol Oils and they boasted the approval of Rolls Royce and one of the major shipping lines. Dad was now in the position that he would have to travel the district for which he would require a car that was not part of the company package.

AUB 82 was the registration of the family's first car. It was a grey 1936 Riley with a pre-selector gearbox and fluid flywheel. It was, by then, thirteen-years-old and, due to its fluid flywheel, had a very distinctive sound - a sort of whine. The driver simply selected the required gear by means of the column-mounted gear lever and then dipped the clutch at the appropriate moment.

Now the owner of a car, Dad set off round the district calling on farms, most of which by now had a tractor of some sort. He would hopefully take an order for at least one five gallon drum or, on a big farm, an order for a forty gallon barrel that would be delivered by a haulier at a later date. At home Dad had built up a small amount of stock, most of which was delivered in a square, tapered, five gallon drum which would be very useful, even when empty of oil. During the day the back seat was removed and, in this space together with the boot, he was able to carry seven or eight drums of Agristernol, which was the grade most suitable for tractors.

In the school holidays I would accompany my father and, when we were approaching a farm across private land, he would allow me to drive the car. I thought this was wonderful. While Dad was talking to the farmers, I was expected to keep out of the way and usually remained in the car reading a comic or drawing, usually animals and horses in particular. It was whilst in the car, which was parked in a field just outside the farmyard, that a large cart-horse that had been quietly grazing nearby, decided to take a closer inspection of this grey contraption which had been left in his field. The huge animal sniffed and snorted and muzzled the windows, then with no warning decided to test the springs on the front end. He placed both his huge front feet on the front bumper and climbed on the car which instantly seemed to sink about a foot. For a moment or two I was frozen to my seat but quickly came up with the idea to blow the horn which fortunately produced an instant reaction from the horse. He leaped backwards and then cantered off down the field, thankfully leaving no damage to the car. I could always tell when Dad landed back to the car whether he had had any success or not. It always showed in his face. I would learn more about that same subject in years to come, but did not know that at the time.

As Easter 1951 grew closer, I began to get excited - I was at last going to be free of school. They had been years which for me had been ruined by just a few of the teachers who, in my opinion, had failed to allow the children in their care the basic right to receive an education free of the constant threat of corporal punishment. Thank God things have changed in this respect. The big day came. I can still remember the feeling of relief and the sense of freedom as I passed through the large stone gate posts for the last time. I was at last going to be able to pursue the love of my life - the land and the animals on it. I was moving on to the next part of my life, and herewith I will try to describe the next fifty years and how I used them.

ELM TREE FARM

Although at the time I left school I had not actually found myself a job, I knew exactly what I wanted to do, which was to work on a farm. I knew also that there were plenty of vacancies and the *Westmorland Gazette* was the paper in which to find them. It wasn't long, however, before my father stepped in. In the course of his travels he had supplied oil to a farm called Elm Tree, in the parish of Preston Patrick, which was owned by Mr Edwin Stanley. Dad had mentioned to Mr. Stanley that his son had just left school and was looking for a job, to which Mr Stanley had replied that he was considering hiring a farm lad and suggested that Dad should bring me for an interview. A meeting took place and I got my first job.

I started work that first day at 6.30am. It was a beautiful, sunny spring morning and I was bursting with enthusiasm, helping with the first job of the day - collecting the cows from the pasture where they were kept during the night. I had arrived at the farm the previous afternoon, settled in with the Stanleys and had an early night.

The brightness of the early morning sun highlighted the green of the hedgerow. The new spring growth, a pale yellowy-green translucent colour, almost choked the hedgerows on both sides of the lane. My new-found energy made me feel so well that I had the feeling I was almost walking on air above the tarmac road. This was the life I had dreamed of for the last few years.

Mr Stanley was not from farming stock but his wife was. He had been a linoleum designer for Williamsons of Lancaster. On his retirement the couple had taken the tenancy of Elm Tree. The Stanleys had two grown sons, Peter and Douglas. Peter had made farming his career and it was mainly he who had persuaded his parents to move to Elm Tree. Douglas had joined the army and enlisted in the Irish Guards. By the time I started on the farm Peter had, for reasons best known to the family, left and Douglas, who had retired from the Guards due to an injury, was running the farm.

On the farm were dairy cows and their following young stock, hens, turkeys, geese and pigs but there were no sheep, which most of the other farms around us had. That first morning I had not needed an alarm or an awakening call. I had leapt out of bed as soon as the bright sunlight coming through my bedroom window had woken me, dressed quickly and dashed outside to find Douglas preparing to bring in the cows.

On seeing Doug and myself at the pasture gate, the cows set off towards us quite happily. A 'how up,' which was the usual call of the dairy farmer when wishing to encourage cows to come in for milking, was all that was needed. One by one they slowly ambled through the gate and up the lane to the cowshed or shippon, as it was called. I had seen milking machines on other farms, but had never previously had anything to do with them. Back at Lickbarrow the cows had still been milked by hand. So Doug, who I later found to be quite an understanding and a cheerful, kindly sort of chap, showed me the basics of using them.

The morning passed with my lack of experience compensated by my eagerness to please. The cows were milked and then returned to the pasture until late afternoon when the same process was repeated. Each milking time, the milk was straight away cooled and allowed to run into the twelve gallon milk churns. Each morning's milk, together with the previous evening's milk, was taken down to the milk stand, a raised concrete plinth by the side of the main road, where a flat wagon from Libby's Dairy would pick it up.

In between the two milkings all the routine jobs would be undertaken. Firstly, after milking, was the feeding of all the other stock and, of course, the mucking out. Following this would be the field work which was very much dictated by the seasons and the weather. By the time I had arrived on the farm cereals, mainly oats and green crops, such as turnips and mangels, had already been sown.

I settled in nicely and the weeks flew by. One of the first arduous tasks that I was put to, was the thinning of the turnips. These were grown from the tiny black seeds that were sown in a continuous line along the top of the ridge. When the plants had grown to three or four inches in height, we would fasten sacks around our knees with strong twine and then crawl on hands and knees along the ground between the stitches (rows) and knock out every plant other than one strong one every ten inches. This process was known as thinning or singling. The sacks fastened around our knees were referred to as specs. I have no idea of the origin of this word, but I do know that in hot, dry weather they caused one to sweat and in wet weather they became clogged up with mud and soon became very heavy. Wet weather was not ideal as the plants that were discarded had a tendency to survive and would have to be grubbed out later. On more than one occasion I have even crawled up the stitches with a corrugated roofing sheet fastened on my back to shelter me from the weather.

The reason that the turnip thinning had to be pushed on even in poor weather was that hay time would quickly follow. Of course everybody hoped for sunny, hot days for hay time and fortunately the summer of 1951 was on the whole a good one. The grass at Elm Tree at that time-was cut with a horse-drawn finger mower converted to work on a tractor by removing the shafts and adding a draw bar. It was called a finger mower because pointed steel fingers separated and held the grass whilst a long cutter bar with sharp segments sliced off the grass just above the ground. After the grass had lain for a couple of days and a lot of the moisture had evaporated, helped hopefully by a nice hot sun, it was turned over and scaled once or twice until it became dry enough to cart away and place in the barn. If hay is not dried sufficiently before being stored inside a barn, there is the danger that it will heat up and even spontaneously set on fire.

By August the meadows had been cleared of hay, and the grass and turnips were growing well. A turnip the size of a man's head was not uncommon - grown from a tiny black seed little bigger than a pinhead. September would see the gathering of the field of oats which, when ready, would turn a beautiful golden colour. In the meantime there were jobs like fence repairs, hedges to slash (cut), which in those days was done manually with a slashing hook, a sharp blade on the end of a three foot shaft. The hedge cutter would swing the tool in a slashing motion cutting off the new growth whilst attempting to keep some sort of shape about the hedge. It was a job that was particularly hard on the arms.

The terms of my employment with the Stanleys were that I would take every alternate Saturday afternoon and Sunday off. My wage was agreed at one pound a week plus my board and lodgings, which were always referred to as my keep. It wasn't much by today's standards but at that time I found the amount adequate. In fact, I do believe that I would have worked for nothing as I was blissfully happy. At the commencement of my employment Mrs Stanley had told me that they didn't pay overtime-but, if at the end of the season, I had worked well, she would give me a treat, this I thought was hopeful and I resolved to earn it.

One of the ideas I picked up from Doug was the wearing of wooden soled clogs. Seeing him in a pair had prompted me to find the necessary 28 shillings and buy some to wear myself. The problem with wearing a boot or clog on a farm was that little bits of straw or small stones have a habit of finding their way inside and, in the case of clogs, the discomfort is really pronounced because there is no give whatsoever in a wooden sole. The best way of avoiding getting foreign bodies in footwear was by taking an old pair of worn out Wellingtons and simply cutting the entire sole away. The tops were then worn like leggings, keeping everything out and also protecting your ankles and legs below the knee. I still maintain that clogs are the most comfortable footwear that anybody could ever wear.

Life was great. Doug was a cheerful boss to work for and was always patient in explaining the various tasks. I had become familiar with all the animals, each of which I found had their own peculiarities and personalities. In the dairy herd there were about 30 cows in milk at any one time and one huge bull. The cows were of the Ayrshire breed, which is a medium sized, rather light-boned breed. Most of them had the characteristic long pointed horns. One fault with the breed was that they were a bit given to being nervous and showed it in different ways.

One of the cows was a rather above average size black cow. Black was not a very common colour in the breed so this cow had been christened Reindeer. She would kick out at you if you went anywhere near her and she could kick forwards, backwards or even sideways. She was particularly difficult to deal with. Another cow was called Big Ben. She was the biggest cow in the herd and, unlike Reindeer, was extremely placid. Big Ben had a tail which had been broken off halfway up when she was young. She would swing her half tail in a vain attempt to swish away the flies; it was more like a base ball bat than a tail and you had to be careful not to get a smack with it when milking her. A number of calves had names that to this day stick in my mind - there was Shiner, China, Ginger and Dinah, all beautiful little creatures.

Harvest time had come, the oats had turned a beautiful golden colour and were ready for cutting. This was done by a binding machine that not only cut the stems laden with ears of corn but tied it in bundles. The long stems of corn would be cut just above the ground, travel up the canvas belt, pass through a knotter and fall out at the back as sheaves, ready to be stooked (propped up) to dry in groups of eight. After being left for a few days to remove excessive moisture they would, like the hay, be carted into the barn. Some time later they would be fed through a threshing machine to separate the grain from the straw.

September passed and the season's work was complete. It wouldn't be long now before the grass stopped growing and the cows and young stock would have to be brought in for the winter. I was looking forward to the little bit of a treat or bonus that Mrs Stanley had promised at the start of the season in lieu of overtime. I hadn't long to wait. One Saturday afternoon when I was to catch the bus at the end of the lane for my weekend off and travel to my parents' home back at Windermere, Mrs Stanley confronted me and told me that she and Mr Stanley had been very pleased with the way I had worked so diligently. I had worked evenings on many occasions and even forfeited a couple of weekends off because the weather had been extra dry and too good to miss at hay time. Mrs Stanley said she felt that a treat was in order. She pressed my weekly wage of one pound into my hand and said: "We would like you to go to the cinema tonight and you must buy yourself some sweets with this." She gave me an extra half crown that was, of course, two shillings and sixpence. I was pretty disappointed, but I had been brought up to be polite and show gratitude, so I took the half crown and said thank you.

As Christmas approached orders for turkeys, geese and chickens came in from customers. These would all have to be killed and 'dressed' in time for the festivities. I had never had anything to do with killing and was happy to leave that part to Doug. The only thing I had ever killed was a perch or two which I had caught in Windermere Lake. Before poultry can be 'dressed' there is the arduous task of removing the feathers or plucking. Large scale enterprises had machines but there was nothing like that at Elm Tree. The first few hours are relatively easy but then the finger tips start to get sore and after a few days they become really painful. One aid to plucking we had was a large electric water boiler that was big enough to accommodate even the largest turkey. If you submerged a feathered bird for a few seconds, it helped to loosen the feathers. Using this technique was very helpful except that you had to be careful not to leave the bird submerged too long otherwise all the flesh would be scalded and would become discoloured with ugly red blotches. Finally the birds were gutted - a messy process - trussed (tied in an attractive position) and finally dusted with white baking flour that gave them a clean pinkish sort of look.

There were, as one can expect on a farm, some amusing and some not so amusing incidents from time to time. I will first relate one such happening that fits the latter category. I had been round the fields once or twice with Doug and one of his friends, rabbiting. For this purpose we used ferret nets and a twelve-bore shot gun. The nets were placed over the rabbit holes of a warren and then the ferret was sent down underground to flush out any rabbits which were at home. Should a rabbit bolt from a hole not covered by a net, it would be shot with the gun. It was all very gruesome, but rabbits at that time were causing a great deal of damage, mainly because of their sheer numbers. This activity sets the scene for the short and very regrettable story that I will now relate.

I decided that in my spare time one evening, I would have a go at catching a few rabbits on my own. I was not qualified to own or even shoot a gun, and so the obvious way to catch rabbits was to trap them. In the buildings I had noticed hanging on the wall a couple of gin traps. These were a strong metal contraption that when stepped on by an animal would release spring loaded jaws about six inches in width. I made my way to a field not too far from the farm, where I had seen lots of rabbits at play. Underneath the hedgerow I found a number of holes with freshly moved soil outside which was a fair indication that they were being used.

Carefully I set the trap and fastened the short chain to a stick that I had driven into the ground and then left the scene. I planned to return to check for victims some time later. Twice I visited the trap that evening but to no avail. Everything was just as I had left it. I resolved that I would wait until the following morning after milking before checking again.

As I walked towards my trap the next morning, I could see something white moving. As I got nearer still my expectancy turned to horror - what I had actually caught in the trap was Mrs Stanley's favourite cat, a Persian called Snowy because of her beautiful fluffy white fur. Poor Snowy was caught by one leg. She had obviously been of the same mind as myself and she too had set out to catch a rabbit. By the time I had run back to the farmyard to break the news, I was upset and in tears and obviously Mrs Stanley herself was distressed. Fortunately Doug was about. He had the task of collecting his gun and putting poor Snowy out of her misery, she was too badly damaged to recover. I never again set a trap to catch an animal. I was just fifteen and, until then, I had never quite grasped the reality between catching living creatures and killing them and the suffering that goes with it, but I have ever since.

Leaving the sad story of poor Snowy and, on a less painful note, I would like to relate an amusing incident that occurred during the warm days of summer. One of the farm's buildings, a large barn, had been built into a hillside on the top side of the farmyard. This meant that the lower part of the building was accessed from the yard. The upper storey had a low ceiling loft which was accessed from the field. The lower level had been converted into pig pens and calf boxes. One particularly hot day a number of young bullocks had been standing in the field, swishing their tails about in an effort to chase away the ever present flies that always accompany a group of sweating cattle. Doug and I were working nearby when we heard an almighty crash that seemed to come from the direction of the pig pens.

Both Doug and I ran towards the building where we were met by a huge cloud of dust billowing through the tall barn doors. For half a minute we could see nothing unusual but, as the dust cleared, a strange sight emerged. There, standing in the pig pen, was a rather bemused bullock and walking round him grunting with indignation was a fat old sow, the rightful occupant of the pen. What had obviously happened was that the bullock had pushed open the door to the loft, and gained access from the field into the loft, probably in an effort to gain some shade from the sun. The weight of the fat bullock had been too much for the half rotten floor of the loft and it had given way. The floor, together with the cause of the incident, had fallen about fifteen feet, the bullock narrowly missing the concrete dividing wall and the pig. Luckily there was no injury to either pig or bullock. The floor was collected up and used for firewood and the door nailed shut to prevent any further calamities.

I had been at Elm Tree for just about a year, had had my sixteenth birthday and, barring one or two little incidents, I had been very, very happy. Traditionally farm workers would consider their employment situation twice a year at Easter and at Martinmas. If their boss, or the farm in general, had not turned out to be as good as they had been led to believe when 'hiring on' or perhaps the food was particularly poor - a bad Tommy Shop - they might move on! In most cases a farm worker, if he was single, would live in with his employer's family. That meant that you were not only answerable to the boss in working hours, but also for the rest of the time you were on the farm premises. You were totally reliant on the family to make your life bearable when living on the spot

24 hours a day. Sometimes things could get a little strained but I had been very lucky in that respect with the Stanleys.

Before my involvement with farming and right up till about 1940 hiring fairs were held for farm workers. They were usually held in the market place of certain towns and villages on specified days. Any person who was looking for agricultural work or any farmer looking for a worker would attend.

There is a story about a young man attending a hiring fair and his concerns about finding the right employer. Though it may be an exaggerated story the underlying theme is very, very real. This particular young man was attending Ulverston Hiring Fair as he had recently given notice to his employer that he would be leaving at Term Time (the name given to the twice annual events). He had been very disappointed with the conditions he had had to endure over the past six months and was resolved that he would do better the next time. A farmer who was seeking an all round worker approached the lad saying: "Noo then, ista looking fer wark?"

"I'y," replied the lad.

"Is 't frittend a work?"

"No!"

"Can 'ta git up av a morning?"

"I'y"

"Wa did ta wark foor last?"

The young chap answered telling the farmer where and for whom he had worked for previously, whereupon the farmer replied: "Reet then a'll just gaa en git thi refrence." He approached the young man's previous employer, whose whereabouts he obviously knew, and arranged to meet in half an hour to confirm the hiring or otherwise.

True to his word the farmer returned to the spot where the lad was still standing. "Reet a've gitten thi refrence and thoo can start reet away." He then continued asking the lad to make an immediate start in his employment.

"Ay," said the lad, "and I's gitten a refrence an all and a's nut gaan to start." The young fellow had, having previously found himself with a bad employer, decided to make enquiries of his own. His findings must have resulted in him deciding this farmer was probably no better than the last one - references can be two sided!

I myself have never been to a Hiring Fair. By the time I got involved in farming in 1951 they had ceased to exist. The last ones were held around about the late 1930s or early 1940s. Practically all the farmers seeking workers would do so by advertising in the local papers; in my case the *Westmorland Gazette*. There would be long lists in vertical columns around 'term time' which still prevailed. The usual advert started: "Wanted, man or strong lad" or "Cowman for large herd." The advert which took my eye was the "Man or strong lad" on a farm which I found out was on the northern side of Kendal and was therefore only half the distance from my parents' home at Windermere than where I was at Elm Tree. The advert went on: "apply to J. Gibson, Helsfell Hall, Kendal."

The next time I saw my Dad I asked him if he knew of this Mr Gibson of Helsfell Hall. He replied that he had called on one occasion, but hadn't managed to sell any oil. I was none the wiser as, for whatever reason, the visit had only been a short one and he had not really had the chance to form an opinion of the man or the place in general. However, I got in touch and made an appointment to meet Mr Gibson.

My prospective employer turned out to be a man of few words and perhaps at that stage, I should have heard alarm bell start to ring, rather like the lad at the Ulverston hiring fair. I should have given more thought to personalities and general mannerisms. The standard mandatory questions were asked: "Was I good at getting up? Was I keen to work?" I was so fired up to widen my knowledge and experience, that I had more or less made up my mind to accept the job if it was offered, even before I attended for the interview. To cut a long story short, probably because nobody with more experience than myself had applied, I was offered the job there and then. I accepted straightaway and was hired. My next task was to inform the Stanleys of my intentions. I would serve a week's notice, take a week's holiday, and then start at Helsfell.

HELSFELL HALL

I had said my goodbyes to the Stanleys, had a week's holiday at my parent's home in Windermere and was due to start my new job on Monday, which meant moving in with my new family who, of course, I had only met on the one occasion. The most practical course was that my Dad would deliver me and my personal belongings on the Sunday. This he duly did.

Here I was, in a strange house, with people I didn't know and expected to stay for at least six months regardless of whether I was happy or not. For some reason I felt a lot more apprehensive than I had done when moving in with the Stanleys. Something told me that things were going to be a lot different, and so they were!

After a night when I had uncharacteristically spent at least an hour lying in bed with my mind working overtime before falling asleep, I was suddenly woken by a sharp voice at the bedroom door: "Michael, let's be doing!" This was followed by the sound of someone running down the wide oak staircase.

I leapt out of bed noticing that the time was quarter to six. Quickly I pulled on my trousers, shirt and stockings. By the time I got down stairs Mr. Gibson had already put on his lace-to-the-toe boots and leather anklets and was making for the back door. Quickly I climbed into my clogs and went outside making for the part of the buildings where I could hear sounds of activity. The boss was hurriedly gathering together the milking units ready for the start of the morning's milking of the 35 or so milk cows which the farm carried.

"Grab that muck barrow and shovel!" he snapped, "and get that ship-pon mucked out." I immediately obliged and wheeled the large wooden wheelbarrow into the building. The steam caused by the heat from the cows could be seen in the dimly lit yard as it flooded from the open ship-pon door. Straight away I began to scoop up the muck which had accumulated over the previous twelve hours and piled it into the barrow, a job which I had done every morning and night for the last four or five months. In the mean time Mr. Gibson landed with a couple of units apparently expecting to find the place clear for him to start milking. Dropping the units he wrenched the shovel from my grasp and virtually ran down the muck grue (grove) sweeping all before him like a miniature bulldozer, scooping up the muck and virtually hurling it into the barrow.

Helsfell Hall which was bought by developers in the spring of 2002.

"You'll have to shape better than this!" he snapped, "You came for a man's job. You'll have to work like one!" The cows got milked that morning. The warm milk cooled in the dairy and ran into the usual twelve gallon kits of that era which, as the last drops passed through the cooler, were whisked away and placed on the milk stand just down the road. Very little conversation had passed between me and my employer that morning other than a few curt instructions and a few unsettling remarks. I now began to realise that I was in the employ of a totally different boss to my last one. It wasn't looking all that good.

I wasn't long picking up the daily routine which was still in it's winter phase with all the cattle still inside. Very soon the earth would start to warm, the grass would shoot up and once more the cattle would be turned out to fend for them selves leaving no mucking out.

The main reason for the headlong rush each morning it must be pointed out, was that both the morning's and the previous night's milk had to be on the stand by no later than eight o'clock or there was a danger that the milk wagon would go without collecting your milk. This would mean a time-wasting journey to Libby's milk factory at Milnthorpe some ten miles or so away.

By the time the milk had gone I had already done over two hours work and I was ready for a drink and something to eat. Breakfast consisted of a large bowl of porridge with milk and salt, followed by several slices of bread and marmalade washed down with a few mugs of tea - all was devoured hastily. I had been used to a more varied diet and, as it turned out, it never varied. But I accepted my lot without complaint.

No sooner had we downed breakfast than the boss was on his feet and issuing instructions. The last job before we went out into the fields was always the fothering (feeding) of the milk cows with hay. Their next feed would be at dinner time with chopped-up turnips. All the stock attended to, attention was then turned to which ever job was priority. A major factor was always the weather and the state of the ground, i.e. firm or wet and soft. Too soft and the tractor wheels would rip up the sward (sod) and damage the grass roots.

Mr. Gibson, or Johnny as he was referred to by most people, (I had always been taught that it was impolite to address my elders by their christian names until asked to do so) was about 36-years-old, slightly less than average height, but powerfully built and certainly a lot stronger than me. I, of course, was only just turned sixteen.

Mrs. Gibson was probably about the same age as her husband. I was encouraged to refer to her simply as Mrs. The other member of the family was their ten-year-old daughter Dorcas, a rather skinny, pale complexioned child. Johnny's father, one Matthew Gibson (Mather), had been

Helsfell House and farm buildings

married twice. Johnny was one of the oldest children of the first marriage which had produced nine children. Mather's second marriage resulted in a further eleven children, the youngest being born whilst I was at Helsfell. It was a remarkable family possibly the largest in the county.

Mather, his wife Hetty, and the children to his second marriage lived about a mile north of Kendal and Helsfell, on a farm known as Toad Pool. The main Kendal to Windermere road in those days ran to the eastern side of the farm close to the house and buildings thus dividing the farm from some of its land. Since then straightening and realignment has caused the road to divide the farm to the west.

As well as Johnny being at Helsfell and Mather being at Toad Pool, Tommy, a brother to Johnny, farmed High Helsfell close by. On occasions such as hay time and harvest time all three farms would pool their labour force and machinery to make the task easier. Tommy was even shorter than Johnny but again he was surprisingly strong, born of heavy laborious work from earliest childhood. To further confuse the reader, Tommy's wife Joan and Johnny's wife Margaret were sisters. Two brothers had married two sisters.

My prime function was to work at Helsfell, but when the necessity arose, I would find myself working on one of the other farms which made a pleasant change. There was always a lot of conversation of great interest. When at Toad Pool come dinner time, we would all troop into the large farmhouse kitchen where there was a long wooden table. Between the table and the wall was a long wooden bench on which all the youngest members of the family would seat themselves. On the other side of the table were a number of chairs and all the men would sit on these.

The lady of the household, Mather's wife Hetty, and a domestic servant, would then bring in two huge enamel bowls of shepherd's pie or Irish stew with dumplings and place several serving spoons in the bowl. These would be quickly seized upon from both sides of the table and pretty soon there would be little or nothing but two empty bowls.

It was unfortunate if any member of the assembled party was at all 'kysty' (picky with their food) because you weren't given a second plate on which to eat your pudding. If you had pushed some of your first course to the side of your plate, there it remained whilst you ate your second course!

Very soon two more large enamel bowls would appear for the same procedure - a number of spoons would dig into a rice or a sago pudding which disappeared in no time at all. In all fairness the food was, to a growing lad, excellent and most welcome as was the conversation. I, with my limited experience of life, had little to contribute but I was a good listener and marvelled at the stories touched on by my elders.

Helsfell Hall itself was a farm of about 120 odd acres made up from a number of medium sized fields, plus a section of land rented off to the local golf course. A lot of the land was 'uneasy' land (steep) and some was only suitable for pasture. Some was excellent meadow ground which would produce a good crop of hay, usually in June, and for the rest of the season it would be grazed .

Whilst I was at Helsfell I did a certain amount of ploughing - turnips and Marrowstem kale were planted, which necessitated thinning by hand, the laborious task to which I have already refered in my experiences at Elm Tree. In the back end and early winter these turnips would have to be lifted and carted back to the farm to be stored in a 'hogg' (a heap covered over with straw or bracken) ready to be fed to the milk cows through the winter. The kale was particularly bad to handle, with stems sometimes as thick as one's arm and growing to as much as four feet in height with a 'bushy' top rather like a cabbage on a stick. It would collect a lot of water which would rain down on you as you were bent double cutting it at the stem. In cold, wet and icy conditions such as they were, it could be a miserable job as your hands soon became so cold that it was nearly impossible to hold the turnip knife. I have to confess that, on more than one occasion, I have urinated on my hands just to get some circulation back whilst cutting kale.

Helsfell, like many of the farms in the area had hardly a hedge on the place. The fields were divided up almost entirely by limestone walls which of course were all dry walled (built without mortar). I wasn't to know it but the repairing of walls which I did whilst at Helsfell would prepare me for an involvement with the same work many years on.

An amusing story occurred one day when I was sent 'thistle bobbing' (cutting thistles) in the farm's 'bull coppie' which was a field around which a particularly high wall was built in which to keep the farm's bull during the summer. At this particular time not only our own bull was in residence but there was also one from both High Helsfell and one from

Toad Pool. My job was to cut the thistles and nettles which sprang up in patches using a 'ley' (scythe). I was to spend the whole of the afternoon until 'doing up time' (milking and feeding time) and then return to the farm.

Now, bearing in mind that I was on my own and there were three rather large and unpredictable fully grown bulls in the field and the walls had been deliberately built high to contain such animals, I recognised that it would be equally difficult for me to get out in a hurry should one of my companions take exception to my being in his field. I wasn't over happy! However, as the bulls tended to graze together and were at one end of the field, I resolved to work at the opposite end.

Over the course of the afternoon the bulls fortunately had more or less stayed in a group and were more interested in their food than in me. They gradually worked their way round the field, I accordingly worked the other way round, being careful to check their progress at regular intervals. By the time it was time to leave to 'do up' I had been once round the field and was just about at the point where I had started off. I made my way to where I had left my one and only work jacket on top of the wall only to find that my companions for the afternoon had pulled the garment to the ground and had spent considerable time chewing it and trampling on it and had left it a green slimy rag. I had to manage without one until my Dad gave me an old one of his.

It was now getting near Martinmas when, by tradition, farm workers moved on to another place or verbally agreed to stay on for another six months. I would have to decide whether or not I was going to stay. The matter was resolved when one day Johnny (or Mr. Gibson as I still addressed him) came straight out with the question: "Are you staying on this term then?" I had known that sooner or later the question would be asked but nevertheless was taken aback at its directness. As I hadn't any other alternative in mind and was somewhat apprehensive about what reaction a negative answer would bring, I 'bit the bullet' and agreed that I would stay on for another term.

Johnny's next question surprised me even more: "You'll likely be wanting a rise then will you?" he asked. "No" I replied. A look of bewilderment came on to the boss' face. "Why's that?" he asked, not able to believe that someone on as low a wage as I was would turn down the chance to earn more money. I stood my ground and gave him my explanation for my reluctance to gain a rise. "Well if you remember" I spluttered out, "at Whitsuntide when I hired on again I was working for 25 shillings and you put it up to 30 shillings and said I would have to get through more work. Well I can't possibly work any harder so my money had better stay as it is!" Johnny looked at me in disbelief and walked away shaking his head. I did stay on and yes, there was another five shillings in my wage packet at the start of the new term!

Despite my staying on the boss' attitude towards work in general did not change. Everything still had to be done at breakneck speed. I had learned to do work as though there was no tomorrow. I was young and fit and getting stronger all the time.

As we crept into the winter the milk cows were brought in from the cold. Dairy cows soon let you know when they are unhappy with the weather. The quantity of milk which they produce drops as they find it harder to maintain their energy levels, burning it off just to keep warm and reducing the amount available to produce milk. Cattle inside inevitably means a lot more inside work. These days it is not as manual as most things are done mechanically. In the early 1950s feed and muck were all handled over and over again by manpower.

View of the top buildings from the north side, looking down towards Kendal. Helsfell Hall is down to the left and the derelict cottage on the right was last occupied by a Mr. Woof and his wife in the 1940s. The shippon in the 'wild cat' incident is the tiny door to the right of the ramp into the barn.

All the cows in milk were kept at the farm but most of the young stock were housed in buildings about half a mile away up the fields near the bull coppie. These were always referred to as 'the top buildings' and consisted of a large barn and several small shippons where the stirks (young cattle) were tied up to 'boskins' (vertical stone slabs). The floor of these shippons was made of rough cobbles and was very uneven. The benefit of this was that the stock got a good grip, the downside was that it was very difficult to keep clean.

There was no electricity supply to the top buildings and, even more inconvenient, there was no water supply so consequently every animal had to be turned out twice a day to drink water from a water trough situated across a field. The morning feeding and mucking out was easiest as you had the benefit of good light. It was the 'doing up' in the late afternoon when the problems occurred. On release the stirks would make a dash across the field to the water trough. Getting them to come back in was sometimes quite a problem.

On one such occasion I had difficulty in getting the stirks in and tied up and when they were finally all in the shippon it was almost dark. I was struggling with arms full of hay having to virtually feel my way between the animals. Suddenly I was aware of something on my back clawing at my neck and shoulders. For a few seconds I was in sheer panic. I then realised that it was one of the feral cats which lived in the cavities in the walls and usually disappear at the sound of a human. For a few seconds I flailed away with my arms and shouted. Fortunately for me the cat then took off and, other than being shaken, I was none the worse. The explanation of this rather frightening experience, I decided, was probably that it had been a cat with young kittens nearby. It had seen me as a threat and had only been defending its young.

Another regular job in winter was carting muck out into the fields. All this, of course, had to be loaded onto a trailer using a muck fork which is a little different to a normal garden fork in that it has long slender tines and is a lethal instrument in the wrong hands. The trailer was pulled by a little, grey Fergie tractor. Johnny and I would load about two tons of muck which would then be deposited in heaps of roughly a couple of barrow loads, about six paces apart and in as straight a line as possible. In order to get the muck from the trailer on to the ground, a 'muck drag' was used - this was a tool rather like a muck fork with its tines bent at right angles to the six foot long slender shaft. To work efficiently two people were required, one to drive the tractor - I usually got that job - and one to do the 'dragging'. As the load was reduced the driver would gradually raise the trailer, a tipping trailer was one of the very few innovative pieces of machinery we had on the farm. You had to be careful not to cause the remainder of the load to go with a rush, all the heaps had then to be spread by hand.

The winter of 1952-53 passed and I decided that come Whitsuntide I would definitely make a change and move on; quite where I had no idea. There was, however, still quite a demand for experienced workers and so I was quite confident that something would turn up. I had learned a lot about farming whilst at Helsfell and, every bit as important, despite Johnny being a hard task master, I have to admit that he had taught me how to work. At times the pressure had seemed unjustified but I now realised that work doesn't get done by simply looking at it and thinking about it.

During the winter we kept our shorthorn bull in one of the shippons. He was a fine animal of the usual roan colour and, like most males of that breed, was rather unpredictable in his behaviour. On one occasion he had been let out into the yard with a cow which was thought to be in service. However she proved to be totally indifferent to the big fellow and his advances. "Waste of time" said the boss showing his usual impatience, "Let's get him back in." Getting the bull back into the shippon on this occasion, when he knew he would be again tied up by the neck away from his lady friend, was to prove more difficult than was anticipated.

Three quarters of a ton of prime beef charged several times round the yard and ran up the alley between the house and the dairy, working himself into a frenzy by scaling a heap of straw and muck round the back by the calf pens, sending it high in the air with his hooves. It was decided that some extra help was going to be needed. Accordingly a phone call brought another member of the family. The three of us, after much shouting and running about, sometimes after the excited animal, and sometimes to get out of his way, finally cornered the by now thoroughly agitated animal in a stall.

Now standing securely tied up Mr. Bull was shaking, snorting and virtually steaming. The three of us were standing in the shippon getting our breath back and considering how lucky we were to resolve the situation without any body getting hurt. "Thank goodness that's over," said our able helper, who had come at such short notice. However his statement

View of the top buildings from the south side showing the tiny shippon windows which were the only source of light.

proved to be slightly premature because unfortunately, just as he passed behind the bull it gave a cough whilst simultaneously deciding to empty its bowels. I will neither go into any further detail as to what happened, nor mention a name, to save a person any embarrassment should he read this account. Suffice to say that Mr. Bull got his own back for spoiling his fun! It was not long after this incident that it was decided that the bull was too dangerous to keep. He went on a one way trip to market.

My father's parents lived in Leyland, Lancashire. Grandad and Grandma Bolton had been retired for quite a lot of years. It was on one of his visits to see his parents that Dad had mentioned that I was ready for a change. It so happened that Grandma, who was a real Lancashire lass and spoke with a pronounced Lancashire accent, had a brother who, after starting out as a cabinet maker's apprentice, had done exceptionally well for himself.

Thomas Hargreaves was my Grandma's brother, and was very much the boardroom director. He owned the Leyland Construction Company, a large civil engineering business, which took on major building and pipe line contracts. He was also a director of Leyland Motors, president of Leyland Cricket Club, and eventually received a knighthood for services to industry.

Anyhow, the relevance of my mentioning my great uncle is that, amongst the numerous acquisitions he had made over the years, was a medium sized farm called Sherbourn House Farm, which was situated just outside the village of Little Eccleston on the Leyland to Wigan road. Grandma must have spoken to her brother because, on hearing of my availability, he had suggested that I make an appointment to meet with him on the farm when he would discuss the possibility of my employment with his farm manager as he was looking for somebody suitable at that time.

The outcome was that, as I was looking for a change and a fresh challenge, which a move down into a new area would surely be, arrangements were made for my Dad to take me for interview. On the appointed day Dad and I arrived at Eccleston and found Banister Lane, the road which we were told led on to Wrennals Lane and then down a cinder road to the farm. My first impression, as we drove through the wide open gateway, was delight. The numerous farm buildings were all attractively painted a shiny black to waist height and above that a rich creamy yellow to the eaves. It became immediately obvious that this was some thing more than just a working farm. It was more of a show farm, an observation which turned out to be correct. Thomas Hargreaves had the place made suitably attractive so that he was able to show his boardroom friends around. It turned out that he himself took no part in the physical

Harry Bolton on the Brough Superior S.S. 80 outside the Kirkstone Pass Inn.

side of the running of the place.

On the left hand side of the yard, as you entered from the lane, stood the farmhouse which could be described as an idyllic country cottage, with multi-paned windows, attractively painted and supported by a well kept garden. Outside the house stood a large black Jaguar car. Obviously, I thought, it belonged to the big boss. From the house emerged a young man in a check shirt and bib and brace overalls. On his head he wore a dark beret. One thing which was immediately noticeable about him was that, despite having a pipe clenched between strong white teeth, he had a broad smile on his face. This, I hoped, was the farm manager.

I was not disappointed. The young man introduced himself as John Schofield, manager of Sherbourn House Farm and followed this with an invitation for myself and my Dad to enter the house where he said his boss, Mr. Hargreaves was ready to meet us.

I had never met Thomas Hargreaves although I had been made aware of his existence from an early age. It was he who, when my Dad was a boy, had assisted Dad to make the beautiful little wooden cabinet which had sat on the sideboard of my parent's home for as long as I could remember. We were guided firstly to the kitchen where we were introduced to Mrs. Schofield, whose name I found out later was Edith. She was of very small stature, very nice looking and with an equally pleasant smile as her husband.

Next we were shown into a rather dark, but none the less pleasant, sitting room where a tall, rather stout, red faced gentleman in a dark pinstriped suit was stood, obviously ready to welcome us. Dad straight away stepped forward and the two shook hands vigorously. "So this is your lad is it then, I've heard about him from your mother." (meaning my Grandma). I stepped forward and rather in awe shook the big man's hand.

I will not labour over the details of the interview but, suffice it to say that, after giving a general resumé of my experience, I was offered the job which I accepted there and then and agreed on a date to start. As I was to live in with the family, Mrs. Schofield insisted that she would show me the room which I would occupy which, it so happened, looked out onto the front lawn, not that a good view came high on my list of priorities.

I couldn't have been happier as we said our goodbyes to the Schofields. My great uncle had left soon after my interview. No doubt he had important business to see to elsewhere. Dad and I had stayed a little longer and had enjoyed tea and scones.

On the journey back home the realisation dawned on me that I would soon have to break the news to my present boss that at term time I would be moving on. I was not looking forward to it. I had not told anyone that I was attending an interview. It had been arranged on one of my days off and as the route back to Windermere passed right past Helsfell, it was decided that Dad would drop me off so I would be ready for work next morning.

After an early night, before which I had decided that I was definitely going to tell Mr. Gibson the news, I rose early and was as usual first up. I had always believed that by so doing I would gain some favour but the ploy somehow had never seemed to work. After the milking we came in for breakfast. When we went out again I plucked up the courage to say what was foremost on my mind. "Er Mr. Gibson, I want to have a word with you." I blurted out. Johnny stopped what he was doing, he must have sensed something a little different in my voice, "I won't be staying on this Whitsuntide!"

The boss stared at me for a moment, no doubt considering his response, which came back harshly: "So you think you can't be done without do you?"

"No" I retorted.

"Well, bugger off then," he said and turned on his heel, "Let's get some bloody work done." I was unable to rationalise my boss' response and the next two weeks were somewhat strained, but I laboured on.

MY MOVE TO ECCLESTON

It was a bright Sunday afternoon when Dad and I arrived at Sherbourn House Farm for the second time, but this time only one of us would be travelling back. I had been thinking constantly about the move since my first visit. In fact it had been hard to think of anything else. I was full of hope that this move would turn out to be a move for the better. Embedded in my mind was the broad smile of John Schofield when he introduced himself and equally the pleasant face of his wife. Surely this was going to be the best thing that had happened to me for some time.

Again the Schofields were there to welcome Dad and I when we arrived and kindly treated us to an afternoon snack. After some pleasant conversation Dad left, his old grey Riley, with its familiar transmission whine, disappearing into the distance up the cinder road. No doubt he would call on his parents on the way back to Windermere and report mission accomplished. Later, after watching John milking and feeding the stock, I sat down to supper and chatted to my new friends who seemed genuinely interested in what I had to say. No doubt they were as amused at my northern accent as I was at their Lancashire drawl. The evening passed and I felt reassured that I had made the right move and that I was going to enjoy the next phase of my career. I fell asleep that night with my head spinning with ideas and expectations.

I awoke next morning in time to hear the footsteps of someone who I took to be John Schofield as he made his way down the creaky staircase. It was obvious from the way he traversed each step that he was making a conscious effort not to waken the other two members of his family - his wife and their beautiful three-year-old daughter who I have not previously mentioned. I could not help contrasting this situation in my mind with my first morning at Helsfell when Johnny had gone down the stairs like an express train. The thought gave me comfort as I quickly dressed and crept down the stairs. As I entered the kitchen John (I had already been invited to call him by his christian name) had already got two steaming mugs of tea on the table and, on seeing me, pushed one across. "I didn't think I would have to waken you" he said, " I could see yesterday that you were keen to get started." That was an understatement but things could wait till I had drunk my tea. This, I thought, is civilised!

It didn't take long to drink up. I had no intention of abusing my new found privileges. I followed John out of the house. "Come with me, I'll introduce you to our other worker," he said. I followed him to where I could hear the clatter of metal buckets which I knew to be in the vicinity of the pig houses as I had visited the buildings the afternoon before. Rounding the corner between the buildings I was aware of a shortish, considerably overweight chap in bib and brace overalls tied at the ankle with string. On his feet he wore clogs which seemed disproportionately small to the rest of his body, as did his shortish arms. "This is Tom," said John, "he lives in the village and comes in daily." I shook hands. Tom Stevens it turned out was, of all places, from London, a fact that was obvious when he spoke. He had moved up north comparatively recently with his mother, finding various jobs. He had been allocated the job of looking after the pigs, under John's supervision. Being of a similar age to myself, we soon found ourselves chatting happily together, despite my sometimes having difficulty in understanding him, and he likewise understanding me.

I had not been working long at Sherbourn House before I became aware of a number of differences in the general approach to farming between Westmorland and this part of Lancashire. The very fact that the skyline was devoid of any hills and those buildings which hadn't been painted showed the red bricks with which they were constructed, instantly reminded me that I was somewhere different. Gone were the grey walls, instead there were miles and miles of hedges. The cows were now all black and white of the Friesian breed, instead of the brown, white, roan and reds of the Ayrshires and shorthorns I had been used to. These breeds were still the only dairy cows about in south Westmorland in those days.

Weeks passed by, during which time I familiarised myself with my new tasks. I had been used to cattle and sheep. Now there were no sheep but there were pigs and battery hens in their place. John was a great help in my settling in. One day Tom, my work companion, announced to his boss that he would be leaving, (there didn't seem to be any recognition of term time around these parts). He was moving back down south. I don't think he had really taken to the Lancashire way of life which I suppose must have been very different from that which he had been used to in London.

Although the farm was less than a mile from the village of Eccleston, I had not yet made any attempt to make a social life for myself or meet up with anybody of my own age. It was only when a replacement for Tom was found that things took a turn in that direction.

Grayham Howard was a lean, wiry sort of a lad of a similar age to myself. He was an Ecclestonian born and bred and he knew just about everyone in the surrounding area. Whilst working with Grayham the conversation drifted round to the activities of Grayham and his friends. It was suggested that I should meet some of them and accordingly a time and a place, the local church hall, was arranged. At that particular time of my life I hadn't really had much success socially. Whilst working at Elm Tree I had joined the Preston Patrick Young Farmers Club and, whilst at Helsfell, the Burneside Young Farmers. I had taken part in a number of club activities such as stock judging, quiz nights and had been to a couple of club parties but on the whole, being of a quiet disposition, I had managed to keep a pretty low profile.

One incident whilst at the Burneside Club had badly dented my confidence. In a previous chapter, referring to when I was at Helsfell, I describe how young stock was kept in outbuildings and that the shippons were dark with no electricity. Well, unfortunately, at one point, a number of the cattle had become infected with ring worm, which is a nasty contagious skin disease which can be passed from animals to humans. Possibly because I had been unable to see my way and to see which animals were infected, I had brushed against one such beast and had got myself a dose of ring worm.

I had nasty red blotchy sores on my cheek and on my wrist which, if left untreated, would grow in widening rings (hence the name ring worm). The cure was to paint the affected parts with a purple ointment which to all intents and purposes looked worse than the sores. Usually the problem is resolved within two to three weeks.

It just so happened that the Burneside Club party was to take place on the day that the doctor pronounced me clear of the infection but insisted that I keep on with the treatment. Everyone around me insisted that I should not miss the party and so foolishly, as it turned out, I went. To this day I remember the humiliation of being treated as though I was a health hazard. I remember how when I sat down for the feed, other members sat at arm's length away from me. I suppose I shouldn't really blame them as most of them would be aware of the virility of the infection. I had tended to avoid social events since then.

Now at Eccleston, for this pre-arranged meeting, I had spruced myself up in my one and only sports jacket, gaberdine trousers, shirt and tie. I gave my shoes an extra polish and set off to walk to the village. It was not hard to find the church hall where Grayham had arranged for us to meet and, true to his word, there he was together with a few of his friends.

The first of Grayham's friends I was introduced to was Rony Danson. Rony worked on his Dad's farm up Braddley Lane. The family had come to the village only a few years previously from The Trough of Bowland. Rony was a big strong lad and, to this day, I have never met a nicer or more sincere friend. I also met Dave Smith who was an apprentice joiner and who was passionately fond of motor bikes and Norman Baxendale who was a coal miner with the nick name Wacker.

Grayham had failed to tell me exactly what the evening's entertainment was to be about. However I began to have my suspicions when a number of girls appeared on the scene. By now a side door in the church hall had been opened and, one by one, the small groups of boys and girls trooped into the building. After a few minutes a rather stout elderly little lady started off a gramophone player. She then attempted to encourage some of the boys and girls to partner up and take to the floor with some success, although no one seemed to want to be the first. As the number of dancers increased to a point that there were more people on the floor than off, I felt a wave of panic sweep over me. I had not prepared for this. What would I do if I was thrust into the arms of one of these girls and expected to dance?

As it turned out it was not a young damsel who approached me, but the rotund red faced little lady who was in charge of the gramophone. She no doubt had noticed that I was a newcomer and my obvious discomfort. My elderly partner was a Mrs. Marsden and the dance she was teaching me was a square tango. Clasping me firmly she guided me through the movements step by step: "Two, three, four, dip." she explained.

I continued to attend the church hall 'get togethers,' soon becoming quite adept at this dancing thing. I even decided that perhaps it wasn't quite such a waste of time after all. My parents were, in fact, experts on the subject of Old Tyme Dancing and were eventually to be responsible for the founding of both the Ambleside and the Windermere Old Tyme

Dance Clubs. I, no doubt, had been a bit of a disappointment to them on this front, having shown no interest. I was now beginning to see dancing as a means of getting to know a few of the girls, some of whom I must admit were beginning to attract my attention for the first time.

During the next few months I found myself with a job which I thoroughly enjoyed, a live-in home with a nice, relaxed atmosphere which I much appreciated, and I had developed a small circle of friends, both male and female. I was approaching seventeen years of age and really felt that I had entered a special phase of my life. On the farm I had made several changes - gone were the corduroy breeches - no one else in farming in these parts wore them. Instead I wore the more conventional bib and brace overalls. My lace-to-the-toe boots were no longer practical as the ammonia in the pig dung rotted the sides, causing big pieces to fall out. I now wore Wellingtons except when working in the fields, when I wore my favourite clogs.

Mine was a mixed role. Sometimes I found myself looking after pigs - some forty sows, their followers (young ones) and a couple of large boars (males). Other times I looked after the milk cows and also the battery hens. Every third weekend was the hardest when on the Sunday one person did the lot. That was hard work!

No doubt the fact that the big boss was a director of Leyland Motors had something to do with the fact that our farm had the contract to remove all the waste food from the canteens of the Leyland factory. John collected it two or three times a week. The swill was treated on the farm in two large steel troughs with steam generated by a coke fired boiler in the piggery, before it was fed to the pigs. The noise at feeding time in a piggery has to be heard to be believed. Hundreds of pigs squealing their heads off whilst trying to gain an extra mouthful more than their neighbour is ear splitting.

One amusing aspect of our swill feeding, with the swill coming directly from a canteen, was that, when one went into the building after feeding time, there would be complete silence, with most of the pigs flat out nursing a full stomach. However, you could almost guarantee to hear a metallic tinkling sound which, if followed to its source, would result in finding a pig with a knife, fork or a spoon in its mouth. The noise would be the metal rattling against the pig's teeth. We picked up literally hundreds of these utensils, none of which were any further use, as they were too badly scratched by the pig's teeth. They had, of course, been swept into the bins by careless canteen workers.

Even after handling the dairy cows for several months, I still found it difficult to recognise every one of them as they were all black and white. I had always been used to coloured cows. One quality that I did appreciate about the Friesians was that, despite being on average about half as big again as the short horns or the Ayrshires, they were far more docile and would only very rarely attempt to kick you. Ayrshires in particular often tried to kick.

On the farm there were about 2000 battery hens. These were kept in row upon row of cages. The hens, although having their movement restricted, were always kept well fed and had an unrestricted supply of fresh water. Hens kept in cages will always be a source of controversy but, for my part, I always thought that on cold wet days the hens in the battery house always looked and sounded a lot happier than those scratching about in the mud and rain and trying to find shelter.

As there was always a lot of animal feed on the farm, it was not surprising that there were also a great number of rats. This is a particularly nasty aspect of farming which is not always easy to deal with, despite having a Ministry vermin controller visiting regularly. Every so often we would organise a rat controlling session of our own. About eight o'clock in the evening one of us would creep around the buildings which housed the pigs, blocking all the drain holes. John, myself and anyone who happened to be available, would then quickly enter the building putting on all the lights and closing the door behind us.

What happened next can only be described as mayhem. Immediately you could see rats of all sizes running from one pig pen to another. Sticks would be brought down on the unfortunate vermin and the farm's wire haired terrier would wait in the central feeding passage catching any rat which attempted to cross in its mouth. It would catch them and with one nip would throw the by then dead rat high in the air and look for another one. It was all very gruesome but so necessary. If such de-ratting sessions had not taken place the rats, which caused so much damage and contamination to feed stuff, would have got completely out of hand.

It was Dave Smith, the joiner's apprentice, who first got me interested in motor bikes. He owned an old Excelsior Auto Cycle, registration number ACK 108, which had a 98cc engine. He was at that time wanting to sell it as he had bought himself a bigger machine. An auto cycle was a sort of cross between a push bike and a motor bike. Dave persuaded me to buy the machine which turned out to be only the first of many bikes which I was to own. It certainly proved to be the least powerful as it was fitted with pedals so that the rider was able to give assistance to the tiny engine when climbing steep gradients. I still have my insurance cover note for that vehicle.

It was inevitable that I soon became dissatisfied with the auto cycle's lack of power and unreliability. Just before I parted company with it, I received notice from the Ministry of Labour and National Service demanding that I report on the 18 February 1954 to Starchhouse Square in Preston to take a medical examination. Duly on that day I set off on my auto cycle in plenty of time to meet my appointment, or so I thought. I did arrive, be it a little late, but not without having to pedal half the distance with an over-heated engine which threatened to seize up at any moment. I was wet through with perspiration.

Quite a lot of my friends had been taken in to do their National Service and I was well aware that there was a strong possibility that I would be joining them. I had more or less resigned myself to have to do the same and decided that I would accept whatever fate had in store for me, despite feeling that the whole business was a waste of time as I was only interested in farming.

After reporting to a uniformed soldier sitting at a desk, myself and a number of young men who were obviously there for the same reason as myself, were told to go into a room and strip down to our birthday suits and leave our clothes on a bench at the back of the room. Next we were taken into a large room around which were positioned a number of examiners who were seated at desks. One at a time we moved round the room and were subjected to various tests, all the time, for my part, feeling as naked as the day that I was born.

As I came to one desk, behind which was sitting a rather plump middle aged man, obviously a civilian, he snapped out a command: "Against the wall." I noticed a measuring stick fastened vertically to the wall and assumed quite rightly that he was wishing to record my height. I stood with my back to the wall.

"Five feet nine" he shouted not even bothering to leave his seat. This was duly recorded by a woman sitting at the same desk. I knew that I

Norwich Union Fire Insurance Society Limited

Head Offices: NORWICH and LONDON

MOTOR COVER NOTE   N.° 741074

Date......3.5.-.1....................1954

Mr. O.R. to .....BOLTON....SIRR...GC....2 ore...HOME.FARM, ECCLESTON

having proposed for insurance in respect of the Motor Vehicle described in the Schedule below and having paid the sum of
....the risk is hereby held covered in terms of the Society's usual form of
..................THIRD...PARTY...ONLY.......................Policy applicable thereto for a period of **Thirty Days**
that is to say from......3....5....3.C....a.m/p.m. on the above date to the same time on the **Thirtieth Day** after such date unless the cover be
terminated by the Society by notice in writing in which case the insurance will thereupon cease and a proportionate part of the Annual Premium
otherwise payable for such insurance will be charged for the time the Society has been on risk.

SCHEDULE

Year	Make	Horse Power or c.c.	Value	Registration No. or Chassis or Frame No. (if known)	Used only for the following purposes
1940	EXCELSIOR AUTO-CYCLE	98 c.c.	£10.	ACK 105	(a) For the Insured's business under a " ..... licence and social, domestic and pleasure. (b) Social, Domestic and pleasure and by the Insured in person for his business, excluding hiring, goods carrying for business or commercial travelling. (c) Social, domestic and pleasure and for the Insured's business, excluding hiring, or commercial travelling. (d) Social, domestic and pleasure and for the Insured's business excluding the carriage of passengers for hire or reward. (e) Insured's business and social, domestic and pleasure — only Insured allowed to drive. (f) Agricultural and Forestry.

† Special Conditions: —

Signed....C....RIMMER....SON...L.m.Lmb.D..

ROAD TRAFFIC ACTS, 1930 to 1934, MOTOR VEHICLES AND ROAD TRAFFIC ACTS (Northern Ireland), 1930 to 1934, AND ROAD
TRAFFIC ACTS, 1933 to 1939 (Isle of Man), AND THE MOTOR TRAFFIC (Third Party Insurance), (Jersey) LAW 1948.

Certificate of Insurance

I hereby Certify that this Covering Note is issued in accordance with the provisions of Part II of the
Road Traffic Acts, 1930 to 1934 and of the Motor Vehicles and Road Traffic Acts (Northern Ireland), 1930 to 1934
and of the Road Traffic Acts, 1933 to 1939 (Isle of Man), and the Motor Traffic (Third Party Insurance), (Jersey)
Law 1948.
    NORWICH UNION FIRE INSURANCE SOCIETY LTD. (Authorised Insurers).
* Strike out descriptions which do not apply.
† State any Excess Condition, Exclusion or Driving Limitation.
    NOTE.—Where no deposit is made omit the words " and having paid the sum of " ....

General Manager

M 154-144-7-53.

was in fact five feet eleven, but thought better of trying to put him right.

Next came a one syllable command: "Eyes." I was somewhat per-plexed by this one. "Eyes," again the word was snapped out. Was this a statement, a command or a question?

"Your eyes, man," he snarled, "What colour are they?" "I don't know," I responded genuinely. I had never thought it necessary to look to find out!

"Well if you don't know who does know?" he said sarcastically.

"My mother," I said. It was the first reply that came into my head, the wisdom of which I regretted the second it left my lips.

"Well bloody well bring your mother with you next time." Combined with my stark nakedness and my apparent dependency on mother I felt decidedly humiliated, but at least it caused a laugh amongst the lads attending, albeit at my expense.

The rest of the day was taken up with different tests and interviews then finally we received a talk from a uniformed officer who was obvi-ously well up in the ranks. He welcomed us into the forces telling us to return home and wait for further instructions. Imagine my delight when, on the 23 February, I received a letter saying that: "following your medical you will rot be required for Her Majesty's Forces." I was nevertheless surprised at being placed in group 1v as I was as fit as a fiddle. I can only assume that it was my eyesight that 'saved' me.

Now knowing that I would be staying in farming for the foreseeable future, I was able to put my mind to the job in hand. It had not been easy trying to concentrate during the last few weeks. However the thought did occur to me that I was being somewhat selfish in my attitude in leaving the fighting, should it be necessary, to someone else but then it had been someone else's final decision anyway! I continued to work to the best of my ability and also started to expand my social life. In order to get around more I decided that I would require a proper motor bike. In the village there was a young chap in his early 20s who was a fitter at the local Carrington and Dewhurst factory. In his spare time he did a bit of wheeling and dealing in motor bikes.

Humphrey Moon operated from a couple of converted garden sheds at the bottom of the garden at his parent's home where he also lived. It was to Humphrey that I turned to buy my first real bike. He had about half a dozen from which to choose. The bike I chose was a single-cylinder twin-port Triumph of about 1930s vintage, quite old even then. The deal we struck was that the bike would cost me fifteen pounds but he would allow me seven pounds ten shillings for the auto cycle. I paid up and rode the bike away. One lives and learns (usually the hard way) with motor bikes. This one was no exception. The Triumph was little better than my previous machine and accordingly I decided that I needed something new or nearly new.

At this stage I turned to my Dad and on a pre-arranged day I met him in Preston at the motor cycle shop of Parish's in the centre of Preston. Dad, of course, had considerable experience of motor bikes. In the shop was a fine array of both new and second hand bikes, most of them way out of my reach price wise. However, we settled for a nearly new Velocette which had only done a couple of thousand miles. The make itself had an excellent reputation for reliability and its appearance, with it's gleaming black paint and huge fish tail exhaust caused me to become excited. I couldn't wait to get astride it and ride it back to Eccleston.

The price of my new acquisition was £115. I had saved a hundred by working evenings for a neighbouring farmer and my Dad made up the deficit of £15. Was I proud riding that bike into the farm yard that day? It never missed a beat all the way back which was something novel in itself. I loved FRN 24. I rode it for many miles including back to Preston a month after buying it to pass my test!

My world seemed complete. At work my efforts seemed to be appreciated and socially I had become quite well known amongst the locals of my age group. I had become a reasonably good dancer which made me quite popular with some of the girls. We used to go to the Saturday night dance, held in the village hall, which sported a first class Glenn Miller style band. In addition I, and one or other of my mates, visited other dance halls such as the Empress at Wigan, the Tudor at Chorley and Park Gates at Blackburn, all of which were accessible due to the new reliable motor bike.

An old adage says that 'pride always comes before a fall' and I guess I was heading in that direction. Certainly, as far as motor bikes were concerned, I had, no doubt, become just a little over confident, sometimes riding faster than conditions allowed. One day John asked me to slip into the village on my bike to get him some pipe tobacco from the village store: "Oh, and don't tell the Missus," he instructed. I believe that at that time his wife thought that he was smoking just rather more than was good for his health. A ride to the store was an opportunity to have 'a burn' on my beloved Velocette with the added bonus that I would get a chance to have a flirt with the proprietor's two daughters, the Marsden sisters, with whom I sometimes danced on Saturday nights.

The ride to the village was uneventful. The shop was too busy to allow much conversation with the girls, so I bought the tobacco and headed back home. My route took me back along Banister Lane which I particularly enjoyed because it had several bends and twists which I would take at speed, completely disregarding the words of wisdom which my father had given me when I first took to the road. He had said: "Always imagine that there is a wood wagon parked just round every bend."

It was not a wood wagon that was parked round this particular bend on that day but the local doctor's car. He was visiting a patient and had 'abandoned' his car (as doctors do) leaving it sticking out into the road. Unfortunately the bit of road on which he was parked was the bit of road which I required to complete my high speed manoeuvre. The result was that, after losing control, the bike and I parted company and I finished up with a broken collar bone which put me off work for the next five weeks. I can't remember whether John got his tobacco or not!

I travelled to Windermere by train the day following my accident and spent the whole of my recuperation period there. During this time my Dad persuaded me that, when I got back to work, the best course of action would be to fit a sidecar to my bike. I believe he, in his way, was attempting to slow me down.

As the time grew nearer for me to return to Eccleston I began to regret the weak moment in which I had agreed to fit a sidecar. Surely side cars were for grandads? Then I started thinking about the advantages. I would have somewhere to put my wet weather gear and I would be able to ask a girl if I could take her home from a dance without first going outside to see if it was raining - yes, perhaps it might not be such a bad move after all!

Soon after I returned to Eccleston I found myself back down Humphrey Moon's garden where, as luck would have it, he had just the thing - a tidy one seater affair with a windscreen and a black canvas hood which was held down with press studs. Humphrey provided the fixing brackets which I believe he made at his place of work, a price was agreed and the 'chair' was fitted.

One of the first outings with my newly fitted out combination came when my friend Dave Smith suggested that we should go dancing to the Floral Hall at Southport which was about an hour's ride away. I had never been to Southport and I doubt if Dave had either, but we had heard that it was a good place if you liked to dance. Now, I thought, this is where the sidecar comes into its own. This would be the big test! The ride to Southport was uneventful, a little slower than I had been used to, but then that surely was the object of the exercise? We were able to park almost outside our venue (those were the days!). Dave climbed out a little chilled but ready for action. I threw my heavy great coat into the cab and my wellingtons into the tiny boot in the rear of the sidecar and in we went.

As we had anticipated the evening went well. There were plenty of pretty girls with whom to dance, all new faces, plus a wonderful band playing all the latest tunes. The evening was a great success and we had about an hour's ride home ahead of us. I also remembered that I had to be up and working by six o'clock and that was now not far away. Whilst we had been enjoying ourselves in the dance hall the weather had taken a change for the worse and we had to make a dash for our transport. Quickly Dave unbuttoned the hood and jumped in. I pulled on my heavy great coat whilst at the same time refastening the hood over Dave's head. Kicking off my shiny dancing shoes I pulled on my wellingtons which had been safely stored away in the most useful little boot on the side car.

"Aaaagh!!" my right foot was suddenly immersed in ice cold water. Water had run off the hood, down the gap between the boot lid and the body of the side car and into my neatly stored wellington. I had a miserable ride home with my right foot getting more and more frozen as the miles went by. I dropped Dave off at his home and then made my way the last couple of miles home, wet to the skin and somewhat disillusioned with my first major trip out with my new outfit. I crawled into bed knowing that in just over four hours I would be up again. Was it all worth it? Of course it was!

Side cars didn't last long after that. When the concerns over the broken collar bone incident had died down and had been more or less forgotten, I quietly reverted back to solo. Some while later, after I had managed a period without incidents, my friend Norman Baxendale, 'Wacker' to his mates, approached me saying that one of his coal miner pals had seen my Velocette and had expressed a wish to do a deal with me. He owned a 500cc Norton International which was a semi-racing bike. The prospect of owning such a machine immediately caused great excitement. I knew the model and had always admired them. I guess my ego must have been working overtime. I knew the macho status which went with owning such a bike and, as you the reader will have already guessed, I went ahead and did a deal.

Another young chap I made friends with had a name I had never previously heard of: John Proudlove. He was a cabinet maker and was engaged to a young lady from the village. John and his betrothed had what seemed to me, in those days, a strange sort of an arrangement. He would go round the dance halls at weekends, often with me, and during the week he would keep his fiancee company.

New Year's Eve 1956 was fast approaching and I had told my friends that I intended to travel to Windermere to see the New Year in. Despite the fact that the weather was bitterly cold at that time, it had remained dry. It was a fair trek and I would have to work until six o'clock that evening, (cows don't recognise New Year's Eve), wash and change into my biking gear, and ride the best part of 60 miles.

My friend John Proudlove heard about my plans and expressed a wish to accompany me, to which I agreed. Everything went according to plan. John, no doubt with his girl's permission (very strange), was ready waiting wrapped up against the cold and, like myself wore a crash helmet, which I had loaned him. We rode off into the dark night. Despite there being no motorways in those days, we made good progress. The big Norton was one of the fastest bikes around at that time and we soon arrived at my parent's home, cold but full of optimism for the night's entertainment .

I knew a lot of people from around the Bowness and Windermere area, including quite a lot of girls. The night was very much a success and both John and I agreed that the long cold journey had been worthwhile. As could be expected, it was after one in the morning when we finally crashed out, only to hear the sound of Dad's borrowed alarm clock going off what seemed like five minutes later. I had agreed with my boss that I would work that morning doing only the essential milking and feeding. There was no alternative but to haul myself from my bed and wake my companion.

After a quick cup of tea and a slice of toast, we crept as quietly as we could from the house and wheeled the bike from the back yard where it had been left over night. We would free wheel the short distance from the house to the main Bowness to Windermere road. The sound of a hot rod Norton starting up was not what the neighbours wanted to hear so early in the morning. The bike behaved impeccably and started the first time I let the clutch out, which was a blessing as there were times when no amount of kick starting or pushing would have the desired effect.

All went according to plan until we started to descend the hill known as the 'House of Correction,' named after the prison and work house which once stood there, down into Kendal. As I rounded the bend not far from the top of the hill, I was met with two bright beams of light which immediately blinded me. The lights on the Norton were not particularly good and did little to assist me to get my bearings.

Desperately I tried to see round the vehicle in front of me which I knew was nearly upon us. I now had little idea as to my own position on the road. Instinctively I turned to the golden rule, keep to the left of a white light and to the right of a red light. BANG, I hit something hard. It turned out to be the near side curb which on impact because of the slight angle at which I hit it, took the front wheel right from underneath me.

My next memory was of sliding down the pavement on my back side which was getting hotter and hotter as layers of cloth disintegrated underneath me. My passenger must have suffered similarly but amazingly neither of us were any the worse, with nothing other than a slight bruising and some gravel rash to parts of our anatomy. The bike meanwhile had slid to a halt and was now laying on its side with the throttle wide open and making a noise worthy of a T.T. rider. I got to my feet and stopped the bike's engine expecting to see the windows of the houses which lined the street being flung open and irate occupants shouting at us for ruining their sleep - miraculously, not a soul stirred.

The cause of our misfortune was a milk man who had been driving up the wrong side of the road: "As he always did," he assured us. When asked why he had not used his indicators to signal his intentions his reply was quite simple: "They're buggered!" After I pointed out that such behaviour was against the law and that I would now require his name and address 'should there be any trouble.' His reply I found even more amazing than his earlier remarks, considering that he had caused what could have been a very nasty accident. "Oh I won't cause any trouble!" I was anxious to get on our way but feared that the bike may have suffered damage. However a quick examination revealed no obvious faults so I fired it up and we got on our way.

I was not very popular when I arrived back at the farm that morning about an hour late. Quite rightly John Schofield had little sympathy for my problems as they had meant that all the extra work had fallen on him. I suppose the whole adventure had been on too tight a schedule and had left no room for any mishaps.

BACK HOME AGAIN

To this day I really don't know why I left Eccleston. I had been happy at work, the people I had come into contact with outside of working hours had always accepted me and, looking back, I would say that those were possibly some of the happiest and least complicated days of my young life. As I was more mobile I had been using more of my weekends off to return to Windermere where I would meet up with quite a few of my friends, some I had gone through school with, and some of whom, like myself, shared an interest in motor bikes. I suppose this link-up with my old friends was the biggest influence in my decision to move back up north. There was another factor to consider, the Schofields had added a little boy named David to their family and I probably felt that I had intruded in their lives for long enough. After asking my parents if I could move back in with them and being told that they were more than happy for me to do so, I made up my mind I would make the move.

The advert in the *Westmorland Gazette* read: 'tractor man required for mixed farm, live out, reply to John Jackson, Gowan Bank, tel...'' Gowan Bank I knew was a farm situated mid-way between the villages of Windermere and Staveley on the route south. The details I learned from a phone call were that the farm was owned by one John Knape, who was a solicitor working in the Lancaster and Morecambe area, and John Jackson was the farm manager. Besides Gowan Bank, which was itself a sizeable holding, John Knape owned another small farm, called Greenhills, at the nearby village of Crook.

An interview was arranged when I met up with John Jackson, or Johnny, as he preferred to be called. We discussed the possibility of working at Gowan Bank literally over a five barred gate. Johnny, a lean but powerful looking chap in his mid 30s explained the 'set up'. He lived in a cottage with his wife and four young children. Another cottage was allocated to the cow man Bob Stables and the third building in the yard, a big house, was used at weekends by the owner Mr. Knape to accommodate his teenage family.

The main concerns at my interview seemed to be my reliability. Was I good at getting up? This was a question which one always expected to be asked when applying for a position in farming. Next came the obligatory question: "Who did you work for last?" Obviously my most recent employer had been someone of whom Johnny would have no knowledge so I explained that my previous employer had been Johnny Gibson. "Well I'll get in touch with him and let you know," were the last words of that meeting.

I had always believed when working for Johnny Gibson that, despite my best efforts, I had never been able to satisfy his insatiable desire for results. Imagine my surprise when Johnny Jackson phoned me at my parent's home to offer me the job. The response from Helsfell had been excellent. Johnny Gibson had given me a first class reference - I must have done something right!

I accepted the job and, after my weekend break, I returned to Eccleston. This time with no feeling of apprehension which I had experienced before giving in my notice at Helsfell. I think in a nice sort of a way the Schofields were probably quite happy to have me move on. They would once more have their home to themselves with no more exuberant teenager coming home in the early hours of the morning. Though I tried hard to keep quiet there must have been numerous occasions when I woke them from their sleep.

I served a short period and then the day came when, with the help of my Dad and his large Humber car, all my accumulated belongings were transported back to Bowness. Dad was now running his own one-man taxi business, hence the big Humber, which he used for weddings, funerals and for general hire. The car was loaded up, I said my goodbyes, started the bike and followed Dad up the cinder road for the last time. I didn't stop behind him for long, the big Norton was not happy at slow speeds when it tended to miss fire and run erratically.

I settled in back at home very easily. I would be leaving the house very early each morning in time to start work at six o'clock on the farm. I had about four miles to ride first so I would have to get myself up at about 5am, swallow a cup of tea, make sufficient sandwiches to see me through the day, fill a couple of flasks, and get on my way. It wasn't going to be easy but I knew I could do it. Meal breaks turned out to be quarter of an hour for breakfast, half an hour for lunch and another quarter of an hour in the afternoon - in other words, barring meal times, I would be working a twelve hour day!

As previously stated, the two cottages were for the manager and the cow man and no provision had been made for out workers so I had to eat my packed meals in the 'provender house' (cattle feed store). In the provender house there was neither heating nor seating. I had to make do with perching on a full sack of cattle feed and put up with the fact that the room temperature was often little different to the temperature outside. These conditions didn't bother me. I recognised they were a step down from those which I had been used to at my previous place of work but I was young and fit and didn't give much thought to the matter.

It was now the spring of 1956. I had just turned 21 and was pretty confident in myself and my abilities. The work which I was doing was similar to work done on any other mixed farm in the area and, despite the fact that the job advert had specifically stated that a tractor driver was required, I was doing a bit of everything around the farm. That was just how I liked it!

In addition to the employees already mentioned, the farm also employed an old chap by the name of Willie Dodd. Willie was at that time just short of retirement age. He was bent with years of toil and was of a scrawny, ancient appearance. He had an aura of life in bygone days and I liked him a lot. Willie had been in farm service all his life, working on farms in and around Westmorland. He had no doubt seen farming in its hardest days when there was little mechanisation and endured conditions which would be considered unthinkable today.

On one occasion when Willie was being chastised for something or other by the farm manager, he expressed his annoyance by stating: "I'll have you know that I was, at one time, the most expensive farm worker in Westmorland!" This implied that he was, at one time, the highest paid farm worker in the county, but did not express the fact too well. "You still are the most expensive man in Westmorland," replied Johnny Jackson, "Get on with your work!"

One day Willie and I were sent to remove some stones which had been hand gathered and left in little heaps on a steep hillside. To do this job we were using a little grey Ferguson tractor, the type which could be seen on farms in any part of the country. Behind this tractor we would use a converted horse drawn cart which now sported a wooden draw bar where previously there had been the shafts. Stone picking, as the job is called, occurs every spring. The frost of the winter forces stones up out of the ground. These have to be removed in order that they don't get caught up in the hay making machinery and cause damage. The field in which we would be working sloped quite steeply from the top to the bottom. The field culminated in a rocky outcrop of waste land which was almost vertical followed by a narrow strip of land little wider than the average garden lawn and then a dry stone wall.

Heap by heap we shovelled the stones into the trailer. Willie shovelled and I helped him as well as jumping on and off the tractor to move it along. We were making good progress. The Fergie tractors were not fitted with a hand brake, but instead relied on the driver pressing down on a sort of ratchet device with his toe whilst depressing the foot brake, which itself was just a crude metal bar. It was very primitive but usually quite effective. However, on this occasion I must have failed to catch the teeth on the ratchet, or perhaps I was in just in too much of a hurry.

Suddenly I became aware that the tractor was moving of its own accord and was gradually starting to turn down hill. Instinctively I dropped the shovel and leapt forward with the intention of climbing astride the tractor. But, to do this, it was necessary to go between the front wheels and the larger back ones, put your foot on the metal foot peg, and swing your other leg over the main body of the tractor. Unfortunately on this particular occasion, the metal caulker on my clog slipped off the metal foot rest and I was left hanging, my left hand grasping the steering wheel and both my legs dragging on the ground almost under the back axle and only inches from the rotating near side rear wheel.

Here I was, half on and half off an out of control tractor, only seconds away from plunging over a precipice. I had to act fast! With one huge effort, still grasping the steering wheel with my left hand and the steel seat pan with my right, I hauled myself up and managed to get into the normal driving position. Only then did I realise that it was too late to try to stop the tractor and over the edge we went. Careering down the face, the wheels hitting and bouncing of the rocks, I hung on for grim death. I was showered with stones as the trailer draw bar snapped and the trailer flew over my head, eventually finishing up on top of the wall below.

The final outcome was that, despite my frightening trip down the rocks, quite remarkably the tractor stayed right side up. I was left still astride the little Fergie, shaking uncontrollably from my experience, the stub of the broken draw bar still attached and stones scattered all around. I must have sat there for a couple of minutes when, upon looking up at the route which I had just traversed, I became aware of poor Willie peering down at me in disbelief. I am sure he expected to see me lying dead. Something must have been smiling on me from above that day.

I am glad to say my run-away adventure had no lasting effects on me - it was certainly due to good luck more than anything I had done to save the situation. I received a rebuke for carelessness for failing to secure the foot brake but, apart from that, the incident was soon forgotten.

I was working long hours but still found the time and energy to attend a hunt ball or two. My favourite night was Saturday when I would go to the Palace, a dance hall in North Terrace, Bowness, where the dance band the Baronettes, played on a regular basis. Every second, or sometimes third, week I would take from midday Saturday until Monday morning off. The Sunday morning lie in was most welcome, especially if I had been out dancing both Friday and Saturday nights.

My Dad's taxi business was doing well and he had become quite well established. Mother helped him by taking bookings over the phone. Unfortunately I wasn't able to help much as I wasn't at home during the day, plus the fact that I hadn't yet got myself a car driver's licence. As well as myself being at home my youngest sister had not yet flown the nest. Both my twin Margaret and my elder sister Marcia were now married. They had had a double wedding and were now living away at Sutton Coldfield and Leeds respectively.

Marion at this time was courting a young chap who worked for Mould and Bloomer's, a private forestry management company. One of the estates which they managed was the Belle Isle estate. Belle Isle is the mile long and longest island on Windermere lake. John, Marion's boyfriend worked on the estate, which consisted of the island and several miles of forest stretching along the Furness fells from the ferry to Wray village, not far from the northern end of the lake.

It was during conversations with John about various aspects of forestry, that I found out that Mould and Bloomer were looking for an additional worker. John suggested that, because of my background of physical work, I might be a good candidate for the job. At first I didn't give much thought to the matter but I had noticed that John seemed to have a lot of free time. He started at eight in the morning, finished at five, and had every weekend off and was not far behind me when it came to pay day.

The more I thought about what had been discussed, the more appealing the job became. I would have more time to go places on my motorbike with my friends. I had recently exchanged my Norton for a Matchless G9 Twin, a beautifully smooth-running superbike of its day. I would also have time to pursue other interests which I never had time for. Another concern had also been bothering me, on farm worker's wages I was never ever going to be able to buy my own farm, even if I worked until I was a hundred. So why then was I working these long hours and weekends? Whether my reasoning was sound or not, I decided that I would let fate decide my immediate future, so I applied for the job and got it.

BELLE ISLE ESTATE, GIRLS AND THE BAND

It was just after Christmas 1957, I had only been at Gowan Bank for about eight months and was now leaving to take up another job. I didn't feel bad that I was making the move after a comparatively short period with the farm. In fact, after Helsfell, I never allowed myself to feel in any way guilty of letting my employer down as I have always given 100 per cent of my ability and only once since walked out on a job. I have always felt that I owe it to myself to make the best of whatever resources or availability is around to benefit me and mine!

The foreman forester for Belle Isle Estates was a chap, then in his mid 50s, called George Carleton. He and his 28-year-old son, 'young George' or 'Geordie' as he was more frequently called, were, besides my sister's boyfriend, the only workers employed by the estate. Old George had been quite a tall chap when younger but endless toil in the woods in adverse weather had caused him to have a pronounced stoop. His whole body had stiffened up, leaving him with a rather strange rolling gait when walking. George was an old man before his time but, despite his lack of mobility, he was able to complete the tasks which his job demanded in his ponderous way.

Geordie was a big chap, broad shouldered and lean. He had worked with his father in the woods since leaving school, apart from a short spell in the Army. As with many father/son working relationships, there were times when they didn't always see eye to eye. Not many days were to pass when the two didn't fall out over a difference in a work related matter.

Harrowslack, the 'hub' of most of the forestry activities, consisted of a house and a cottage. George and his wife Annie, a rotund cheerful little lady, together with their son Brian, who was an apprentice boat builder, lived in the large house and Geordie, his wife Joan and their baby son Terry, lived in the cottage which was tucked in behind the big house. From the front step of George's house, you could see a fantastic view looking easterly to Belle Isle, Bowness and the hills beyond. Below the houses, down nearer the lake, a large corrugated barn like building stood. This was the saw-mill where, on particularly wet days, we would work sawing huge tree trunks into planks, making fencing posts or sawing off cuts into firewood or pit props to be used in the coal mines. To saw these large pieces of timber we used a rack bench which was effectively a moving

The author, aged about 22, pictured at Harrowslack Saw Mill.

table with a slot running the full length through the middle. This allowed the circular saw blade to slice off planks as the table was wound forward by the person in charge.

On most working days, the team would travel to one or other sections of the forest areas which constituted the Belle Isle Estate. Very occasionally this would include the island itself, which was more or less covered in woodland, apart from the only house on this mile long piece of land. The house is unique in that it was built entirely round - every room had a radiused outer wall. This was the home of the owner of the estate, a Mr. Edward Chance-Curwen. The Curwen family had made their fortune coal mining in north west Cumberland.

Looking back on our daily excursions into the woods now makes me smile. As a rule, Geordie would drive the large 'Fordson' tractor which was fitted with a powerful timber winch, hooked on behind was an old converted horse cart, similar to the one which I had nearly wrecked in my runaway escapade at Gowan Bank. Into this trailer would be loaded all the saws, axes, billhooks, chains and other equipment which we were likely to need for the day's work. It also contained our boxes of sandwiches, flasks etc. - there were no snack bars in the middle of the forest.

Now, the amusing facts - as well as ourselves perched up on the tractor mud-guards, into the trailer would jump a large lurcher dog call John Boy, a pet sheep which had been reared by Annie, George's wife, and a large black cat which curiously had six toes on each foot. These animals would appear from nowhere when they heard the tractor bark into life and jump, with no extra encouragement, into the back of the trailer. They would travel to wherever we were working, hang around all day and then travel back late in the afternoon. Often our route would take us along the road by the lake shore and it was amusing to see the looks on the faces of visitors when they saw us pass as we looked something like a mini Noah's Ark.

One thing that I found appealing about forestry work was that it was always varied. Sometimes we would be thinning the plantations (roughly speaking this is the cutting down and removing of every other tree). Some plantations had grown together so tightly that they were nearly choking each other. By cutting out half of them it gave those remaining a chance to grow. I was always fascinated with the change. The breeze would once again pass through the trees and the sound was almost like a sigh of relief at their new freedom. At times it was very eerie. Often as we passed through the trees we would catch sight of deer, usually the little roe deer, but occasionally a big red stag, which in rutting (mating) time would make a tremendous noise, calling its harem together and warning off rival stags.

Other jobs, such as planting saplings, bracken cutting and ring fencing, added to the variety. It was necessary to erect a high fence round an area which was to be planted, hence the name 'ring fence'. Had you just gone ahead without a fence, the deer would have eaten the tops out of the young plants as fast as you could have put them in the ground. Deer invariably do their raiding of plantations during hours of darkness. Planting was done in the winter months and then, as the tiny young trees start to grow in the spring, it is necessary to cut the bracken from around them. This was done, of course, by hand. Each worker would have a thin stick, about two feet long, which had a fork in the end, making it rather like a long handled catapult. With the stick each young tree was located in amongst the bracken, pinned down with the forked end, and then with a sickle (a sharp, curved blade) all the bracken around the tiny tree was cut off at ground level. The process was repeated travelling along the rows of plants. Very occasionally a plant got chopped off, but only occasionally, or there would have been questions asked.

Bracken cutting was possibly my least favourite job. The worst aspect was that by chopping off the brackens and weeds you also disturbed all the insects which lived in these plants, such as ants, flies and midges which would bite incessantly and cause irritation to your skin.

One job which I particularly enjoyed was the cutting down and extraction of thinnings. The first thinning was undertaken around fifteen to twenty years after planting. In the case of larch or spruce plantations, the trees would be by then about 20-25 feet high and six to eight inches thick at the base. Light weight, one-man operated power saws were just starting to become available and George had managed to persuade the estate managers to provide one. The one we had was a Swedish make called Jobu, and it was quite an innovation.

When cut, the thinnings were dragged from amongst the standing trees by hand with a short light weight chain with a noose on the end. This was slipped over the thick end of the thinning which by then had been 'denuded' of its branches, leaving only a 20-25 foot pole which was then physically dragged to the nearest clearing, using a short wooden stick for a handle to avoid the chain cutting into your hands. On the level ground a great deal of effort was required, but on the steeply sloping ground you would find yourself running to get out of the way as the tree gathered speed and slid after you. This task either fell to myself or Geordie; George was not mobile enough.

After sufficient thinnings had been gathered together in a clearing they would be loaded onto a two wheeled timber bogie dragged behind one of the early T.V.O. (tractor vapourising oil) Fordson Majors down to the nearest main road. It was from this point that the thinnings would be re-loaded onto a timber wagon. Some would end up as pit props in the coal mines, some were made into fence posts while the thinnest went to the garden centres for ornamental fencing and the like. Nowadays a lot of young people talk about going to the gym for a work out. I doubt if many of them would bother if they had a job involving dragging lengths of timber around on the end of a chain all day for a living!

As we moved around the forest, we would establish temporary base camps. A sort of crude hut was made by driving a few posts into the ground and covering the roof and the sides in with a few sheets of corrugated iron. When a heavy downpour occurred, we would retreat to this shelter which was always damp and draughty. Sometimes the wind would change direction and drive the smoke from our nearby camp fire into our hut making us cough and our eyes water.

George was the consummate woodsman. He would find a nearby stream or even the merest trickle of water, form a funnel from a bit of tree bark and place it in such a way that it would direct the water into a small kettle strategically placed underneath. Later, at break times, he would boil the kettle on a constantly burning wood fire. I wasn't very keen on George's tea, it was usually strong, black and rather unpalatable.

One day, after eating my sandwiches and swallowing a cup full of George's strong brew, I decided to use the rest of my break to have a wander further up the wood. Following the tiny stream which ran past our camp, and from which George had been drawing the water to make our drinks, I travelled up through the closely grown larch trees which I knew we would soon be thinning and thought to myself how much more easily they would thrive when we had sorted them out. Suddenly about half a mile from our camp I was horrified to come across the rotting carcass of a roe deer lying right in the middle of the stream. My stomach turned to think that we had been drinking water which had first passed through this putrid mass. Needless to say I reported the matter as soon as I returned to where we were working. George just smiled: " It'll be alright, it'll add a bit of body to it," was his comment. I stuck to my flask from that day on!

Working together in a small group, isolated from others, relies on each member being able to get along with the others. In our group's case John, my sister's boyfriend, had left Belle Isle employ soon after I had started, (not in any way because of me I hasten to add) and there was now only George, his son Geordie, and myself to carry out all the work. It was a case of each of us having to rely on the others' strengths and knowledge, not least where safety was concerned. I was short on the experience side but prided myself that I was quick and eager to learn, attributes which I think both of my work mates seemed to recognise. I enjoyed a very good relationship with both of them. Both father and son were well versed in all aspects of forestry work and I do believe that therein lay the one flaw in the operation.

It was an unfortunate fact that on occasions things didn't always run too smoothly. George, with all his years of experience, seemed to find it hard to accept that his son was similarly capable of tackling jobs and finishing them to a satisfactory conclusion, albeit by going about it a different way. One day when we had collected together a large number of thinnings which lay in a rather inaccessible part of the forest, the two men were discussing the best route to get them out. Geordie, who after all would be driving the tractor, wanted to take a certain route, and his father another, at the same time he inferred that Geordie didn't know what he was doing.

An argument ensued in which young Geordie, uncharacteristically in a fit of rage, hurled the axe which he had been using to 'bough out' thinnings, as far as he could down the wood and stormed off in the opposite direction. Some minutes later the father turned to me with a mischievous grin on his face: "Daft bugger, we'll see him hingin up in a tree yan of these days." I have to say that such shows of disharmony, however infrequent, used to make me, not wishing to take sides, feel decidedly uncomfortable and unhappy at George's apparent indifference to his son's feelings. The dreadful irony of this account came home to me when, a number of years later, I heard that Geordie had in fact taken his own life.

About the time that I had started on the forestry, I had taken advantage of the fact that my Dad's saxophone was lying unused in its case. Dad had retired from playing with Arnold Baron's dance band when he started his taxi business. I hadn't touched a violin since leaving school to start farm work when I was fifteen, but with music seemingly still in my blood, I had started of my own accord to teach myself the sax. Like my father, Arnold had left the music business and was now the landlord of the Brook Side Inn, in Old Lake Road, Windermere.

Following the retirement of Arnold and my father, the remaining players continued to entertain the public under the name the Baronettes, travelling to the various villages around the district for hunt balls. They also still played regularly every Saturday night at the Palace in North Terrace, Bowness.

It was whilst on one of my Saturday nights out at the Palace that, during the interval, I struck up a conversation with Desmond Atkinson, the alto sax player with the band. I had known Desmond from being a small child and, during the conversation, I told him of my efforts to learn to play using Dad's sax and that I had practiced a number of popular tunes of the day. Desmond's response was that I should take my instrument along and sit in with the band the following Saturday. Knowing that my instrument was a tenor and that Desmond's was an alto I was aware that if I could play sufficiently well, there was a fair chance that it would sound quite nice. I didn't need asking twice! With the agreement of the rest of the members of the band, I arranged to have a go before the crowd arrived the following Saturday for a trial. No doubt my Dad's reputation as a musician had influenced the arrangement!

The following Saturday, true to my promise, I turned up at the dance hall with my saxophone nicely polished. Not quite knowing what to expect, I had brought with me a few small band scores (sheet music written to accommodate the instruments of a small band) which I had sent away for. After handing out the appropriate copy to each player, I settled down ready for my very first attempt at playing with a real live band, in the knowledge that at least I had practiced my part over and over at home.

After playing a few numbers I was pleasantly surprised as to how well my contribution had fit in with the overall sound. The rest of the band must also have felt the same way because I was asked to join them again the following Saturday night, which was just what I had hoped for. Accordingly the next few Saturdays came and went, and I found myself staying on stage for longer and longer sessions. By this time I was beginning to play from the band's own sheet music and was becoming reasonably competent. Not surprisingly there came a day when I was asked if I was prepared to accept a booking for one evening during the week. I really felt my efforts were beginning to pay off. I would be paid £2 for about four hours work and it was work which was more like pleasure - this couldn't be bad! I was only getting £8 for a full week's work in the forest.

Each morning, to get to my job at Harrowslack, it was necessary to cross the lake from the eastern shore to the western side by ferry boat. I had the journey timed to a T so that I left the house, had a swift ride on the Matchless, and arrived just in time to catch the ferry. On a few occasions as I rode off the boat, amongst the people boarding for the return journey, there was a rather pretty girl. But, as the boat did a quick turn around, I never got the chance to speak to her. This daily sighting went on for weeks, until one night I attended a dance held in Hawkshead Village Hall. I was there not in the role of musician playing in the band, but simply as one of the lads out for a night's entertainment. I had not been in the hall for long when my attention was diverted from watching and listening to the band, (playing in a band myself had focused my interest in musicians in general) and I became aware that one of the girls on the opposite side of the dance floor was the girl who I saw each morning boarding the ferry.

As the band struck up I approached the young lady and I asked her for a dance, an invitation which she accepted with a pleasant smile. I was pretty sure that she had recognised me, but in all fairness, if she hadn't, it would be understandable as she had only seen me with my crash helmet on, at least as far as I was aware. During the evening I spent quite a bit of time talking to this pretty girl who, it turned out, was called Brenda. We spent so much time together that, when the band announced that they were about to play the last waltz, she agreed to dance it with me and then allow me to walk her the short distance home.

The following Monday morning, on alighting from the ferry on the western shore, there was Brenda waiting to board. On this occasion I was prepared - I had positioned myself and my bike in such a way that allowed me a couple of minutes, time enough to arrange to pick her up

The Jack Hartley Quartet at Windermere Hydro.

on a certain night and take her to the cinema in Kendal. The film *Rock around The Clock* made round the American band Bill Haley and His Comets had just taken Britain by storm, and was being shown at the Kendal Palladium. It appeared that Brenda was as keen as I was to see it.

On the appointed night I crossed the ferry for the second time that day, and rode the four miles or so to Hawkshead where Brenda was waiting, suitably wrapped up in her warmest coat. I had acquired a spare crash helmet which I had taken with me, and which Brenda donned with some amusement. The journey to Kendal was pleasant, the temperature was just a little below freezing, but at least the weather was dry. I suppose the film lived up to our expectations, I don't really remember, but I do remember the cold ride home. Whilst we had been in the cinema the temperature outside had dropped several degrees. I had to ride with extreme caution as patches of ice had appeared. By the time we had ridden the near twenty miles back to Hawkshead, we were both frozen to the marrow.

Arriving back at her home Brenda, knowing that I still had the journey back to Windermere to make, asked me if I would like a hot drink and assured me that it would be OK with her parents. It was an invitation which I was happy to accept. Brenda produced two mugs of hot tea and then went up stairs presumably to inform her parents that she had arrived back safely.

I had been in the house for about five minutes and had just started my drink when I heard steps, which I presumed to be Brenda's, descending the staircase. "Do you usually come into people's houses uninvited?" I spun round to see the figure of a man in a one piece vest and long john combination standing at the bottom of the stairs. "When I want someone in my house I ask them in," he said. I was completely taken aback but still managed a reply: "I'm sorry sir, Brenda thought it would be alright, but I'll go if you don't want me here." He, after a little more remonstrating, and with Brenda near to tears, suggested that I finish my tea and disappeared back upstairs.

By now I had taken stock of the situation and had started to see the funny side of things. It was midnight and I was in a stranger's house against his wishes and he had been standing there in his underwear remonstrating with me. I had been respectful but that didn't stop me smiling to myself as I drove back round the head of Windermere lake on my journey home.

I saw Brenda again the following morning and she apologised for getting me into a situation with her father. I assured her there was no apology needed and she told me that her Dad had actually said that he liked me. Strange world isn't it? I did see Brenda again on a number of occasions, she really was a sweet girl, but eventually we went our own separate ways.

GETTING FRUITY AND CATTLE FEED

The spring of 1959 came after a long, cold, wet winter. Mud and ice had made it difficult to extract timber and thinnings from the woods and repeatedly dragging thinnings down the forest tracks had made them into a quagmire. Now the better weather had arrived, trees were shooting out their new growth and the larch trees in particular looked magical with their pale green needles forming an almost translucent canopy over head. The brackens were bursting from the ground in their relentless efforts to smother everything else that dared to try to take root any where near them, including the tree saplings which we had planted in the back end. We would soon again be slashing them back in the annual fight for control.

Much as I enjoyed working out in the open air (I hadn't really experienced anything else since leaving school) I had felt for some time that there was something missing, but I wasn't able to put a finger on it. My Dad told me that he had had a conversation with the manager of W. B. Andersons, a wholesale fruit and vegetables distribution company, which was based at the railway station next to the taxi rank. The manager, whose name was Alan Black, had told Dad that he was urgently looking for a wagon driver salesman. Dad, who said that I was 21 and keen on driving, suggested that I at least have a talk with him. I had at this stage not long passed my driving test in Dad's car, and jumped at every opportunity presented to me to get behind a wheel.

After my meeting with Alan Black I became convinced that the 'something' that was missing from my normal daily life was quite simply people. Since leaving school as a shy retiring sort of a lad, I had gained confidence enormously. Working away in woods and fields, often on my own, sometimes with the same one or two people, I was not satisfying the side of me which needed contact with different people. I needed more challenges and this was certainly going to be a challenge. Was I up to it I thought?

Despite the fact that I hadn't driven a vehicle of any size, and I knew nothing whatsoever about selling, I was in touch with Alan Black and agreed to take the job. Had I been married I might have had to think a little bit harder before agreeing, but I didn't have a mortgage and had only myself to support. On the first day of my new job, I was sent out with one of the established drivers, a chap called Reggie Milburn.

Reggie had been with the company for several years. Incidentally the firm's claim was that they distributed fruit and vegetables from the Mersey to the Clyde. This was, of course, only one of the company's smaller branches .

The vehicle allocated to Reggie was a Guy Otter, which I suppose would carry about four tons, and must have been at least ten years old even then. Before moving off, the vehicle was stacked high with sacks of potatoes, crates of vegetables and boxes of fruit. Up to then I had never realised just how many varieties of these products there were. I had always believed that an orange was an orange and an apple was an apple, and that was that - how wrong I was!

As soon as the Guy was loaded and we had collected price lists and invoice books from the office, we set off on the pre-determined route. We would be calling on shops, travelling retail fruiterers, hotels and school canteens and in fact any establishment which was likely to require a reasonable amount of the products which we had to sell. Slowly we worked our way round on this my first day, and the next day was exactly the same, except in a different area.

As we visited the various establishments, Reggie introduced me to the proprietors making it known that I would be the person who would be looking after them in the future. It was then that it really began to sink in how responsible a job I had taken on. I was going to be the link between the company and the customer. It was going to be my responsibility to see that they got the right produce and they would lose out if I made mistakes. I was going to have to learn and learn quickly!

After four days with my tutor at hand, I was allocated a vehicle, a little Guy Chieftain, very similar in size to Reggie's wagon. I remember the radiator sported a Red Indian chief's head on top of the filler cap which I eventually painted in bright enamel colours. It looked fantastic and drew a lot of attention - but I digress! From this point I was on my own. Weeks and months went by. The first few days had been difficult but on the whole I soon got into the swing of things. By far the hardest part of the job was the fact that the prices of the produce changed daily. Head Office would phone up each morning and notify the manager of the changes, he in turn would give us a price list which we were supposed to then memorise. Our clients were not impressed if we had to constantly refer to our list!

I was with Andersons for about two years during which time I probably met more people than I had met in the previous twenty years of my life. This side of the job really suited me. However, the fruit side of the business (and let's face it, that's what the job was all about) was, or a part of it was, a constant irritation. Many of our customers were small one man businesses. I would come along and sell them, say, a box of pears on a Thursday or a Friday. If they had not sold them all by closing time on Saturday, come Monday morning the pears would be running out of the box. Perhaps I was over sensitive but, as I knew they had probably lost money on the deal, I would feel guilty. Ridiculous, I would tell myself, but with the next half box of rotting fruit, I would feel just the same.

Just around the corner from the shop of one of my customers, who fell into the category of small shopkeepers to which I have just alluded, was the warehouse of Whittakers, the hay, straw and animal feed merchant. It was a firm of long-standing and was old-fashioned in its approach to business, as were its farmer customers. I happened to be aware that Whittakers were in need of a delivery man and on this particular day, when I had been looking at a box of over ripe fruit, I slipped round the corner and had a discussion with the manager, a Mr. Key.

John Key was a particularly nice chap. He was an ex-farmer, having given up farming when an accident with a bull had left him with a damaged back making it impossible to continue. I didn't take a lot of convincing that the job on offer would suit me. The thought that I would once more be dealing with the farming community rather appealed to me and there would be no more worrying about rotten fruit! I left John Key agreeing that I would serve notice at Andersons and start work for Whittakers immediately afterwards.

Whittakers had only recently been bought out by the Liverpool family firm of Samuel Stergen and Sons. The staff at Windermere consisted of John Key, an elderly chap who I can only remember as Albert and now myself. I replaced a young chap who had only just left to work for the local council on road maintenance. Part of my job would be taking the firm's wagon to Sefton Corn Mill which was owned by the Stergen family and was situated just on the outskirts of Liverpool. There I would load up with animal feed which had been manufactured by them, and bring it back to Windermere where it would be either delivered direct or put into store.

The wagon at the Windermere store was an old petrol-engined Commer flat bed with a rather battered cab and doors which had been knocked and strained on many occasions and didn't fit at all well. About three times each week I would climb into the cab at about six o'clock in the morning, shut the doors, and then from the inside, fill the gaps with empty feed sacks to protect me from the cold draughts. I had a two hour journey with no heater to keep me warm.

Nowadays wagons have power steering, air conditioning, hydraulically sprung cabs and seats, tape decks and every creature comfort. In the 50s most wagons ware Spartan with few extras and even worse, essential components such as brakes were very poor on a lot of the vehicles. At that time there were no motorways. The first in Britain, the bit round Lancaster, had not yet been built and it was necessary to pass through all the towns and small villages on my route to and from Liverpool.

It was on one such journey that I was to receive a fright which I would never forget. On this particular day I had arrived at the Sefton Corn Mill, loaded a full load of 200 hundredweight sacks (ten tons) of cattle feed, neatly roped and sheeted the load to make it safe and weatherproof, and had set off home by about nine o'clock in the morning. It was often the case that I would arrive there in good time but would find myself waiting in a queue to be loaded. This morning, for once, I had flown through.

The first part of the journey back was uneventful. I was about to pass through the city of Lancaster, which at that time still had a two way traffic system round the centre. Down past the Royal Infirmary I went, bearing right towards the Town Hall Square and on, down the hill, towards the bridge which would take me over the River Lune. Because I had a full load I deliberately kept the speed down, knowing that just ahead of me was a zebra crossing which, as it came into sight, I noted was seething with pedestrians, crossing from both sides. I was by now down to a mere crawl.

Now almost on the crossing, I was virtually standing on the brakes with my back-side clear of the seat, doing no more than walking speed. Still the wagon refused to come to a halt. Within seconds I was reduced to a state of blind panic while the unsuspecting pedestrians, who were no doubt blissfully unaware of the impending danger, were milling about in front of me. In what seemed like slow motion, and as if helped by the hand of God, like the parting of waves, a gap opened up in front of me and my wagon passed through without incident. To say that I was relieved would be a mammoth understatement. I must have turned white as a sheet and I was still shaking when I arrived back at Windermere, vowing that I would never again find myself in such a situation!

Despite my experience in Lancaster, and after making a forceful complaint to my boss, which resulted in an overhaul of my vehicle's braking system, my passion for driving, especially larger vehicles had not diminished. I remember the days, as a young child, when visiting my grandmother at No. 10 College Road, I would climb over the wall into the piece of semi-derelict land owned by Smith's Garage. The garage stored old carcasses of scrap wagons and cars to be cannibalised for parts on this piece of land. Once over the wall, I would spend hours sitting in the driving seat of the biggest scrap vehicle I could find, my imagination running wild. In my mind I was driving a huge timber wagon dragging trees out of a forest, perhaps an omen of what was to come?

One day, when I was outside my parent's home, a close neighbour, a chap called Nick Holt, who was the owner of a small garage, approached me to ask if I was interested in doing a bit of extra work driving a bus which he owned and was mainly used at weekends for transporting cricket and football teams around the district. The bus had seating for some 29 passengers and to drive it I would require a P.S.V. (Public Service Vehicle) licence. I of course didn't hold one at that time.

To cut a long story short, I agreed to borrow Nick's bus and attempt to gain a licence. An application for a test was made and finally a date and time for an examination was set. I was to collect the bus and travel to Kendal where I would meet up with a Ministry of Transport examiner. It turned out that the tester was a Mr. Parkinson who, firstly introduced himself, then instructed me to drive around the town, himself sitting in the seat immediately behind me.

Mr. Parkinson I realised right from the word go, was a no nonsense sort of a chap. There was no idle chatter, just straight forward instructions. The test culminated in a reverse into a narrow side street. I must have driven satisfactorily because, still showing no emotion, he advised me that I had passed. Seemingly Mr. Parkinson had a dual role, as he also doubled as a vehicle examiner, the purpose of which was to ensure a vehicle's road worthiness. As soon as he had completed the necessary paperwork, and given me a pass certificate, he turned his attention to the bus.

For the next half hour my examiner, now 'wearing the hat' of a vehicle inspector, subjected the bus to a rigorous investigation which culminated in me being presented with a long list of faults which he had discovered, most of them, it seemed to me, of a minor nature. It didn't really seem fair. Nick had been kind enough to lend me the bus, I had come away with a licence, and Nick finished up with a list of jobs which would have to be completed within a specified time.

One of my routes when at Andersons had taken me to the Grange-over-Sands and Flookburgh area. On the route home I had often called at a garage at Newby Bridge which had a small retail shop. This garage was owned by a Mr. John Battersby and his wife. A lot of the trade for the shop came from customers who had stopped to fill up with petrol and also from a caravan site in the woods behind the garage. I had supplied the Battersbys with small quantities of fresh fruit and vegetables.

At some stage I came to realise that Mr. and Mrs. Battersby had a daughter, actually two daughters and a son. One daughter, the eldest, whose name I learned was Wendy, particularly drew my attention. Wendy was eighteen years old and was training to be a hair dresser in the little town of Ulverston, which lay about half way between Newby Bridge and Barrow-in-Furness. She was all but out of her apprenticeship and would soon be a fully qualified hair dresser. Now playing regularly at the Saturday night dance at Bowness, it wasn't long before I saw Wendy with a group of her female friends on the dance floor and I decided to make it my business and approach her.

Although I played regularly with the Baronettes on Saturdays and some nights during the week, I was not getting paid for the Saturdays. I treated that night as an experience night. This meant that I could leave the rest of the band for the last half hour of the evening whilst they continued playing. I was then free to have a dance or two myself. I could hardly have done this if I was being paid!

One of these Saturday nights I had been dancing with Wendy and learned that the following day she and her group of friends would be congregating in the area of the steamer pier at Lakeside at the foot of Lake Windermere. I had not long since bought myself a car, a Woolsley 16 of 1939 vintage, and suggested that myself and a friend of mine would meet with the group and that we might possibly go somewhere for a ride.

Just as arranged, I and a young chap called Keith Jeffrey, who played the trumpet and who had also started to join the Baronettes on Saturday nights, rolled up in my cavernous 'limo' and met up with Wendy and four or five of her friends. After a bit of light-hearted chatter, it was decided that the whole of the group would pile into my car and that we would go to Grange-over-Sands where we stayed for most of the afternoon and, as young people do, we had a thoroughly fun time which ended with me making arrangements to take Wendy to the Royalty Cinema at Bowness one evening the following week.

Despite my passion for motor bikes, I was beginning to realise that a car was a far better proposition for dating girls. It removed any concerns that I might have as to delivering my date back home wet through and usually vowing to have nothing to do with either the bike or its rider again!

One day John Key, the manager of Whittakers, the firm for whom I worked, told me that there was a strong possibility that the Windermere warehouse was going to close. It was then that I decided that I would try to put my P.S.V. licence to good use. I had not been asked too often by Nick Holt to help him out with his private hire business. It so happened that, just at that time, I heard that the Ambleside firm of Brown's Motors was looking for coach and bus drivers as the holiday season was almost upon them. The licence which I held allowed me to drive a vehicle fitted with up to 29 seats, so I decided to make an approach to the firm.

BROWN'S FUNNY LITTLE BUS

Stan Faulkner was a big heavily-built chap. I should think at that time he would be in his late 50s. He and his son Alan ran Brown's Lake District Tours which had been founded by the Brown family way back in the coach and horses' days. Stan and his brother had taken over the business after charabancs had replaced horses. Browns, at the time I made my approach, had five tour coaches on the road. These, I was aware, had seating for 41 people and I would therefore, under the terms of my existing licence, not be eligible to drive one. Perhaps I would be allowed to upgrade my licence?

In addition to the tour coaches, Browns also had a licence to operate a bus service which ran between Ambleside and the ferry on the western side of Windermere Lake, passing through the quaint little village of Hawkshead. The two buses used on the Hawkshead bus service, were both Bedfords. One was an old bull-nosed Duple-bodied Bedford, and another Bedford which I later decided would not have looked out of place taking prison work gangs out to break stones on the roadside. I have no idea how many had applied for the vacant bus driving job, but I do know that when I enquired about the position, I was immediately taken on with the promise that, after a short spell on the Hawkshead service, I would be given the opportunity to take a further test to qualify to drive a coach. I was now a bus driver!

On the first day of my new job, I was to do the driving and Alan Faulkner the conducting, the taking of fairs and issuing of tickets. I was of course to learn where the official stops were. On the second day, I had the lot to do. I was left on my own which I have to say didn't bother me. The passengers, most of whom were local, were very friendly and went out of their way to keep me right. The rest of the passengers were visitors to the area.

It didn't take me long to find that I had a natural aptitude for the job. It was great - I was meeting and dealing with people, something I found I was good at. I was somewhat amused when it occurred to me that in my previous job I had had to lift every hundredweight of my load on and off the vehicle and now my load walked on and off by itself, with only occasional help from me!

For most of the time I found myself driving the old bull-nosed Bedford, the like of which would later be used in the James Herriot's vet films, vastly over-bodied and under-powered. It would crawl up the Ferry Hill like an old tortoise, the back axle whining away, but always keeping going and in a curious way, fun to drive. I soon realised that this bus service was different to any other bus service I had ever come across. None of the regulars expected to get a ticket - these were a nuisance! Some of the regulars expected to be picked up and put down outside their own homes, and even more irregular, some would expect credit and would say: "I'll pay you at the weekend." To some extent I went along with these arrangements of convenience and I can honestly say that I don't think I was ever let down by any one defaulting on an arrangement.

One of the unofficial tasks which was expected of the driver was the carrying of parcels to be delivered on route. For this purpose the two front seats had been removed and, surprisingly, this service was provided free of charge, although most parcels were accompanied by a chocolate bar or the like

One particular parcel, which I well remember, was a large box of newly baked meat and potato pies which were handed to me by the proprietor of a bakery in Hawkshead. These pies were renowned for their succulence and were to be delivered to the Sawrey Hotel ready for the hunt ball which was to take place that evening. The box was made of strong cardboard and was fastened with a length of strong twine. It probably containing five or six dozen of the golden treats and the aroma soon spread down the bus.

In a previous paragraph I explained the tendency of regulars to want to be dropped off near their homes and, on this particular trip, there was an elderly lady who I knew would expect this extra part of the service. Meanwhile I, possibly intoxicated by the scent of the pies wafting around me, had completely forgotten about this dear little soul and had driven straight past her usual point of dismount. It was not until she had made her way down the gangway to a point just behind me and shouted the word "STOP" into my ear that I remembered her.

The very sharpness of my passenger's voice provoked an instant reaction. I stamped on the brake pedal which, under normal circumstances, would only have caused my seated passengers to rock slightly forward. There was of course one passenger who was not seated - the lady who had just shouted in my ear. She, unfortunately, was caught right off balance and, after grabbing at the vertical hand rail at the top of the stairwell, she did a full 180 degree turn and finished up in the parcel area, and yes, you've guessed it, she sat on top of the box of pies.

Obviously my first concern was for the dear lady, who thank goodness, was absolutely unhurt, after all she had made a perfect soft landing. She assured me that she was none the worse and trotted off back down the road to where I should have dropped her in the first place. Next my attention turned to the box of pies which was now somewhat concertined into about half its original height. I lifted the parcel by the string and noticed brown gravy running out from the corners. There was little that I could now do but deliver it to the hotel and hope that they would be able to salvage something from the situation.

One day in the week on the bus service always proved to be chaotic. This was what we always called baby weighing day. On reality it was clinic day when the district nurse would have all the mothers bring their babies to the village hall to check on their health. Needless to say, one baby equals one pram, and my bus was ill designed to carry a large number of prams. Some of them didn't fold up as they practically all do today. That day was always difficult but we seemed to have a good laugh, even though the schedule always went haywire!

The first bus of the day left Ambleside at 7.30am, usually travelling empty to Hawkshead, where instead of carrying on to the ferry, it turned round and returned to Ambleside. It was timed so that all the people from the village who had jobs in Ambleside could get to work. During the winter months, on reaching the tiny hamlet of Outgate, the bus would be met by a burly farmer who, despite the majority of seats being taken, would board the bus dragging a huge sack of hay behind him, as far down the gangway as room would allow. The reason for this procedure was that he owned a couple of fields further down the road in which he kept a few cattle and he was taking them their food for the day. This procedure was accepted by the rest of the passengers, most of whom knew the farmer and were happy to exchange pleasantries with him.

It is one thing dragging a large soft bag of hay down the gangway of a bus, but it is another thing pushing it back out. When the bus reached the point where the farmer was to disembark, the chap had to rely on the good nature of the rest of the passengers to help him out. By the time I had dropped the workers off in Ambleside and again set off for Hawkshead there, sure enough, standing at the roadside, was the farmer, the sack rolled up neatly underneath his arm, the only evidence of his journey, the trail of hay seeds down the gangway of the bus.

Right from the start of working for Browns it was my intention to move on from the Hawkshead bus service and onto the tour coaches. I had got as far as upgrading my licence to any single decker, which meant that if coaches got longer, as they did, I would be entitled to drive one. However no amount of asking had got me any further on that issue.

At this particular time in Windermere two coach tour businesses operated out of the village, or rather one was in Windermere and the other about a mile nearer the lake in Bowness - Mallinson's Lake District Tours in Windermere and Silver Badge Motors of Bowness. Imagine my surprise when one morning Teddy Mallinson, one of the partners in the former mentioned company, knocked on the door of my parents' home, where of course, I was then living, expressing a wish to speak to me.

Teddy had a daughter Jennifer who was a close friend of my twin sister Margaret right through her grammar school years and had remained so. Although I had never spoken to him, he was well aware of my family and evidently of me!

"I would like to discuss a proposition with you," he started, "I understand you have a P.S.V. licence and that you are currently working for Browns." I was somewhat surprised that he knew so much about me. I was also quite flattered that he should be talking to me. Mallinsons, I knew, were the uncrowned kings of coach tours in the Lake District.

Teddy went on to outline the company's strategy and the fact that they bought two brand new tour coaches each spring, ran them for one season, and then sold them off in the winter. These were facts which everybody in the local coach tour industry knew, but none of them had been able to work out how such a capital intensive programme could be financed!

"My partner and I operate a system whereby I drive one coach for a half-day tour, whilst he manages the office. For the second half of the day, my partner drives and I manage the office. This means we require someone to drive our second coach." I had heard unconfirmed rumours about Mallinsons losing their driver, but at this stage of the discussion, I decided to let Teddy tell me what he wanted me to know!

"This brings me to the reason for my being here." I had already guessed the 'reason' but was never-the-less somewhat perplexed as to why it was me who was being approached; why not someone else with a lot more experience? "Subject to you meeting with and gaining the approval of my partner, I am here to offer you the job of full day tour driver with Mallinsons."

As I have already indicated, Mallinsons enjoyed the reputation of being the top tour company and by far the most professional. I really was flattered that they had chosen me from all the drivers in the area. I can only conclude that, as they didn't know me personally, it could only have been the impeccable credentials of the rest of my family and our forefathers who had been established in the village for several generations and who were a reliable lot.

I now had a dilemma on my hands. This job would only be seasonal, from Easter until the end of October, whereas my present job was for the full year. There was however an incentive whereby, if I was to accept the job, I would receive a retainer of half my summer's weekly wage during the winter. This would allow me to seek temporary work, even if it wasn't well paid, and return to Mallinsons for the spring. The thought of working from my home village and a brand new coach instead of the old Hawkshead bus made my decision simple - 'no contest.' If I could meet with and agree with Teddy's partner, I would accept the job!

A few days after the original approach, it was arranged that I would meet with Teddy Mallinson and his partner, who in fact was also his brother-in-law, one Harvey Leigh. The meeting was to be at Teddy's home in Woodland Road in Windermere. Whereas Teddy was a tall gaunt sort of a chap, Harvey was of only average height but also of slender build. On every occasion I had ever seen both gentlemen they were always immaculately dressed in dark pin striped suits and both men wore thick,dark rimmed, glasses. Together in this environment they seemed slightly intimidating! Later I learned that Harvey was the son of a former vicar of Rydal. He was considered by some to be rather upper crust and spoke with a rather high class accent.

The interview was as I had expected. There were questions about myself and how I considered myself in the reliability stakes, my knowledge of the Lake District, the various points of local interest and my driving ability. Strangely I got the impression from some questions they asked, that they were particularly interested in my temperament. Perhaps there was a reason?

The outcome of the meeting was that their offer of the job was confirmed and that I accepted it. I left the house delighted but with Harvey's last remark puzzling me: "I do hope that you won't try to bully us!" Strange, but I was to understand the meaning of his words some time later. My task now was not going to be either agreeable or easy. I was not looking forward to handing in my notice to Browns and I knew it would not be accepted without some sort of backlash. I was not wrong!

The next day I went on time to work as usual. I drove the old Duple-bodied bus out of the company's garage and onto the bus stand in the Market Place where, as often was the case, there were no passengers for the first run of the day to Hawkshead. I had decided that, rather than putting off the time when I broke my news, I would speak to either Stan Faulkner or his son Alan on the first occasion that I saw one of them.

In a strange way I had come to quite like the bus service and certainly the majority of the people who used it regularly. I was sure that most of them appreciated me and I began to wonder just how long I would have continued on that route if I had not had this approach from Mallinsons. However, there was a whole new adventure waiting for me just around the corner so I had to move on. It was mid-day when my opportunity came. I had returned to the garage to take my lunch break and saw Alan was fuelling up one of the firm's taxis.

"Could I have a quiet word with you?" I asked. " I will be leaving you in a couple of weeks. I have got the job as Mallinsons' driver. Alan's normally expressionless face didn't show any change. He carried on the job that he was doing without making any comment. There, I had got it off my chest, but I knew that was only the start of things. Quite rightly I guessed there was more to come - I wasn't going to get off without a good bit of explaining.

Sure enough, within minutes of Alan going back to the office the phone on the wall rang. "You're to go to the office straight away" was the message I got from one of the other drivers who answered it. I obeyed this instruction but never-the-less felt a bit like the condemned man marching to the gallows.

"What's all this then, you're going to drive for Teddy Mallinson?" Stan had already got himself into a confrontational mood. "I've kept you on all winter and now you're going to leave me when it's nearly Easter!" There was some truth in what Stan had said. I had worked for him all winter but then I knew that he would be taking on additional drivers, who also would be leaving other employers who had kept them all winter; this was an area of moving, seasonal workers.

At first the boss appealed to my better nature: "I want you to go back to Teddy Mallinson and tell him you've reconsidered things, and that you've decided to stop with Stan Faulkner and thank you very much."

"But I don't want to stay here!" I replied.

"Well you're a rotter then!"

I put forward a number of reasons for making the move which was advantageous to me, but to little avail. The boss wasn't convinced that my needs were as important as his.

"Now look here my lad," said Stan placing his hand on my shoulder. "I know that I can trust you enough to send you anywhere," he said with a change of tack. "I know that at the end of the day you'll be best off stopping where you are with me, now don't you agree?"

" It's no good, I'm sorry if you think I've let you down, but my mind's made up!"

The stand off must have lasted at least half an hour and it was time to take the next bus out to Hawkshead and the ferry. Despite the altercations in both directions, I do believe that both the Faulkners and myself would shortly part company with mutual respect. Certainly for my part, I respected Stan and his son who had a business to run and, in those days of full employment, it couldn't have been easy to retain staff.

It was while serving my notice that I learned, through the grape vine, the true reason why my new job had become vacant. Apparently Mallinsons' regular driver, a chap in his late 50s called Bill Carter, who I had seen on many occasions, but had never actually met, had apparently been suffering from depression. Being a single person, Bill was able to avoid working in winter, just as Teddy and Harvey did. However, for whatever reason, he had chosen to take his own life. On finding out the truth I was left thinking that I would much rather have gained my new job in less tragic circumstances.

MALLINSONS

Mallinson's Motor Tours was started originally with one car in the late 1920s by Teddy Mallinson himself. He would ply for hire on the promenade at Bowness offering to take the tourists on trips around the lakes. In those days most of the tourists would have travelled in to the village of Windermere by train, not many would have their own car. Some would stay in Windermere village itself, whilst others would prefer to be nearer the lake and would find excellent accommodation in one of the many hotels, guest houses or bed and breakfast establishments.

Teddy eventually persuaded his new found friend, Harvey Leigh, who had not long married his sister Jessie, to join him in the business. Harvey had just received a substantial inheritance from his Uncle Charlie, a successful timber importer. With the business now on a sound financial footing, and with Harvey's business acumen, Mallinson's Motor Tours was founded, expanding to four large open touring limousines with three, sometimes four, drivers.

The Second World War interrupted the expansion of the business. In

Mallinsons' bus pictured in the Duddon Valley from the eastern side of Corney Fell.

any case there would have been few tourists who would have required the service. Both Harvey and Teddy were seconded into the war effort in local factories. Immediately after the war ended, Teddy, now married with three children, a daughter and twin sons, and Harvey and his wife who had no children, (they would remain so), embarked once more with the tour business.

Whilst growing up, I well remember visiting my grandma at No. 10 College Road, which was situated a mere two hundred yards from Mallinson's office and vehicle stand. I vividly remember the bustle of strangers and watching them climbing into the huge gleaming Packhard open tourers. Every day in summer seemed to be blessed with brilliant sunshine then. I was not to know that a few years on I would be driving for this very same firm taking out not seven people at a time, which was the maximum those vehicles could accommodate, but 41.

It was in the mid 50s when the seven seater cars requiring a driver apiece became no longer viable. Although charabancs had been around for at least 30 years, it was only now that the change over became inevitable and Mallinsons got its first two coaches. The first of these coaches was 28 feet long, seven feet six wide, and carried 36 passengers.

By the time I had served my notice with Brown's, Mallinson's were close to the time when two brand new 41 seater coaches were to be collected from the Plaxton body works at Scarborough. The maximum size of coaches had by then increased to 30 feet long and eight feet two and one half inches - a curious figure but not too wide for the country lanes of the Lake District. It is a width that still stands to this day. My final day with Brown's passed, and after a short break, I boarded the train together with Teddy Mallinson who of course I had only spoken to on two previous occasions. We were to travel to Scarborough, stay in a hotel overnight, and arrive at the works mid-morning.

During the journey I took the opportunity of finding out as much as I could about what would be expected of me in the coming season. Teddy was a very talkative chap, slightly disadvantaged by the fact that he was partially deaf. He overcame this by indicating to people to speak into a 'receiver' sticking out of the breast pocket of his jacket. Possibly because of my interest in what my new employer had to say, the journey seemed to fly by and in no time at all we were booking into the hotel. We joined other guests in the bar where I began to see Teddy's extraordinary talent for gaining people's attention and entertaining them. Next morning, following a hearty breakfast, we made our way down to the Plaxton coach building factory where we were met by the management who obviously viewed Teddy as an important customer, judging by the copious amounts of coffee and biscuits we were offered.

For my part, the excitement came to a pitch when it was decided that it was time to go into the factory. I was finally going to meet up with the vehicle of my dreams, the vehicle which I would be guiding round fifteen to twenty thousand miles of mainly Lake District roads in the next seven months.

There they were, side by side, still on the factory floor - two gleaming pale blue and silver coaches. They were the very latest in design and every bit the best of British craftsmanship, except that where were the seats? Where was the rubber flooring? Even the huge windscreen was still missing! I needn't have worried, in the space of the next couple of hours, an army of workers, each with his own specific task descended on the two vehicles. Teddy was quite unperturbed, he had seen it all before and spent the time with the management. I was fascinated with the whole procedure and discreetly watched the metamorphosis, taking great care not to get in the way.

I don't think that I will ever forget that experience of climbing into the driver's seat of that particular coach on that particular day. I had driven everything from the beaten up wagon of Whittaker's to the ancient buses of Nick Holt and Brown's Hawkshead service, and here I was driving back to Windermere in a BRAND NEW vehicle. For the first few miles I gloried in the scent of new paint, newly crafted wood, fabrics, sealants and polishes around me, ever aware of Teddy following a safe distance behind me. At the same time it occurred to me just how much trust had been placed in me. Neither Teddy nor Harvey had ever even driven with me in so much as a motor car, let alone the thousands of pounds worth of luxury of which I was now in sole control. I resolved, there and then, that I would prove to them for as long as I was in their employ, that their trust had not been misplaced.

Arriving back at Windermere, a journey which thank goodness was uneventful, both vehicles were parked up for the night in the firm's garage in Chestnut Road. I had very quickly felt totally at home driving, and had no concerns for the hard season ahead. In fact, I could hardly wait to collect my first passengers. It was my job to see that both coaches were on the stand outside the office, washed off and cleaned right through, plus filled up with fuel and oil, in time for the first passengers to board. The full day tour (the one which I would be taking) left the office at 10-15am to collect the last of the passengers before departing at 10-30am. This meant that I had to make a start cleaning around 7am, 'do the business', dash home to get washed and changed ready for the tour. This didn't leave a lot of time to spare, however it worked!

Mallinson's had a policy of not allowing passengers to book specific seats. If anyone particularly wanted a certain seat, they were advised to get there early. It was a system which I soon found out, worked perfectly well - 'behinds reserve seats.' Whilst Teddy and I had been away at Scarborough, Harvey in anticipation had managed to get together half a coach load of passengers for a thirteen lake tour. Seldom would the first few tours of the season be fully booked, but at last I was going to get on the road.

The arrangement on that first trip out, was that I would do the driving while Teddy would accompany me and act as courier. I already knew the Lake District but not the exact route of the tour and he would introduce me to the proprietors of the various stopping off places which the firm used. Passengers all collected and off we set. From the start I recognised the skill which Teddy had of capturing the attention of people and bringing a smile to their faces. At the hotel in Scarborough he had, within minutes, converted complete strangers into an audience eager to dwell on his every word. He was a natural entertainer and would be a hard act to follow.

Strangely enough, I don't remember a lot about that first day trip round the thirteen lakes. I suppose I would be too busy filling my head with all the details which Teddy was relating to the passengers over the public address system. His knowledge of the district and countless experiences had been gained over many years and thousands of miles of touring the Lakes. I didn't intend to make myself into a carbon copy of Teddy, but felt that I would be foolish if I didn't take this opportunity to glean the most interesting aspects, the bits you would never find in a book, and then build up my own repertoire for the future.

Barring a couple of stops at view points, the first on the shores of Coniston Lake, followed by one on the eastern side of Corney Fell, our

Mallinsons' bus pictured on the western side of Corney Fell on the west coast of Cumbria with the Irish Sea in the background.

main break was in the little village of Gosforth, on the west coast of the then Cumberland ,where we took lunch at the Globe Hotel which was owned and run by Mr. and Mrs. Coupe. I met them for the first time that day but I was to visit the Globe later on many more occasions!

The next part of the tour took us down to Wastwater, England's deepest lake, which is overlooked for most of its length on the southern shore by the massive scree beds simply known as the Screes. The lake itself on most occasions looks as black as ink, so much so that it is joked that you can fill your fountain pen from the lake. I learned later of one point where you can park a car, blow the horn, and in return hear the most amazing echoes, which sound like a thousand trumpeters, as the sound waves bounce from one rock to another and reverberate around the range on the other side of the lake.

We then had to return back through Gosforth in order to get to Calder Bridge where we left the coast road and headed over the open expanse of Cold Fell and down through Kirkland, then on through Lamplugh leaving the A66 and making our way down the Vale of Lorton into the Buttermere Valley. At the point where Crummock Water comes into view, a palpable atmosphere came over the party. I doubt if any of the travellers had ever been presented with such an awesome display of beauty, the softness of the panoramic picture before them could not have contrasted more with the harshness of the view from Wastwater which they had seen only two hours earlier.

On down the valley we went, round the rocky outcrop of Rannerdale Point which juts out into the lake, and would later cause passing difficulties on so many occasions when a thoughtless visitor parked his or her car in the designated passing place only, and sat on a rolled out car rug eating sandwiches and watching everyone struggle. Another half mile, and we arrived at the tea room at Croft Farm run by the family of Robbie Jackson, who also farmed the place. The tea room always had available fresh cream teas, and home made scones.

The last lap of the journey took us back up the valley to join the Whinlatter Pass, but not before travelling a little further to Gaitsgarth at the foot of the western side of the Honister Pass, which unfortunately was too steep to negotiate safely, but would have taken us over to Borrowdale and Keswick. However we had the opportunity to look down into the waters of Buttermere Lake, which again, in contrast to Wastwater's inky depths, gave off a luminous green glow which has always reminded me of my childhood when we used to crawl along the boards under the steamer pier and look down into the green depths below.

Over the Whinlatter Pass and we again joined the A66 for a short time until we reached Keswick. We were left with the remaining twenty miles back home with views of Bassenthwaite, Derwent Water, Thirlmere, Grasmere, Rydal and finally Windermere Lake. We returned at the usual time of 6.45pm and the tour had gone without a hitch.

Easter and Whitsuntide passed and we were then into the busy part of the season which would last through until September, before tailing off into the end of our season in October. I continued taking out all the full day trips whilst Teddy and Harvey accommodated the half day ones. On Saturdays, which was the day when most of the tourists either came into the village or went home, only one afternoon tour went out, which one of my bosses would take and I was sent 'on hire' to the Ribble Bus Company who required extra transport to move passengers about. Sometimes this would take me as far afield as Liverpool or Manchester. Very occasionally I would travel empty to Blackpool, pick up a load of passengers, and return them to Glasgow or Edinburgh where I would stay the night, and do the same journey in reverse the next day. I would then be up first thing again Monday morning, clean both coaches then I would go out and round the thirteen lakes.

Mallinson's were agents for seven major travel companies who, for a commission, booked customers in advance of their arrival. Many of these people were from overseas. On any one tour I might have visitors from half a dozen different countries, often from the Commonwealth. I took every opportunity, during stops, to make myself available to answer questions, most of which related to the district and the environment. I felt, to some degree, qualified to answer, as I had experience in both farming and forestry, which proved of great help.

With regard to presentation, I have already suggested that both in mine and many other peoples' opinion, Mallinson's were the most professional tour company around. The coach roofs were specially designed with extra glass in so that it was possible to see the mountain tops regardless as to which side of the vehicle you were seated. A public address system allowed the driver/courier to give out information, (when appropriate). I was well aware of the danger of talking too much and becoming an irritation!

Another facet of the firm's approach to professionalism was that, when in charge of a coach, the drivers were expected to wear long white cotton coats, which were laundered regularly. This was the one aspect which I preferred to be without. I wore mine, all be it reluctantly, but often removed it when I got to my first stop. I felt the coats were terribly out of date. I did not, however, object to the removable white cover on my peaked cap.

My first summer with Mallinson's was nearly over. I had worked a seven day week solidly from Easter doing the thirteen lakes on Mondays, Wednesdays and Fridays, Ullswater and Appleby on Tuesdays and Thursdays and either an afternoon eight lakes tour or a Ribble hire job on Saturdays. On Sundays I did a Coniston and Langdales afternoon and evening tour. In short, what with driving and cleaning, I had given my all and, by October, after completing over 18,000 miles of mainly narrow, twisty roads, without so much as putting a scratch on my vehicle, I was ready for a break and I felt that I had earned it. At the same time, I had enjoyed every minute of it.

Regardless as to whether or not customers had been found to buy the now redundant coaches, Mallinson's shut down and new coaches were ordered for collection in late March the following year. I was delighted that a number of customers who had travelled with me had taken the trouble to write expressing their gratitude. Apparently I had helped to make their holidays a success. This made me feel that I must be doing my job something like right, and helped reinforce my boss' belief in me!

With my job finished until the next season, I decided to take off in my car. I would still be driving, but I would have no schedule to keep. London was my choice, having relations with whom I could stay for a while. It would be a complete contrast from my beloved lakes, but it would do me good. I'm sure it did, but after a couple of weeks I had had enough and headed up north again, spending a few days with my twin sister Margaret at her home in Sutton Coalfield. By then I knew that I could never be anything other than a country lad and within three weeks I was back amongst the hills. On my return I was contacted by Teddy who asked me to deliver the two coaches which had been sold in my absence, curiously to a customer based only a few miles from Scarborough where they had been built. I was happy to oblige.

My task completed and my holiday behind me, it was time to sort myself out with a temporary job for the rest of the winter. I had been giving quite a bit of thought to the matter and had decided to make an approach to my ex-employers, Mould and Bloomers, the forestry management people. I had decided that coach driving, being a rather sedentary occupation, would be better replaced with something a little more physical for winter. I had put on weight and this would be a good way of getting fit again. Accordingly, I sought out Archie Galloway, who was the then proprietor, who of course knew me and my capabilities. As I hoped, I was well received. I knew that Archie was the perfect gentleman and would appreciate my enquiry whether or not he had any thing to offer me.

With the approach of Christmas, I knew that there would be a lot of activity in amongst the Christmas trees and that Mould and Bloomers themselves were responsible for supplying a considerable number of wholesalers from their nursery near Harrowslack (the Belle Isle estate saw mill). My meeting with Archie, a tall, lean, angular man who was very knowledgeable and well spoken, proved to be positive. All the extra seasonal business would soon be in full swing and he was glad of an extra pair of hands and especially of someone who knew something about the business. He had already taken on a few students who were on their seasonal break but, with the best will in the world, they weren't able to work without first being shown the ropes. The result of my meeting with Archie Galloway was that I was able to make an immediate start. He was also happy that I would be returning to my summer coaching job and would keep me on until the end of March.

Forestry work, since the Agricultural Wages Act came into force, has always been subject to the same wage structure. I would now be receiving the same wages as I would had I been working on a farm. However, at the same time I would be receiving my retainer from Mallinson's and together they constituted a really worthwhile package - things were looking good!

As I expected, I worked the whole of that winter. It was the winter of 1961-62 and I worked, firstly amongst the Christmas Trees and then fencing and planting. Some of the work was within the nursery and some was on various estates. One job even took me to the golf course at Alderley Edge, near Wilmslow in Cheshire. Here we erected small enclosures, placed at strategic points on the fairways, and then planted them with appropriate types of young saplings. I never did learn whether that project had turned out successfully or not. For sure we didn't make a hole in one any more easy to achieve!

Although my relationship with girls at that time was somewhat sporadic, I was seeing quite a bit of Wendy, the daughter of Mr. and Mrs. Battersby who owned the Newby Bridge Filling Station. Wendy was no longer working at Ulverston, but was working in a hair dressing salon in Windermere village for a Miss Inglis. She was now a fully qualified hair dresser. I had given up the playing in the dance band, not because I was bored, but because it was just not possible to be driving all hours and take on bookings to play with the band. It was pretty well a straight forward choice - the music or the job!

In no time at all it seemed, the new season was upon us. Archie Galloway was aware that I would soon be leaving and there was no problem naming the actual day when I would be leaving. I timed my departure so that I would have a few days break prior to once again travelling by train to Scarborough with Teddy for the new coaches.

At the start of the 1962 season, the two new vehicles having been collected, things were pretty much the same as the previous year. There

were full day tours during the week and half days, evening tours and private hires at the weekend - it all made for a very full programme. In those days certain rules had been brought in about driving hours, although in the whole of my P.S.V. career, I was never asked to produce any documentation relating to the matter! Months went by and there were amusing little incidents like an American lady asking: "Say, driver, where is the powder room?" It was not an unusual question, except that we were on the top of Corney Fell at the time!

On another occasion we were parked alongside another coach party on the shores of Coniston Lake admiring the view. The driver for the other firm, who was talking to me at the time was approached by one of his passengers, obviously an American, recognisable from his clothing. The man said: "Driver, I'm a lecturer in botanical studies at the such and such university and I can't for the life of me think of the name of that tree." He was pointing to a tree a little further up the shoreline.

"Ay mi lad," answered the driver, who incidentally prided himself on his broad local accent, which I suspect few of his clients would understand, "Ay, mi lad it's a wooden yan." Although not very helpful, and not the answer which I personally would have chosen, I did see the funny side of things. I doubt if the American gentleman even understood his answer. He might even have spent some time looking up in his botanical encyclopedia the Latin name for "Ay-mi-lad-a-wooden-yan."

During the summer of 1963 my relationship with Wendy developed further, and we became engaged. Obviously it was impractical to get married until the back end as there was no way that I could take a break until then. We set the date for 19 October. This we thought would allow us plenty of time to look for a home. As it was, it would be Wendy who would have to do most of the organising and house hunting as I was so desperately busy and only saw her in the evenings.

As it turned out it was late August when we finally settled for the property which was to be our first home. It just happened to be a short walk along the road from where I was then living with my parents. Howe Cottage was a pretty little house in an elevated position overlooking the top end of the village of Bowness-on-Windermere. In fact the view extended way beyond the houses over the lake, and took in the full arc of the mountainous skyline beyond. It was a view to die for! The ground floor had two small living rooms, both with windows looking out at the view just described. Also on the ground floor was by far the worst feature of the property - a make shift kitchen which had been bodged onto the end of the house. The kitchen seemed to have been built from whatever materials had been lying around at the time, including bricks, blocks, window panels, corrugated iron sheets and bits of timber . The kitchen would definitely be the first project to tackle.

Fortunately the rest of the house was more or less original and very substantial. There was a narrow staircase which turned back on itself which led to two decent bedrooms and a toilet/bathroom. Finally, up an incredibly steep short staircase, again turning back on itself, was an attic bedroom the full width of the house. The view from this room, helped by its elevation, was nothing short of breath taking!

Outside there was a decent sized garden which was fairly steep, rising in a constant incline from the cul-de-sac road below to the cottage above. A narrow local slate stone pathway connected the cottage with the road. We felt the property, with a little bit of attention, could be made into something we could be proud of. Howe Cottage had been owned by a Mrs. Robinson who had an antique shop in Bowness. We had agreed a purchase price of £2,500 and the property was ours, subject to a mortgage of course! We thought it would take for ever to pay back £2,500. We also had to pay for the honeymoon. Between us we had saved the grand total of £500. This would have to go for our deposit on the cottage.

OUR WEDDING AND A ROCKY START

Our wedding took place in the tiny little church nestling in the trees in the village of Staveley-in-Cartmel. Wendy had been brought up in the nearby village of Newby Bridge and had attended the quaint little school next to the church in which we were to be married. Later, at the age of eleven, she moved on to the Victoria Grammar School in Ulverston.

Shamefully I don't remember a lot about the actual wedding ceremony. I guess all the excitement and nerves were probably the reason for that, but one thing does stand out in my mind and that was how the church itself had been so beautifully decorated out with fresh flowers. I also noticed that Wendy and the bridesmaids looked so beautiful against the background of the lovely old church.

My best man was a young chap with whom I had been friends for a few years, and for whom I had played the same role that he was about to perform for me. I was his best man six years to the day previously. John Pearson had married his wife Ivy at the church above the village of Allithwaite and now the couple and their children lived and farmed at Borderside Farm, Crosthwaite.

Following the ceremony, our reception was held at the Newby Bridge Hotel. The reception was supervised by the owners, Mr. and Mrs. Steel, who put on a wonderful banquet during which some telegrams were read and speeches made. In all it was a a wonderful occasion. Mid-way through the afternoon Wendy and I made our get away. We had considered touring Scotland in my old Wolsley, but instead decided to hire a Morris Minor, only half the size and hopefully with only half the thirst for petrol. Our first night was spent in Moffat. We had no pre-booked accommodation and no schedule to keep. I had had enough of schedules for the time being.

Our travels that week took us through Braemar and on up to Inverness and along the northern shore of Loch Ness. We went on down past Fort Augustus and Fort William to Oban on the west coast. We had stayed in a number of hotels and guest houses one of which comes to mind for an amusing feature. It was when we were only a mile or so out of Braemar, famous for its Highland games, that we came into the tiny village of Tomintoul and decided that a certain cottage with a vacancy sign in the window looked particularly inviting. Accordingly we booked in and were amused when we were shown the toilet, the only one in the house seemingly. When wishing to use the said toilet one opened a door and were immediately faced with six or seven steep and narrow steps. The room was so narrow that it was possible to touch both walls at the same time. The crowning glory was that at the top of the steps, for all the world like a royal throne was the toilet pot. We have had many a laugh about it since. After staying the last night in Edinburgh we headed back to Bowness to spend our first night in our new home.

It took only a few days and nights to settle in. I guess we were fortunate that my parents were close by and we were able to call on them for the bits and pieces which inevitably were found missing, usually when all the shops were shut. I had been unavailable right up to the big day, so it had very much been left to Wendy to set up our home. I would now be around a lot more to help sort things out.

Being a married man with a wife and a mortgage was now all the more reason to get myself once more gainfully employed. Should I again approach my good friends at Mould and Bloomer's? The idea had occurred to me that perhaps I should try something else. I enjoyed estate work, but there were plenty of other jobs around. An advert in the *Westmorland Gazette* stated that a local quarrying company urgently needed a dump truck driver for their Kirkstone quarry. On many occasions when I had been 'on tour' crossing over Kirkstone Pass, I had looked across at this quarry and wondered just what was involved in the extraction of the beautiful stone. Perhaps this was my opportunity to find out and any knowledge gained would come in useful should a tourist happen to ask me a question on the subject.

After weighing up the options available to me, I decided to apply for the job, and subsequently attended an interview with Mr. Harry Fecitt, the owner of both Kirkstone Quarry and the stone processing works at Skelwith Bridge where I attended my interview. After a few questions about my driving background, I was given the job together with a time and a place to report for work. By the time I actually got started with Kirkstone Quarries Ltd. we were into November and winter had come with a vengeance. I was to be at the Market Cross in Ambleside on a Monday morning at 7.15am where a wagon would pick up all the workers. That morning turned out to be the coldest and foggiest morning so far that winter.

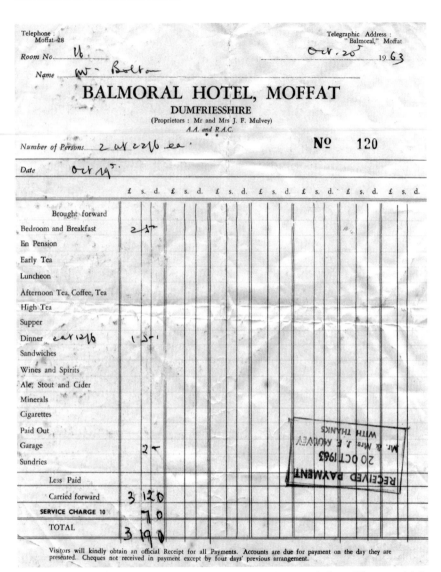

		Telephone : Moffat 28				Telegraphic Address : "Balmoral," Moffat

Room No. 16

Oct. 20 19 63

Name W - Bolton

BALMORAL HOTEL, MOFFAT
DUMFRIESSHIRE
(Proprietors : Mr and Mrs J. F. Mulvey)
A.A. and R.A.C.

Number of Persons 2 at 22/6 ea.

№ 120

Date Oct 19.

	£ s. d.	£ s. d.	£ s. d.	£ s. d.	£ s. d.	£ s. d.	£ s. d.
Brought forward							
Bedroom and Breakfast	2 5 -						
En Pension							
Early Tea							
Luncheon							
Afternoon Tea, Coffee, Tea							
High Tea							
Supper							
Dinner 2 at 12/6	1 5 -						
Sandwiches							
Wines and Spirits							
Ale, Stout and Cider							
Minerals							
Cigarettes							
Paid Out							
Garage	2 -						
Sundries							
Less Paid							
Carried forward	3 12 0						
SERVICE CHARGE 10	7 0						
TOTAL	3 19 0						

RECEIVED PAYMENT
20 OCT 1963
Mr. & Mrs. J. F. MULVEY
WITH THANKS

Visitors will kindly obtain an official Receipt for all Payments. Accounts are due for payment on the day they are presented. Cheques not received in payment except by four days' previous arrangement.

As the works truck climbed the steep hill out of the village, which stretched the three or so tortuous miles to its summit opposite the Kirkstone Inn, already mentioned in my account of my father's employment with the RAC, the freezing fog thickened leaving the truck headlights barely able to penetrate the gloom. The road was well named 'the struggle.'

By the time we had left the tarmac road and wound our way up the rough quarry road into the work's yard where every one dismounted, it was about 7.30am, the official starting time. All the regular workers made their way to their respective places of work but I was left to seek out someone who could help me get started. A pleasant chap, who I only remember as Cedric the foreman took me in hand and explained that I would be working out of the 'top' quarry (there were two quarry faces) and accordingly I was pointed in that direction.

The top quarry was around 1500 feet above sea level, and I was unable to see more than a few yards in front of me, and that only because of the one or two arc lights sparingly positioned on masts amongst the rocky terrain. Above me, beyond the reach of the diminished lighting was an eerie, inky, blackness. I was now beginning to realise that I was in an 'hostile' environment of which I knew nothing. Little was done to alleviate my concerns when I was 'introduced' to my truck, an enormous but somewhat dilapidated scow ended (open backed), half cabbed dump truck. It was obvious, even in the limited light, that the thing had seen better days.

I was no happier when I climbed into the one man cab and found the interior semi-derelict. The seat was basic and in a terrible state of repair. The broken and none existent dials and gauges told their own story of abuse and lack of maintenance. I was not expecting a masterpiece of machinery such as I had been used to driving, but I had hoped for something better than a rival for the worst farm tractor I had ever had to drive.

It was not a good start, however I followed instructions and started up 'the beast' and drove it across the quarry floor to where a large tracked loading shovel was waiting to load me with pieces of raw rock which had obviously been blasted out of the quarry face and now lay in a giant heap where they had fallen. I was to learn later that only certain top quality pieces are selected. The rest are transported across the quarry floor and dumped down the spoil heap - this was to be my job.

The truck shuddered as each shovelful of rocks landed on its back, some pieces weighed two or three tons each. Very quickly I was loaded with in the region of 25 tons or so, and was immediately instructed to dispose of the same over the edge of the tip. I had prior to loading been shown the tip, or more correctly had been shown where the tip was, as it was still dark and foggy, making it quite impossible to see anything beyond the row of roughly placed railway sleepers which designated the tip edge.

Gingerly I drove across the quarry floor, I could feel by the floating sensation that the truck was at its maximum carrying capacity. There was no luxury of power steering on this vehicle - I had to heave at the steering in order to turn to reverse. Having backed to the tip edge, I applied the hand brake and searched out the lever which would put the the tipping rams into gear. I was, to some degree, conversant with the procedure of using tipping machinery, having used farming equipment, but I had never used anything on this scale. I was completely taken aback by the speed at which the huge steel body rose in the air, quickly reaching the pivotal point where the full load of rocks started to slide. Up to this point I had remained seated but was rewarded for my efforts by being suddenly jerked violently skywards, resulting in my head banging against the cab roof. What had actually happened was that one of the larger rocks had jammed half way down the body. The weight of the larger part of the load was by then beyond the pivotal point and caused the front of the truck to lift two or three feet off the ground. Fortunately the load had then freed, allowing the front of the vehicle to drop heavily back down to the ground.

As the morning progressed, the daylight came and the fog lifted and I was able to see the layout of the quarry. I had by then driven several times between the quarry face and the tip edge, and was now able to see beyond the railway sleepers and down the man made scree bed of loose rocks tumbling for hundreds of feet down the fell side below me. Looking further I could see the twisty 'struggle' and the occasional car, some ascending and others descending - either way they looked like toys and seemed to be hardly moving.

Later that day, I was approached by one of the regular quarry workers. He said: "I've been watching you when you're tipping and, if I were you, I wouldn't stay in the cab." He went on to explain that in the past they had lost two dump trucks over the edge through them flipping over backwards when their loads jammed half way out. He continued: "One was fairly recently, you can still see part of it sticking out of the rocks," and he pointed down the tip. Sure enough when I looked down to where he had indicated, you could see a large balloon tyre already all but buried. From that point on I never stayed in the cab whilst tipping, instead I chose to set the rams into gear and stand well clear.

When I had applied for the driving job in the quarry, I had been under no illusions that it would be a soft touch. I was well used to a tough life having roughed it on farms and in the forests. The fact that my cab had no heater and there were no 'creature comforts' I could live with, but when an air braking system, designed to run at a minimum of eighty p.s.i. (pounds per square inch) only reached a pressure of 40 p.s.i., and that was before you touched the brakes, I began to have my doubts as to whether I should be there at all.

Things for me came to a head when I was asked to take a number of 'clogs' (large pieces of stone) down to the saw sheds where they were to be sawn into slabs. On my first journey down the incredibly steep slope from the quarry face down to the sheds, my truck jumped out of four wheel drive and I had to use the brakes excessively to regain control. By the time I came to a halt, I realised that the air reservoir was practically empty and any further use would have emptied it, possibly with dire consequences...

Following this incident, I made complaints but to no avail and nothing was done to improve matters. So reluctantly, after only about three weeks, I decided that enough was enough, at least as far as I was concerned. I did feel some disappointment and half felt that I was being a quitter, but my stronger sense of self preservation won the day and I left. Only a few days later I learned that the very same truck I had been driving had turned over at just about the same place that I had nearly run away. Mercifully the driver escaped serious injury - I felt vindicated!

By now Christmas was only days away. I satisfied myself that I would catch up on a few jobs about the home, and when the festivities were over I would look for work of some sort. I didn't like the thought of Wendy working and me not, despite the fact that it would only be three months until I took up my summer driving again. That Christmas, the first Wendy and I had together, was one to remember. We had lots of friends round; it seemed so much nicer to be able to invite them into our own home rather than just meeting them in a pub. I suppose I was quickly becoming what is known as a home bird enjoying evenings in by our old fashioned open hearth fire.

The weather that January was particularly atrocious and I began to think about the wettings and chills that come with working outside for a living. Perhaps it might not be a bad idea to find an inside job to see me through until Easter? Jobs were plentiful and I thought there must be someone who wanted a bit of temporary help inside out of the wet and cold. I visited the Labour Exchange (now the Job Centre) to see if I could find something.

On my first and only visit to a labour exchange I met Bronc, Andrew Hardy to give him his proper name, a giant of a man at around six feet four or five and eighteen stone. Bronc was rather in the same position as myself. He worked seasonally on the motor launches, his father owned shares in the Waterhead Motor Launch Company based at the head of Windermere Lake. After a casual conversation, we both realised that we were more or less looking for the same thing, something just to put us on until Easter. It was not surprising therefore that when the desk clerk suggested that we might wish to apply for a vacancy that had arisen in Kendal for unskilled bench hands, whatever that might be, that Bronc and I decided to follow the job up.

"Can you read a drawing?" was the first question we were asked. We had decided to make a joint approach regarding the job and the interviewer seemed happy to go along with us. "No problem mate' was Bronc's swift reply. I had already realised that my new companion was a man with a direct 'no frills' approach to conversation.

"Well for the moment all I can offer you is bench work, but machine work might follow if you prove to be the right applicants." "We'll take it," replied Bronc, not even looking in my direction.

After what must have been the shortest interview on record, Bronc and I were taken on as bench hands with Gilbert Gilkes and Gordon, who I have since found out enjoy the reputation as one of the world's finest manufacturer of water pumps and turbines. We were shown around the works, including the area where we would be working, and asked to report at 7.30 on the following Monday morning.

The ease with which we had been allowed to join the payroll of G. G. & G. soon became apparent when on the first morning we were put to work 'de-burring' at one of the benches. This, very simply, involved the taking off of the rough 'burrs' or sharp bits of metal which were left on the pump castings after they had been machined on a lathe. For our part, we found ourselves standing at a bench with a wooden handled steel file and a handful of emery cloth and the instructions to remove all traces of roughness.

I can honestly say that, despite having done a number of what might be considered by some people to be boring, repetitive jobs, nothing I had done before came anywhere near to being as dull as this. I was never-the-less prepared to see it through despite the fact that there was no relief from the sheer boredom. Fortunately, after a couple of weeks persever-ance, Bronc was drafted onto a pillar drill and I to a milling machine. Obviously neither of us had had any experience on these machines but after some tuition we were left to do some of the simple machining jobs. Fortunately there were two time served chaps, John Baron and Alan Guy, who worked close by me, who were most helpful and readily forthcom-ing with advice.

One thing that did emerge in my few months at that factory was that, despite the machine work being very interesting, I found that being sur-rounded by four brick walls was just too oppressive. As I left on my last day to once more take up my summer job, I vowed that I would never again do a job which kept me inside all the time - I never did! Working day in, day out, operating machines and building wonderful pieces of equipment wasn't for me but I left much the wiser for my short experi-ence. I have nothing but admiration for people working in factories though it is something which I personally could not bring myself to do.

At home Wendy and I turned one of the two bedrooms on the first floor into a hair dressing salon. We had fitted it out with a tiled floor, basin, a large mirror on the wall and to add to the professionalism, a brand new hydraulic chair and hair dryer. The reason for Wendy's change over from employed to self-employed was that she was expecting our first baby, and felt that she would have more control over when she worked this way.

I was quickly back into my stride with regard to Mallinson's Motor Tours. It was the 1964 season and as hectic as usual. Harvey, as forward thinking as ever, had ordered diesel coaches as opposed to the quieter running petrol engined ones. His reasoning was that, as diesel became more popular, there might come a time when petrol driven vehicles would be harder to dispose of. This move proved to be a wise one. At first I must admit to being a little sceptical as our passengers had often remarked to me: "How nice to ride in such a quiet vehicle." I wasn't too disappointed as it turned out!

By midsummer I was beginning to give more and more thought to our baby which was due at the end of September. Was it to be a boy or a girl? When would Wendy give up her hair dressing? Was I going to be around at the time when she needed to be rushed to the maternity hospital? That would be an interesting scenario. I found myself worrying that I would be just moving off on tour with 41 customers when I got a phone call to let me know that Wendy was in labour. As it turned out Wendy surprised us all and on 30 August 1964, a month early, gave birth to a beautiful blonde haired little boy, who was later to be christened Miles Harvey Delmar Bolton.

As the number of tourists using our coaches dropped, the firm put on an extra tour - a five day excursion into Scotland which was largely patronised by local business people who had been too tied up with their various business interests to consider holidays earlier on in the season. As an annual event it was extremely popular and we always departed with a full coach. This Scottish tour was always taken by Teddy, he had been doing the same trip for many years, long before I joined the firm and often with many of the same clients. Once again Teddy's superb gift as an entertainer came into play.

Teddy's 'party piece' was that for the whole of the tour , he would wear a kilt and all the regalia that goes with it, of which I am not qualified to comment other than he really looked the part. On previous occasions I had helped see the tour off. Teddy had his own way of 'warming up' his charges, one was that, underneath his kilt he would wear a baggy pair of silky knickers to which were attached all sorts of amusing baubles and trinkets including fluffy toys. His party were in hysterics even before they boarded the coach! I was of a more reserved nature and was quite happy to laugh with them, but could never have been the central figure like Teddy. I was quite happy to hold the fort back at home.

This year there was something different about Teddy's departure. The passengers were just as excited, Teddy was there as usual in his regalia and he was going through his routine just as usual, but the sparkle wasn't there. It almost seemed that he was forcing himself to perform. Harvey had also noticed the change but was reassured that everything was OK and that Teddy had everything in hand. So the tour departed.

It was later, when I returned from my day tour around the lakes, that I learned the news. It was news that was to change not only the fortunes of myself, but would also bring about the demise of a tour company which was supreme in its role of guided tours in the Lake District. Teddy had been taken seriously ill.

Being in charge of a coach loaded with passengers is not the place to be feeling ill. Just as with any other job, people turn out for work feeling perhaps one degree under the weather. Teddy had been faced with such a situation and had tried to shrug it off. It hadn't worked and he had been taken into hospital in Edinburgh with a suspected heart condition and a local driver had then been recruited to continue the tour. As things turned out, Teddy had to remain in hospital for several weeks. I saw the season out doing all the driving leaving Harvey to manage the office.

The situation was that Teddy was completely out of action. He was in his early 60s and Harvey was almost 65. They were very comfortably off financially and there was little or no reason for them to carry on in business as it would necessitate the hiring of another driver and an office person for the following year.

The decision was made to close the business. The two coaches were sold off as usual and the office and coach stand in Ellerthwaite Square and the garage in Chestnut Road would be offered for sale. The business, including the tour licences would also be available. I had considered the possibility of taking over the firm myself, but gave up the idea as it would involve me having to borrow a small fortune, a risk which I could not justify. As things turned out, the coaches were sold out of the district, and both premises were sold to Silver Badge Motors, the firm who worked out of Bowness. They were generally accepted as poor relations to Mallinson's, at least as far as touring was concerned.

Following the take over of Mallinson's business I spent the winter of 1964-65 again amongst the Christmas trees, (no inside brick walls again for me!). This time I had no retainer to supplement the flat forestry wage. I began to think about looking for a more lucrative source of income. My dilemma was solved when in the March Brian Wilson, the son of the owner's of the Silver Badge company called one evening at Howe Cottage. He had been authorised by his father to offer me the position of additional driver with the firm. As was expected, by adding Mallinson's business to their own, it was necessary to involve one more driver. Obviously it was not necessary for me to justify my ability for 'my old job' and, after a little negotiation, it was agreed that I would fill this position.

Once more Easter came round, and yet again, I took to the driving seat of a tour coach. This time though it was not a brand new silver and blue one, but an older maroon and grey one. There was no question that I had been spoilt by the old firm and I had revelled in it! More or less straight away I realised that things were going to be different. The approach of my new boss to business in general, lacked finesse. A booking of specific seats system was employed and on too many occasions this led to the same seat being allocated twice, usually because of confusion between the Bowness and the Windermere office, causing some rather unwelcome disputes. I completed the season, never as happy as when working with Teddy and Harvey, and left in the back end with neither a job nor a retainer.

Just before I finished my season with Silver Badge, I met up with my ex-boss Alan Faulkner. He, having lost his father, was now in charge of the family firm of Brown's Motors in Ambleside. During conversation it was mentioned that I was shortly to be requiring a job, and Alan was wanting another driver. It was not really my intention to drive for a living through the winter. I had learned that a more physical approach suited my health better and I recognised that sitting on my backside permanently was not the best way of keeping fit. However a job was a job, and I agreed to join Brown's for the second time in my life.

The reader might be excused if he/she is now confused as to why one firm appears to be finishing its drivers and another is seeking them. The answer is simple. In the case of Brown's Motors, they had an all year round policy. They took on all types of private hire work, including a contract with the Charlotte Mason Teacher Training College to take trainee teachers to schools all around the district. This would happen in the early morning and they would then be collected in the late afternoon. Besides the school work, Brown's had a thriving private hire business, involving work travelling all over the North of England, as well as trips as far afield as London and beyond. They had half a dozen coaches and kept as many drivers.

My old favourite, the Hawkshead Bus Service, had been taken on by the Ribble Bus company. There wouldn't be any "I'll pay you at weekend" with them, and parcels would now have to be paid for. A lot of the driving was late night/early morning work and I was now the newest employee and would, for the time being, move to the bottom of the pecking order, at least as far as 'good' jobs were concerned. Some jobs were more likely than others to yield a decent tip.

Weekend work usually involved taking football or rugby teams and their supporters to matches. Getting there was no problem, it was getting them together for the return journey which often proved the challenge. Without a doubt it was the rugby teams who caused the most chaos. After playing an afternoon match, it invariably followed that the visiting team would have a shower, then a feed, and then join the home team in the club house for a drinking session which could last an hour or it could be a marathon finishing around midnight. By this time most of the players, and often some supporters, would be much the worse for drink. It was on one such occasion when I had driven the Kendal A team to play against Workington that heavy drinking delayed our departure.

Time and time again I had attempted to gather the team together. Club rules of staying only long enough to be sociable had gone right out of the window. Eventually, with what I took to be the full contingent, I set off home. At one point I had to stop at a set of traffic lights, simultaneously I thought I heard the vehicle's sliding door open and then shut. Half a mile further up the road I became aware of what had happened: "You'll have to stop and wait for my mate!" drawled a burly young chap, his speech slurred and his eyes glazed over, "he's running down't road after us."

I pulled up and looked 'down't road.' Lo and behold in the distance, seen in the light from the street lights and a few passing cars, could be seen the naked figure of the missing player. The opening and shutting of the sliding door which I had heard was when a number of players had pushed the poor chap, in only his birthday suit, out into the cold night air. Our involuntary streaker arrived at the coach puffing and panting, no doubt more sober than he had been a short while before. This was only one of a number of 'tricks' which the rugby lads performed. I of course, had to refrain from any form of alcoholic drink and got much ribbing for doing so, but fortunately I was never on the receiving end of any but minor tomfoolery.

Brown's company policy, for the main part, was that each driver was allocated his own coach. Wherever that coach was booked to go, day or night, that driver drove that coach. The unfortunate spin-off of this arrangement was that if you had been out with, say, a party to Manchester and arrived back at two in the morning, you were still expected to be available to pick up again the same morning even if it was an early start. As I lived in Ambleside I had to drive back to Windermere before I could get my head down which added to my problem.

As I had left the Silver Badge in October and started more or less straight away with Brown's, and following that worked through Christmas, by the July of 1966 with eighteen months driving without much more than a few days off, I was beginning to feel pretty tired. I was rather more tired than ever before. As a rule, when feeling tired, I simply shrugged it off, telling myself not to be so soft, something I had learned during my farming days.

It was after I had had three particularly long runs over to the North East that things came to a head. The first trip took me over to Scarborough, a coach from there had broken down and I was given the job of taking the party home in the late afternoon. Following this, with short local trips in between, I found myself in Thropton near Alnwick on the east coast of Northumberland with the Burneside Academy of wrestlers. Finally, after two extremely late finishes in the early hours of the morning, I was sent with the local fans to the News of the World Darts Championship held in Tynemouth. It was again going to be the middle of the night before I would be finished and back home. I really was feeling the pace.

However I delivered my rowdy, happy, good natured party at the hall where the event was to take place. I wasn't the least bit interested in the game and satisfied myself with a walk around the neighbourhood. After returning to the coach an hour or so later, I settled down with a newspaper, it was going to be a long night. Cat napping in a stationary coach in a car park is not necessarily the best place to rest, invariably you will be constantly disturbed and, if you do manage to nod off, you will wake up frozen. This trip was no exception. I had nodded off, it was about ten in the evening and when I woke I was cold and hungry. I was just about to leave my coach and make my way to a small chip shop which I had spotted not far down the road, when I suddenly realised that I hadn't a penny in my pocket, not so much as a bean. I had left home in such a hurry that I hadn't picked up my wallet. Here I was over a hundred miles from base, hungry and penniless!

Ahh, I thought, I know the answer - the back of the seats. When cleaning out the coaches, occasionally we would lift up the passenger seats and practically every time some loose change would be found. This was always claimed by whoever did the cleaning, invariably the driver.

Systematically, starting at the front, I began working my way backwards. I reached the middle seats with no luck and, by the time I had reached the back with only the full width, five seater left to check, I was beginning to think that I would be going the rest of the night hungry. Perhaps stupidly, I was too proud to seek out any of the party to 'cadge' a few shillings.

With an extra heave I managed to dislodge the most awkward seat on the vehicle and there in all its glory was the most beautiful ten shilling note (50p in today's money). I was home and dry. I bought my fish and chips and enjoyed them, but I did spare a thought, wondering when the seats had last been lifted and which unfortunate individual had lost the ten bob note. Oh well, one man's loss is another man's gain. I only hoped that the rightful owner didn't have to do without his or her supper.

It was four in the morning when I finally got to bed. Two members of the party had not returned to the coach and had delayed departure by nearly an hour. We finally left without them. I learned later that they had met up with girls and had stayed overnight.

I had many amusing little incidents from time to time and all of them helped to make my job a happy one, but the sheer volume of work was definitely beginning to have its effects on me. I wasn't enjoying my job any more, every trip seemed to be a chore, this was not me! One morning I was asked to go to the Christian Holiday Fellowship establishment, 'Monk Coniston' just outside the village of the same name. I was to collect a party of guests and to take them to Grasmere where the famous Grasmere Sports were taking place. Having collected these people I headed back on a route which brought me back to Ambleside and then on through Rydal to the sports field.

As I passed along the road over looking Rydal Lake, only a couple of miles short of my destination, I started to feel really strange, almost as though I was about to blow up, it was a feeling as if electricity was being passed through my body. This was not good. I had around 40 passengers on board and I was feeling decidedly ill! In an attempt to gather myself together I leaned towards the side window, sliding it open as far as it would go. I gulped a lung full of fresh air which seemed to give some relief; all this with the vehicle still in motion.

Within minutes we were outside the sports field and my passengers were alighting. They all seemed unaware of the drama which had been going on, however, as I climbed light headedly down the coach steps to see them off, one older fellow did approach me to ask: "Are you alright?" I answered that I was, probably pretty unconvincingly, but it sufficed enough for him to allow me to board the empty coach once more and drive cautiously back to the firm's garage where I was supposed to make ready the vehicle for another party outing. I knew then that this was not going to happen.

As I drove into the garage, it seemed a re-enactment of the situation six years previously. Alan Faulkner was again standing by the fuel pumps just as he had been when I presented him with my notice before moving to Mallinson's. It was a different story I had to tell him this time.

"I'm sorry Allan, I won't be driving any more today," I said, "there's something really wrong with me I'm afraid." Alan looked at me and straight away realised I was ill. " I think I'd better get you home," he said and immediately instructed one of the firm's taxi drivers to do just that. I had always considered myself a pretty robust sort of a chap until that day, but here I was on my way home, half way through a day's work and unable to continue and with as much energy as a 90-year-old. I knew that whatever it was that was wrong with me wasn't going to be fixed over night. I was right on that score, and the way things turned out, I would never again drive another coach or a bus.

SOME CHANGES AND A JOYOUS OCCASION

Obviously when I arrived home, no doubt looking like death warmed up, Wendy was taken aback. She had probably noticed that I wasn't at my best, but like myself had put it down to tiredness. A phone call call was made and, within the hour, I was in Dr. Robin Hall's surgery.

"I know what's wrong with you," said Dr. Hall. I'd only been in the room for a minute but evidently it was long enough to make what turned out to be an accurate diagnosis. "You have got nervous exhaustion." I had been preparing in my mind a whole list of symptoms with which to bombard the man, but evidently my normally fresh complexion now replaced by an ashen grey one, combined with my general persona must have told him all he needed to know.

A discussion as to what treatment would now be required ensued, before I left with a prescription for a supply of 'dozzy pills' (the name we gave to the sedative drug which was prescribed) with instructions that I should rest, eat good food , and then rest more. What happened next can be best described as a long haul. For the next couple of months I was able to do little different than follow my doctor's advice. I was constantly drowsy with hardly the energy to climb the stairs. I would rise from my bed in the morning and feel that I wanted to climb back in again an hour later, I really felt that my world had collapsed in around me!

My illness came to a head in August 1966 with the incident whilst travelling to Grasmere. By the Christmas of that year I was just starting to have a few better days. During this time I was almost totally dependent on Wendy, not only as far as looking after baby Delmar and myself, but she was now the only bread winner. After only two weeks off sick my wages had ceased to be forthcoming, (in fairness I hadn't been back at Brown's quite a year) but we now relied on my flat state sickness pay and the income from Wendy's little business to pay the mortgage and all the other on going expenses which occur in a household.

My reliance on Wendy I suppose helped spur me on most to get myself sorted out. My inability to provide for my family hurt me and I was determined to do something about it. By my 30th birthday, on the last day of February, I really felt that things were beginning to turn for the better. I was getting around a bit, I was going for increasingly longer walks and doing the driving when we visited Wendy's parents at Newby

Bridge. But, perhaps understandably, in the back of my mind was the fear that all would suddenly come tumbling down around me again if I did just that tiny bit too much.

My Dad came up with a suggestion that, if I was to get myself a suitable car, he would be prepared to hand over the over spill from his taxi business. The jobs which he would normally have to hand on to someone else could be accommodated by me, it would be a help to him and possibly something of an income for me. The idea seemed a good one, perhaps this would provide the route back to once more being in a position of standing on my own feet. With no more ado, an old but very tidy Humber Super Snipe was purchased; I can't remember how it was paid for. I set up somewhat apprehensively as a private hire person - a special licence would be required before I could set up a separate taxi business - and for the first time in my life I was now self employed.

That spring, as well as helping my Dad out with his business, I gathered together a number of regular clients of my own, mostly it seemed elderly ladies who wished to be taken into the village on shopping trips, or maybe to be taken to their friend's home for afternoon tea. Most of them came over as rather genteel and extremely pleasant ladies, all of which helped to boost my confidence. I began to get back some of the

The author pictured with the Humber Super Snipe taxi.

sparkle which, though I say it myself, had helped me become quite popular amongst tourists on the coaches. As well as private hire I was soon to be fortunate enough in obtaining both a council taxi licence and a place on the railway station taxi rank. This allowed me to join my Dad and the dozen or so regular taxi drivers who plied for hire from that point.

My first real test came in August 1967, when an elderly couple approached me asking for a quotation to take them down to Torquay in Devon, a round journey of nearly 800 miles which would have to be done in two days. I now had a dilemma - should I just say that I was unable to give a price? That would be like running away from my problem or should I give an over the top estimate which would then in all probability rule itself out? No, I had always been true to myself, I was not going to start going down that road!

When you are as ill as I had been, you know the things that you can't do. When you are starting to feel well it is more difficult to be sure of the things that you can do. When a letter arrived to say that my estimate for the trip was accepted, I decided to confirm the booking and hope for the best. As things turned out I completed the trip down, stayed the night in an hotel, and returned home the next day without incident. I also had a booking for the same trip in reverse a month later to bring my clients home.

Summer and autumn had been pretty busy. Our bank balance had improved and I was very nearly back to myself health wise. I had not found it too difficult to wean myself from the use of my dozzy pills which I understand is sometimes a problem. Fortunately I am one of the world's worst at remembering to take medication, besides I believe that the less toxic substances one introduces to one's body the better. In all, it is fair to say, that things were now looking pretty good, despite the fact that taxi work had diminished with the onset of winter.

During my visits to the railway station and whilst waiting on the taxi rank for fares, I had come in contact with a young chap called David Blezard whose father, like my own, was also a taxi proprietor. The Blezard family were just about the longest established taxi people in the village. David Blezard had started his own independent business as soon as he was eligible to drive a car legally. By the time I had met up with him he was 24 years of age and had six or so years of business under his belt.

It was in conversation whilst waiting on the rank that the subject of the availability of work came up. David, like myself, had left school at fifteen and had spent a couple of years with the landscape gardening firm of Thomas Mawson & Sons and had gained some experience in outdoor work. We both agreed a lot of time was being lost waiting for fares. There were too many taxis available in winter for too few jobs. We also agreed that we, as practical hands on chaps, could make better use of our time. Accordingly we placed an advert in the good old *Westmorland Gazette* seeking general estate type work. Hopefully this would produce a much needed boost to our incomes.

The advert worked well and produced several jobs which David and I were able to accommodate in amongst our much diminished regular work. It wasn't long before we both realised how well we worked together, each quickly recognising the other's strengths and weaknesses - we proved a good team.

A few years previously, whilst I had been working in the nursery of Mould & Bloomers, I had persuaded my father-in-law to buy and have me plant 4000 Norway spruce (Christmas tree) saplings. They were by now at the stage where they could be harvested and sold off. An arrangement was worked out whereby, as I had done the planting, and if David and myself provided the labour, we could collect the most suitable trees, market them, and we would split the proceeds equally three ways.

Whilst the approach of Christmas once again heralded a time of excitement, Wendy and I had something much more joyous to look forward to. December was to be the month when we were expecting our second child. Just as before Delmar's birth, Wendy was continuing with her hair dressing. I had reservations but that was Wendy - never looking for a soft option! After making a few enquiries, it was decided that the outside market at Barrow-in-Furness would probably be our best bet to dispose of several hundred Christmas trees. We approached the Market Authority and a pitch was booked. Everything was going to plan, except for the small matter of transport - how would we get several hundred trees to Barrow Market - in a taxi?

A stroke of luck led us to find out that a semi-retired local farmer had a rather beaten up old Bedford dormobile, (a van with windows) which was for sale for the princely sum of £15. The vehicle was bought, a cheap insurance arranged and we were in business. Straight away we commenced cutting the trees and fastening them in bundles of five in order to reduce their volume. We had limited space available but at least the van had a roof rack on top enabling us to practically double the normal load. The following day was market day. David and I were up early. we had been advised that in order to claim our pitch, we would have to be at the market by 7.30am, otherwise we might miss out. The weather was kind to us, cold but dry. We had loaded the van the day before, now all that was necessary was for us to get ourselves there.

As we had expected, we were not the only people at the market selling Christmas trees and, after a few hours, we were rather disappointed to find that we didn't seem to be doing just as well as some of our competitors. The main reason we worked out was that, unlike most of the others, we were not offering branches of holly for sale as well as our trees. The bright red berries seemed to make the opposition's stalls so much brighter than our own. Not to be perturbed, we resolved that when we returned the following day, we would have some holly. Quite where we would get it was going to be the problem.

That evening David phoned round a few of his farmer friends and met with some success. We were hoping to find some ready cut but this was not the case. We were offered some but unfortunately it was still on the tree. Knowing that getting to Barrow for that early start was crucial, we had only one option open to us. If we were to have holly on our stall, we would have to get out even earlier and collect it ourselves. So saying, at four o'clock the following morning we headed out to the area of Crook where the holly was to be found. With still more than four hours of darkness left, this was not going to be an easy exercise. A comprehensive description of where the field with the holly could be found had been given, so we had little difficulty in getting to the right place. The problem lay in that we were only able to get the vehicle to within 50 yards of the spot.

A number of Christmas carols refer to the holly bush but none that I have heard of mention holly trees. Our holly however, turned out to be at least twenty feet up in the air, and we had to get some down. In our capacity as estate workers, David had already shown a reluctance to climb up trees and, on weighing up the situation we were now faced with, he said: "I'm not bloody well going up there!" To save the day, it was me who finished up the tree. Reasonable heights had never really bothered me. David remained on the ground and shone the torch to direct me to the boughs with the most berries which I clipped off with a large pair of secateurs.

By the time we had gathered together what we believed to be sufficient of the festive greenery and carried it to the van time was getting on. We had topped up with trees at Newby Bridge on the way home the night before, and now had to stand on the wall to stack the bunches of holly on the very top. Job done, we set off up the lane with the van now looking like a war-time Zeppelin on wheels, nearly twice its normal height.

By now it must have been just after six o'clock. Travelling down the narrow lane the headlights seemed to bring the walls either side of us even closer. The rest of the world it seemed was still asleep! However, just short of the point where the lane joins the main road leading in the direction of Barrow, we both became aware of a set of headlights ahead of us coming in our direction. As the lane at this point was still only fractionally wider than the van it became obvious that either we, or the oncoming vehicle, would have to give way. One of us would have to reverse to the nearest wide spot. Still the headlights came on. I happened to be doing the driving that morning, and it was I who muttered a curse under my breath: "damn fool, should have waited!" It wasn't a damn fool however, it was a police patrol car, out looking for poultry and Christmas tree thieves who were operating in the county. Now, with our vehicles stationary, bumper to bumper and blocking the lane, nobody was going anywhere, at least for the moment.

"I reckon you think you think you've got yourself a fair cop here," I said to the officer who had exited his vehicle and was now stood beside the open sliding door of our van.

" Don't give a damn as long as we get one apiece," he said nodding towards his mate who by then had joined us.

"No problem, I think we can manage that," I said confidently in the knowledge that David and I were acting totally legitimately. A couple of nice tidy trees were sought out, together with a few well berried stems of holly and the gentlemen in blue went on their way. On the face of things it might have appeared that the strong arm of the law had been a little lax, however I knew that the officers had recognised both David and myself and were no doubt aware of our backgrounds giving them little concern as to our legitimacy.

We spent a further few days at Barrow Market. The addition of the holly proved very worthwhile and our stock of trees and holly was disposed of practically to the last berry. Whilst at the market we had observed the other traders, some of whom had provided us with some great entertainment. One cheeky chappy in particular, a fellow with a 'Cockney' accent, had arrived in an old bread delivery van. "Come along ladies, come and see these beautiful Cartier wrist watches, sit on your wrist like pieces of royal jewellery, not like a tin of John West salmon. I'm not here today and gone tomorrow! I'm here today and gone tonight!" The same chap was selling cheap miniature radios. All day people were returning them 'not working' he would fob his customers off with all sorts of excuses. His patter was highly amusing to listen to, a real professional!

During the whole of my involvement with the Christmas trees I had a constant anxiety about how things were going on at home. Wendy was due to give birth to our second child virtually at any time. I knew that she was being watched in my absence, but nevertheless my thoughts were constantly drifting back to how she was progressing and I was leaving the stall every few hours to phone home (no mobile phones in those days!)

"It's a boy!" I shouted, "It's a boy!" I didn't care who heard me. The lady on a stall nearby beamed with delight: "Congratulations," she said, as did David and several other stall holders who had realised what the commotion was all about. I now had another son, later to be named Simon John Harry Bolton. He was born on 15 December 1967 and I was walking on a cloud!

Christmas passed and Wendy got back into a routine of looking after our enlarged family, which meant fitting her hair dressing customers in with all the other jobs. I was busy with a mixture of taxi work and little walling, fencing, tree felling jobs and the like. Altogether it could be said that we were a pretty industrious lot.

My friend and then part time work mate, David, was quite an expert with considerable knowledge of the various makes and models of cars about at that time, a fact that leads me into the next part of my story. David and his brothers had been in the habit of following various car auctions which meant trips down to Preston, Blackpool and even as far as Brighouse in Yorkshire. I had never heard of such places let alone ever been to one. However one evening I was invited by David to travel with him to Cottam Street, Chorley, where every Tuesday evening just such a sale took place.

The experience of attending Chorley Auction that evening proved to be a real eye opener. Cars of all descriptions were driven into a building where an auctioneer, sitting on a raised rostrum, immediately commenced taking bids from dealers and private buyers. The speed with which they were disposed of, and the knock down prices left me stunned. As we drove home, a plan to try to capitalise on this newly discovered potential source of profit making was hatched. We would buy a car, check it over and polish it up, splitting the cost and hopefully some profit two ways. We would do all this of course in our spare time. Over the next few months we managed to buy and sell quite a few cars profitably!

During the spring and summer of 1968, I was busy with the taxi business and Wendy with her hair dressing and looking after the family. The boys were both thriving and developing their own personalities. Most Sundays we were able to get down to Wendy's parents where the children were able to take advantage of the tarn and swimming pool in their large garden. On the face of things everything was going well. I was more or less back to good health and I should have been fully contented, but I wasn't. Always in the back of my mind was the thought that I had built up quite a successful little business, but, I didn't want it! I suppose I had had few options open to me when I took on with taxis and, had my health not broken down, I would probably have still been coach driving. But that was in the past. Taxis had served their purpose and I was now open to a new challenge.

Just about this time the Ministry of Transport were starting to build the road which we now know as the lower stretch of the Cumbrian section of the M6. The by-pass round Lancaster was already completed and in use. The new section between Carnforth and Penrith was, for the purpose of construction, to be split up into a further three sections and allocated to three separate main contractors. The southern end, Carnforth to Crooklands, was awarded to W. C. French, the middle section, Crooklands to Tebay, to John Laing Construction, and the northern stretch, Tebay to Penrith, went to Christiani Shand. Having gained these contracts, the major contractors would then involve smaller companies who would further sub-contract the work out.

It was when I met up with a young chap who was already working on the central section of the project which I have just described, that a seed of an idea started to grow. This young fellow, together with a friend had bought a wagon each and were now engaged in hauling stone from the quarries to various parts of the section. In order to carry out the first phase of the project, Laing's had appointed an agent who would be in charge of hiring all the haulage. The agent was a firm called Tattersall and Gorton. It was to them that I made an enquiry with regard to the possibility of getting work and the necessary licence. The enquiry proved positive - they had already engaged around 40 wagons and were looking for considerably more!

For a week or so the idea that I might buy a tipper wagon and go hauling stone on the motorway mulled around inside my head. This I was sure was more me. It was a challenge and I was looking for a challenge! I obtained some haulage rate figures, estimated what it would cost to keep a wagon on the road and how much I would need to turn over to make a reasonable profit. I soon realised that there were so many factors to be taken into consideration. In the end it was down to two options - I either had a go or I didn't!

With Wendy's nervous approval, I answered an advertisement in the *Lancashire Evening Post* regarding a Leyland tipper which was for sale. I had again contacted T. & G. Associates who had assured me that I would be granted a 'B contract licence' and that they could provide me with any amount of work. I felt reasonably happy and went one step nearer to what could only be described as a radical change of direction.

Following up the advert I found myself in the village of Warton which lies a little to the north west of Carnforth. The vehicle which I was going to look at was an oldish Leyland Comet and the owner was about to take delivery of a new Leyland. This gave me some assurance that at least he couldn't have had too much trouble with his present Leyland! I was not disappointed when I first set eyes on the vehicle for sale. It was pretty much as it had been described although the owner had failed to tell me that, although the main body was metal, the tail board and sides were wooden, a detail which I was later to find out was all too relevant. Apart from this, a reasonably comprehensive road side appraisal revealed nothing other than normal wear and tear.

Now the moment of truth - the owner, by the way, had informed me that the advertised price of £180 was now £200 as, since I had been in contact, he had had several further calls. One had offered to buy the vehicle unseen! I knew that, because of all the activity in the area, he was probably telling the truth. It was now make your mind up time.

"I'll have it!" There, I'd done it - there was now no turning back! I paid the £200 and got a receipt, the documentation and two sets of keys. I assured the now ex-owner that I would return later to collect my new acquisition. Today £200 seems like peanuts, but at the time it was the maximum that I could have paid for the wagon bearing in mind that I also needed funds set aside for the running of the thing. I guessed that it would be a week or two after getting started before any money would come in my direction, a guess that was to prove right.

In the next few days I was able, in amongst my taxi work, to find time to arrange insurance and set the wheels in motion with regard to getting my contract B licence, which, surprisingly, landed through our letter box almost by return. Under the terms of my licence I was now able to haul stone and other materials for and on behalf of John Laing, within a fifteen miles radius of Lowgill. These conditions, as it turned out, were all too relevant. The big day came and around six in the morning I climbed into the driving seat of the big Leyland. It was a tidy old thing and a credit to its last owner. I had been instructed to go to Dillicar Quarry which I knew was on the side of the Kendal to Tebay road just before the road dropped down into the Tebay Gorge. It was there that I was to join the many other tipper lorries who, like myself, had been hired to haul the raw rock to the various points of new road already under construction.

On arrival I reported to the weigh bridge where every ton of stone had to be weighed before removal from the quarry. The contractor paid the haulier not by the load but by the ton. The driver obtained a weigh ticket every time he left the quarry loaded. No ticket, no payment! My first job was to establish my vehicle's tare weight, that is the weight of the empty truck. After that it was just a question of deducting the tare weight from the total or gross weight of the loaded vehicle to establish the amount of stone on board.

Inside the quarry was a hive of activity. Hundreds of tons had been blasted from the hillside and were being loaded onto a succession of wagons by a huge N.C.K. rapier face shovel. Its huge steel bucket scooped up two or three tons of rock at one go. Three or four scoops and a blast on the operator's air horn told the driver that he was to move out. Any driver a little slow in reacting was given a second longer blast signifying the operator's impatience and also that he was probably on a bonus for tonnage loaded out of the quarry! The sound of the air horn reverberating round the rocks brought back memories of the sounds from the scree beds on the far side of Wastwater back in the Mallinson days when I blew the vehicle's horn, but no time to dwell on that!

Although I had had the short experience of working in Kirkstone Quarry, I was not prepared for the furious pace at which the work was carried out at Dillicar. After a few days it became apparent just how indifferent the regular Laing employees were towards the influx of none Laing people; the gangers and the plant operators (excavator drivers) were the worst culprits. One occasion which directly involved myself, typifies the callous regard that the gangers had for the owner drivers, who struggled to move sometimes as much as a couple of hundred tons of rocks a day each, from the quarry face to the dropping off point. I had just loaded about ten tons of rocks, been weighed, and was now waiting my turn to tip my load.

At this point a ganger was directing wagons, two at a time, to reverse two abreast depositing their loads on the edge of an in-fill which was to form the foundations of the motorway. A huge bulldozer would then, with one pass, sweep the two heaps over the edge. Unfortunately the ground on which my wagon stood sloped badly to one side, with the result that, when the body was some two thirds up, it became apparent that any higher and the wagon, now leaning at a precarious angle, would tip over. I had no alterative but to lower it quickly. By now, because of the delay, the ganger was becoming decidedly agitated. I unfortunately found that, because of the twist in the body, it would go neither up nor down.

"Get this bloody thing to hell out of the way!" shouted the now angry ganger in his rich Irish accent. "Get it moved or we'll bury the **** thing!" I was beginning to become flustered. The twin tipper rams were working one against the other and refused to react to the controls. There was only one thing left for me to do as I was holding the whole job up. Very slowly I inched forward towards more level ground, the wagon, with its full load of ten tons of rocks was immovably jammed, swaying precariously in the air just behind my head and threatening at any moment to tip the vehicle on its side. The threat to bury my truck had been a very real one however, as it turned out, I just managed to gain level ground. The tipper mechanism was then able to function and I found an alternative dumping ground.

The loaders were no more kindly disposed. With the huge loading shovels they were able to lift some tremendous rocks and made very little effort to place them down with minimum impact, resulting in a huge amount of damage to the hauliers' vehicles. Some of the chaps I met and talked to had left good businesses believing that they were going to make good money. A number of them had bought brand new wagons, I suspect in most cases with £3000 or so of borrowed money, and were now seeing their acquisitions bashed to bits in front of them!

After a few weeks I had gathered together quite a lot of weigh tickets which I had submitted for payment. I had done some calculations and was beginning to realise that the haulage rates were not really enough to cover costs. I had been forced to replace the wagon body as the sides had virtually disintegrated being made only of wood. I had had to replace springs and tyres and, with fuel costs, the whole thing was doing not much more than breaking even. In addition the conditions in which we were operating were atrocious!

When the hauliers had finished a section, all the rough rocks which form the base of the road had been put in place and the rough work was done. All of a sudden a fleet of yellow cabbed wagons bearing the name Laing appeared and started to ferry full loads of the white crushed little stones from Pennington's Quarry. There were no jagged rocks dropped from out of the sky for them. The granulated stone was quietly loaded, none of it bigger than a fist and there were no uneven roads of raw rock for them to drive over ripping their tyres to bits. It was now obvious what the game plan was. Laing's and all the other main contractors let all the mugs rip their equipment to bits on the rough work, and when the easy bit came with little risk, they used their own trucks.

By now the realisation that I wasn't going to make any decent money whilst up on the motorway had sunk in. Under the terms of my licence I wasn't able to work anywhere else or for anybody else. I couldn't blame anybody else, not even John Laing - they were only going about the job as economically as they could. I should have gone further into the whole thing before making my move. Strangely I wasn't too bothered. I had a gut feeling that a solution was not too far away. As it turned out it was lady luck who decided to intervene at this stage of the haulage saga by allowing me to come into contact with a haulier called Lenny Muscroft. Lenny was in his late 50s and had been operating a one man tipper haulage business from a small yard at Longlands in Bowness, not very far from where I lived. Lenny's wagon was a rather old Dodge tipper, well serviced but well worn. It wasn't worth a lot, but what he did have, that was valuable, was a B licence with few restrictions, which allowed him to haul practically any material for any customer, within a 100 miles radius from his base at Longlands. There was at that time little chance of me, or any one else, obtaining an open licence. Lenny told me that he was considering retiring from haulage to further his life long interest in engineering and suggested that I should buy him out. I decided that I would try to take him up on his offer.

The asking price for the business was £1,250, apportioned as follows: £800 for the good will, £250 for the wagon and £200 for a bulk diesel tank plus fuel and oils. The licence would be transferred with the business, subject to Ministry of Transport approval. On 2 July 1968, with the help of a bank loan, I agreed to purchase the haulage business known as John Watson & Sons' (Lenny's predecessors) and Lenny agreed to sell. The money was paid, and I was then in a much improved business, free from the constraints imposed by my existing licence and free from the cruel (on the vehicle) conditions of motorway construction.

The day after the deal had gone through, I was in the saddle and it was all systems go. I had now to justify a bank loan. Lenny had two main customers - the Windermere Sand and Gravel Company and Pennington's Quarries of Kendal. Both companies were owned by the Pennington family of Kendal. As would be expected by anyone taking over a business, an agreement had already been established with the customers that they were prepared to allow me, the new owner, to carry on where my predecessor had left off.

My first port of call that morning, with Lenny in the passenger seat, was the Sand Wharfe on the shore of Lake Windermere where the plant workers were responsible for extracting sand and gravel from the bed of the lake. They would pass it over a series of large vibrating sieves and stock pile it in its different grades. After Lenny introduced me to the key men, I was loaded, weighed off on the weigh bridge and left the the plant heading for Kendal with ten tons of Windermere sand on board.

Despite the Dodge being rather old with a high mileage, I was delighted to find that it pulled better than the old Leyland which I had by now disposed of. We were soon at Pennington's works at Kendal where the load of sand was to be delivered. The set up there was that the sand (or gravel) was to be deposited in one of a series of bunkers from where it would be taken by conveyor belt to a concrete batching (mixing) plant.

From there it was taken by mixer wagons to building sites etc. We deposited our load and then reported to the transport office to be given further instructions as to which materials to load out of the quarry and where to take them.

The rest of that day and the days that followed, were taken up collecting loads from the Kendal or the Windermere plant and delivering them to various sites around the district. It was an absolute doddle compared with the harsh motorway conditions, with very little stress on either man or machine. I soon began to believe that I had made a good move.

Months passed by without too many hitches at work. At home baby Simon was now nearly a year old and was turning out to be a particularly handsome little fellow. He now had a beautiful head of dark curly hair and big round eyes, and from the start showed that he had a will of his own. Delmar, or Del as he was now beginning to be called, showed an amazing stamina much preferring to push a pram rather than ride in it - he was happy walking miles. Having only two main customers made book keeping quite a simple affair. All that was required was to keep a record of each delivery and bill the customer accordingly. The account was a monthly one and often took several weeks before settlement so, in order to improve cash flow, I decided to seek out a few smaller customers who would hopefully provide work which could be done at weekends.

One private job I inherited with the business, was one which could be said fitted into the category of a labour of love. It was the emptying of the waste bunker at St. Martin's Church in Bowness. The bunker itself was built from a number of table size slabs of slate stone fastened together vertically. It was into this receptacle that all the dead flowers from off the grave stones were thrown, together with empty cardboard boxes, waste paper and, worst of all, lengths of string which made it extremely difficult to drag out with a garden fork. Two or three times a year, the rubbish was loaded onto a truck, and now the job fell to me.

On the appropriate Saturday morning, I drove the old Dodge down to St. Martin's Square and parked alongside the wall adjacent to the bunker. I spent a couple of hours loading the rubbish then drove to the local municipal tip, and disposed of same - a good job done. Come Monday morning I was up early as usual and straight down to the sand wharf where I loaded with sand. It was just a routine morning and I arrived at Pennington's, drove up to the sand bunker and emptied my ten ton load of best quality sharp (coarse) sand. Five minutes later I had a sudden rush of blood to my head. Where were the fork, the shovel and the yard brush? What had I done with them? I had finished my rubbish removal job on Saturday, but had I removed the tools from the back of the wagon when I returned to base?

I got my answer when I quickly made my way to the work station which lay underneath the huge concrete sand bunker from where sand and gravel were directed up long conveyor belts to various parts of the works. Johnny Barker, the man in charge, was busily trying to wrestle my garden fork from the jaws of the control chute which fed the sand onto the long endless nylon belt. He had spotted the foreign body just in time and stopped the plant.

I dread to think what it would have cost me that day had the fork come another few inches out of that chute and had Johnny Barker not seen it and stopped the plant. The prongs of the fork would have, in all probability, ripped the belt all the way round. In the end, the rest of my equipment was extracted, and I got off with a caution. The incident could have got me banned from the works and lost me my main customer.

By December 1968 new legislation was coming into force. They were introducing a new system of 'plating' of all haulage vehicles, whereby they would all have to meet certain standards in order to carry specific weights. My concern now was that my old Dodge, despite being quite able to carry a ten ton load, would soon be down rated to a pay load of perhaps as little as seven and a half tons. As I was paid by weight not by the load, the loss of capacity would render the vehicle non-viable. I could be doing the same amount of work for as much as thirty per cent less. The reality was that I would soon be faced with two options - either to buy a wagon that fitted the new criteria or do the unthinkable!

After looking around and getting prices for new wagons and scanning the pages of the adverts, I heard about a vehicle which was for sale in the Carnforth area. This was the area where I had bought my first wagon; there are several quarries in that area so it was not surprising there was a reasonable supply of lorries for sale. The vehicle I arranged to see was a K. M. type Bedford. It had done a couple of thousand miles, was as good as new and the asking price was £2,200. A new one at that time would have been about twice that price. Again I faced a dilemma, should I or shouldn't I? Oh well, this must be what being in business is all about. I had little choice, so let's get on with it, with the help of a further loan I bought the thing!

It was some months after putting my new acquisition into service that one morning I was given a load of three cubic yards of wet concrete to deliver to a building site at Annisgarth in Bowness. We hauliers didn't really like taking wet concrete in an open wagon, especially a distance as far as Kendal to Bowness, some ten miles, as the vibration from the road causes the water in the mix to separate from the rest of the mix, resulting in the concrete drying out while still in the truck. Under normal circumstances, concrete would be delivered in a rotating mixer, but none were available.

At this point in time house building was going through a boom time. The trade was on fire and this particular load of concrete had to be delivered come what may. I arrived at the site and was directed to where foundations had been dug for a new property whereupon I routinely opened the tail gate, put the hydraulic tipping mechanism into gear, and waited for the rush of concrete when the tipper body got high enough. When the body had reached the full extent of its travel and still nothing had come out, I realised that I had a problem on my hands. The weather had played a part in the problem, being exceptionally warm and dry.

My load of concrete was now a good way to being half set! Ten tons of the stuff was suspended up in the air in the back of a near vertical wagon body; it wasn't a lot different to when I was struggling to tip up on the motorway. Going underneath a raised wagon body, even an empty one, is not a practice that is recommended and under a ten ton load is even worse! However drastic situations call for drastic measures and somehow the concrete had to be dislodged. I seized a fifteen foot ladder which happened to be lying nearby. This, I thought, could be the instrument which would save the day. Grasping the ladder vertically, I prepared to ram the underside of the floor of the body - surely this would release the fast drying load?

Ferociously I lunged upwards with the ladder hoping to hear the sound of sliding material followed by the shudder of the truck as it and its load parted company. Unfortunately the only sound I heard was the crack as my left thumb caught the extended neck of the diesel tank. I dropped the ladder and grasped my left wrist and stared at the damage. My left thumb had broken completely through and was now touching my wrist, held only by the skin and tendons.

Whilst I sat on a pile of bricks feeling decidedly 'woozy', a digger was summoned and the almost hard concrete was dragged from the vehicle with the digger bucket. By the time this was done I had somewhat recovered from the initial shock and, with one hand, drove the now empty wagon to my Bowness garage. My father then took me to the accident department at Kendal Hospital where my thumb was re-set and my wrist and hand put in a plaster cast.

After a few days, my hand ceased to cause any pain and I was able to drive again, though I had to take great care not to catch my thumb. In the few days which I had been incapacitated, I had really had time to take stock of my situation. One thing which had come to the fore was that I was rather vulnerable in that I relied so much on the haulage of other peoples' materials. I thought perhaps I could make some adjustments to my business which would broaden the services I had to offer.

As I travelled around delivering materials to the various projects which were going on around the district, I found myself being fascinated by how the various pieces of ground were transformed from being just a plot of land into groups of dwellings of various sizes. The whole process fascinated me. I found myself dropping off my load and wishing I could stay and join in the process rather than having to dash off to get another load to take somewhere else. In a sense these people were creating something out of nothing.

One day when I arrived in the Kendal Quarry, a little later than usual as I had been delayed waiting to be loaded with sand in the sand wharf, I was approached by the managing director of the quarry who, to his credit, was not a boss who came in in the middle of the morning and sat in his office. He was always right there on the job from first thing when the plant started up in the morning.

"And where the hell have you been? I wanted you here first thing! I'm going to get more wagons of our own and then you hauliers can go to hell!" No doubt the boss was just having a bad morning. It must have been very difficult trying to keep things running smoothly, but the message was there. I was vulnerable, having pretty well all my eggs in one basket.

Following my run in at the quarry, I began to think of a way of diversifying my little business, preferably in such a way that would utilise the assets which I already had, i.e. my wagon and my garage/workshop. By this time I had moved my base to Crag Brow in Bowness, ironically it was the garage which had previously housed the Silver Badge Coaches which had moved to Mallinson's Chestnut Road garage. Again I found myself scanning the for sale columns of the *Westmorland Gazette* and the *Lancashire Evening Post* for ideas.

It was from the latter paper that I read of a firm who were wishing to dispose of an International Drott, which I knew to be a form of bulldoz-er/loader. I had toyed with the idea in the back of my mind of mixing excavations and earthmoving with haulage for some time and I thought this Drott might be the answer. A phone call confirmed that the machine was still for sale. It was owned by a very successful haulage contractor by the name of Cecil Davidson and the machine was on a demolition site in Southport. I made an arrangement to meet Mr. Davidson at his depot near Chorley so that I could view the Drott. It was my good fortune to have met a young chap called Gordon Campbell who was an excellent self-taught mechanic and a good all-rounder. Gordon agreed to travel with me to give his opinion on the machine.

On arrival at Chorley, I was most impressed to see the standard of the wagons parked up in the yard. It would be no exaggeration to say that they were without exception immaculate. I was also equally impressed when Gordon and I were asked to climb into Mr. Davidson's car, or rather his car and a half. His personal transport was a big shiny American beast which was about twenty feet long. It ate up the miles to Southport effortlessly and gave the impression that one was floating on water.

My first sight of the Drott was as we drove onto what had been a large demolition site. I say had been because all that remained of what had obvi-ously been a number of large buildings was an area about the size of a foot-ball field with only a few heaps of broken red bricks remaining. Perhaps at this stage it would be appropriate to describe in a little more detail what a Drott is. It is simply a sort of tractor, in this case weighing around eight tons, which has a large bucket (scoop) on the front, and a counter weight on the back. The Drott is both capable of digging out and lifting and load-ing earth or stones onto a wagon and relies on caterpillar tracks to move about. Gordon started up the machine, moved it backwards and forwards several times and went through the motions with the front end digger. All seemed to be in working order and a deal was struck.

A few days later I was free to collect my Drott. I would have to travel down to Southport empty and load the machine myself. My wagon was legally entitled to carry ten and a half tons so there was no problem there but just how I would get the thing on the wagon I wasn't sure. Well I would sort out that matter when I got there.

Although I had driven all sorts of wheeled vehicles before, I had never so much as sat in a machine on tracks. I arrived at the site and found things, including the heaps of broken bricks which I had now decided were crucial to my plan of action, were exactly as when I had been there previously. I had no problem starting the Drott, and spent a while trying to familiarise myself with the controls until I reached the point where I knew only experience would teach me further. I removed the tail board of the wagon and commenced to bull doze some of the heaps of broken bricks that lay about up against the rear of the wagon. I was trying to form some sort of a ramp up which I could drive the machine.

When I considered there was sufficient spoil banked up behind the wagon, it was now time for the moment of truth. My Drott was down here and I wanted it up there. Could I manage to get it loaded without a mishap? With the tipper body half raised in order to continue the constant gradient of the make-shift ramp, I gingerly eased the Drott forward. Gradually the front end started to rise and point towards the heavens. I had already decided that, once under way, my best policy was to keep going rather than attempt a jerky stop start approach.

The whole distance of travel must only have been about twenty feet but, by the time I was nudging the front of the wagon with the nose of my machine with the raised digger bucket extended high in front of me, it seemed as though I was up in the gods. Fixing the hand brake I stopped the engine and climbed down onto the ground. I'd done it! All that remained for me to do was to replace the heavy tail board, and lower the body of the wagon. I was to repeat this performance again many many times. It soon became nothing more than a simple chore, but I never again put the Drott on facing forward as I realised my mistake on that very first trip. With the machine facing forward the ton weight digger bucket was suspended above the wagon cab, not a good idea if the hydraulics burst or the truck was in a collision. After that first time I always reversed on.

GLENBURN, SON NUMBER THREE AND MUCK ON THE ROAD

By now with the boys growing bigger, our little cottage seemed to shrink. Wendy started to get ideas about moving to a bigger house. Howe Cottage had served us well, but it was time to move on. Wendy had for some while felt that she would like to try her hand at bed and breakfast. Her grandmother had been quite successful and now she felt she would like to have a go. The tourist industry was booming and, at weekends in particular, we would see tourists driving round and round desperate to find accommodation so finding guests would be no problem.

When a large house called Glenburn came on the market things started to happen. The house stood beside the main road which ran between Windermere and Bowness (and the lake). It was ideally situated to catch passing trade. Mrs. Bruno, the widowed owner, had used the house for the very same purpose.

Glenburn was a very impressive property, built in the Edwardian style, from a mixture of beautifully dressed red sandstone and random local slatestone. From my point of view the place would benefit from opening up a little. Although there was plenty of garden front and back, cars had to be parked on the driveway and good parking would be paramount if the place was to be used effectively as a guest house. Everything about the place had a feeling of being solid and built to last. The house was originally built as a gentleman's residence but was now to be put to a different use. Putting in an offer for Glenburn might, on the face of things, have seemed a bit reckless as we had not yet sold Howe Cottage, but this is just what we did. The offer was accepted. However I had not done this without a great deal of thought and, as I will now explain, a little bit of forward planning.

The next door property to Howe Cottage, separated from us by a high stone wall, was a rather large house which, like Glenburn, had been turned into a small but rather nice hotel named Howe Villa. The conversion had been done by an industrious chap called Norman Hammond and then sold on to a couple of very nice people, Peter and Marjorie Bergin. Although Howe Villa was a very nice place to stay, the property had one major problem - it had no official car park and had to rely on the generosity of the management of the Windermere Hydro, a huge hotel nearby, for guest parking. It was a rather unsatisfactory arrangement. The

Villa's garden was quite large and could easily have been turned into a car park, but the exercise would have been pointless as they had no vehicle access.

Soon after I bought my Drott, I had opened up the bottom of our own garden and had made it into a car park. I had done it in such a way that, with very little effort, the dividing wall between the two properties could be taken away and next door's land could be converted for parking. My theory was that they would have to buy our house! Well that was the theory, would it work? The following day I kept an eye out for Peter. I knew he spent quite a bit of time in the garden and was not disappointed. I was determined that when I approached him I would try not to appear to pushy. If I acted casually I thought, I might stand a better chance of getting my asking price. However the speed of his reaction left me flabbergasted.

"Just thought I'd let you know that our house is on the market as from today Peter" His initial look of surprise soon gave way to the look of a man with a purpose. "How much will you be asking for it?" he enquired.

"£6,000," I replied, "and, if you're interested, I would include taking down this wall and tarmac the bottom of your garden in the deal." The next reply came swiftly, "Give me five minutes." With no more ado he shot off up his garden. Peter's five minutes was just that. I had gone back in the house to make Wendy aware of what I had said, and had only just sat down when there was a knock on the back door. It was Peter.

"I've spoken with Marjorie and we'll have it!" were the first words he said. "We're prepared to give you your asking figure and, if you will take down the wall and sort the parking out, that'll do us." We shook hands on the deal. There was no commission to pay to estate agents only solicitor's fees. My forward planning had worked, thank goodness.

The first job on the agenda after we had settled in at Glenburn was, as I had anticipated, the sorting out of the car parking. Fortunately as I was in the haulage/earth moving business, this didn't present any sort of a problem. I immediately set about removing a section of front lawn which was very poor, and replaced it very tidily with a tar macadam surface. Now we had room to park four vehicles comfortably.

In the house we were beginning to get used to the extra space with wide staircases and high ceilings - all a complete contrast to the cottage. With a lick of paint to freshen some of the rooms, we were very soon open for business. Our first guests were two South African boys who were quite amused when we told them they were the first paying guests we had ever had! At the rear of the house was a large garden, around fifty to sixty yards long, which culminated at the end with a steep slope down to a beck (stream). In my head I had plans to convert some of the land into further car parking, but this was going to have to wait until I had a 'slack' time at work. This area of the garden was shortly going to cause me the fright of my life.

It had been raining solidly for close on a week and I had been having great difficulty in getting on with my work, which at that time was mainly digging trenches in the road for the then Lakes and Lune Water Board. The constant deluge had caused a temporary shut down of their operations and I found myself at home wall-papering the living room. During a lull, Wendy had decided to walk up to the village to call at the bank and a few shops. Simon, who was always strong willed and not easily persuaded, decided he would rather stop with his Dad and play with his toys.

Half an hour or so after Wendy left, I realised that Simon, who had been rather quiet, was no longer close by. Quickly I downed tools and set about looking for the four-year-old, dashing through all the rooms on the ground floor, then on the first floor shouting his name. I started to panic - had he got outside? I ran into the front garden, there was no Simon. While I was running round like a headless chicken the men from the local refuge disposal department landed at the house.

"Have you seen a little boy on his own around here?" I asked.

"Not me," answered Kevin a chap I had often spoken to on other occasions. By now I was being joined by the other men and we made our way to the bottom of the garden where the sight that greeted me made me feel sick. At the bottom of the steep sloping banking, where the usual babbling stream was, there was now a dark brown raging torrent swollen ten times over by the constant deluge.

"He's a gonner if he went in there," said Kevin insensitively. Despairingly I knew he was right. As if a life-line had been thrown to me, a sudden thought came into my head. Had Simon had a change of mind? Perhaps he had decided that he wanted to go with Wendy? It was just a chance. I ran to my car and sat off at a break neck speed after Wendy. My usual regard for the highway code was the last thought in my head. Almost on two wheels I rounded Woolley's corner and followed the one way system round the village.

My car had hardly come to a halt before I was out of it. The bank staff must have thought it was a bank raid as I crashed through the swinging doors. I had only one thought in my head and was oblivious to all around me. All I could see before me were two children with their mother, one with light wavy hair and a smaller one with dark curly hair. To say that I was relieved to see little Simon would be like saying that I was glad the world was still going round. Just minutes before everything had collapsed around me, no words can describe the anguish I suffered in that short space of time. Without giving an explanation for my behaviour, or saying a word even to my wife, I turned and walked slowly from the building then drove the short distance home at a ridiculously slow speed. I was totally drained physically and emotionally.

The following morning, with the rain still coming down in buckets full, I ignored the half papered living room and set off in my wagon for the village of Far Sawrey where at Bruce Dixon & Son's sawmill I bought twenty or so ten foot posts which, together with a roll of wire mesh I already had, were used that day to build a tall and substantial fence across the bottom of the garden. I had had my warning, I wouldn't get a second chance.

Gradually I was finding that I was doing more on the excavation side than the haulage. This suited me as I had more control over which work I took and I found that I had a natural ability for that type of work. Soon it became apparent that more jobs were coming in than I could handle on my own. I had already bought an additional wheeled machine, a Massey Ferguson excavator (like a J.C.B.) and now had to consider buying another one if I was to employ someone to help me. With house building and road excavations at an all time high, it was not going to be easy to find a good driver/operator. Whilst I had been running out of Pennington's Quarry, I had met up with a young chap called John Bethel. John drove one of the ready-mix trucks and had always come over as a friendly cheerful sort of a lad as well as being very good at his job.

During one of our conversations John told me that he was a little bit fed up with his job and that secretly he really fancied a go at digger driving. This fact had remained in my mind, so much so that, as I was now ready to take someone on, I straight away thought of John and contacted him, offering to give him sufficient tuition to get him started. John, like myself, had started his working life on a farm, so I knew with tractor and truck driving experience, he would have little difficulty in picking up the basics. After that only experience would make him into a real expert.

We agreed on a wage and John became my first employee.

Earth moving can at times be a pretty rough job and shifting hundreds of tons of earth about can have its problems. One such occasion remains in my memory and I have to smile when it comes up, although it was decidedly unfunny at the time. In the middle of Bowness there is a steep hill called Helm Road. It runs directly from the top of the equally steep Crag Brow up past the Hydropathic Hotel to the private Matson Ground Estate. In February 1971 a road widening scheme for the lower part of this road was taking place. I had become involved and was responsible for digging out the banking on the side that was to be widened as well as loading and removing all the surplus.

As was often the case, the job was being hampered by persistent rain. In fact the constant moving of vehicles and plant, had made the ground into a sea of mud. The manager of the hotel arrived and registered a strong complaint saying that: "The mud was being carried on vehicle tyres and from his car park into the hotel." Something had to be done about it. There was nothing for it but for me to try to scoop up the mud and try to get rid of it. After several passes of my Drott bucket, I had scooped up several tons of the brown porridgey slurry and deposited it in the back of my wagon. It would now be possible to cover the excavated area with some of the nice white gravel lying in heaps

HO/RT/1 MEMORANDUM
Road Traffic Act, 1960

Date 1/8/24 197 Time 11-10 a.m./p.m.
Name M.R. MiLES R.M. Bolton
*Driver/Passenger/Other
Address 149 Crag Walk.
Windermere

Accompanied *Yes/No
Registration mark of vehicle 91F 442F
Type of vehicle Bedford Lorry.
L Plates *Yes/No
Purpose for which vehicle was used Business

Police station at which { *driver's licence / certificate of insurance / test certificate }
is to be produced Windermere

Issued by Pc 348 Brown
Police station Windermere
Police force Cumbria
*Delete as necessary

NOTE.—The Act provides (in sections 225 and 226(1)) that a person who has failed to produce his licence or certificate of insurance or test certificate when required shall not be convicted of the offence if the document is produced within 5 days (IN PERSON in the case of a driver's licence) at a police station specified by him when its production was required.
Dd.136296 K3200

CUMBRIA CONSTABULARY

Telephone Kendal 22611	**COUNTY POLICE STATION**
Our Ref. U10/89/71	Busher Walk
Your Ref.	KENDAL
	Westmorland

23 February, 1971.

To:

> Mr M.R.M. Bolton
> 149 Craig Walk
> BOWNESS-ON-WINDERMERE
> Westmorland

Dear Sir

I have to inform you that I have received a report against you for a motoring offence(s) viz:

Insecure load

at Kendal Road and Windy Hall Road, Bowness

on Thursday, 18 February, 1971

No further action will be taken in this matter, but I am to inform you that, if you are reported again, it may be necessary to take proceedings against you in respect of the later case.

Please acknowledge receipt of this letter.

Yours faithfully

[signature]

nearby. This would tidy up the mess and placate the upset hotel manager.

With the road cleaned up for the time being, I now turned my attention to the load of slurry. I had to get rid of it and the only practical solution was to take it to the local refuse tip which was a couple of miles away. The route to Lindeth tip took me down the steep Crag Brow and through the main shopping area of the village, round the Royal Corner and into St. Martin's Square, over the zebra crossing and up the constant climb to the Crook Road. As I passed Brantfell Garage, which was owned by Norman Askew, an old friend of my father's and from where as a child I got my first bike, I reflected on how well the Bedford was pulling.

As I hit the steepest part of the hill, just opposite the entrance to the footpath to Brant Fell (Steep Fell) from where one of the finest views of the lake can be seen, I began to get a very uneasy feeling. I should have been changing down through the gears and be either in bottom or reaching for crawler, but I wasn't. Was the load lighter than I had thought? The answer to that question was answered when I looked in the rear-view mirrors. Down the road behind me I could see a brownish trail of what I immediately recognised as my thick brown slurry. Climbing from the wagon I just could not believe my eyes. After examining the back of the wagon, I realised that the swirling action of the slurry had forced the tail gate over the lugs which would normally keep the back shut, and allowed the load to slither out.

With no other course of action open to me, I turned the now near empty wagon round and headed back the way I had come. The whole affair got worse - the further I got into the village the thicker the deposit of the thick brown slime got. Other road users were weaving in and out in an attempt to avoid the mess. By the time I reached the point where the slurry had first burst forth, the scene looked as though a herd of wild buffalo had rampaged through the place. I was going to need some help to get out of this one. It took a team of three men and myself with brushes and shovels and a couple of strenuous hours work to put the mess back on my wagon. Fortunately the rain had stopped otherwise the nightmare would have been even worse.

As I expected the strong arm of the law appeared and I got booked. I was given a ticket by P.C. Brown. This was followed by a cautionary letter - no further action was to be taken which was a great relief. No doubt

The author pictured August 1973 with his new Poclain digger at College Road, Windermere, only 50 yards from where he was born.

the fact that I organised the cleaning up helped my case.

For the next couple of years things went on pretty well as we had hoped. Wendy, who was now expecting our third child, was fully occupied running the home and her guest house enterprise. She employed some part time help, particularly in the mornings, getting breakfast over and cleaning the rooms, not to mention getting the boys off to school. I was now employing three full time and one part time men. I now had four diggers, my wagon and a couple of tractors with fitted winches, but more about them later.

By the beginning of June 1973, Wendy was showing signs of not being quite as well as she should have been. This was not perhaps surprising as she was the world's worst for not standing back and letting other people do the hardest jobs. However her role in the running of things was suddenly curtailed when, on a visit to the pre-natal clinic, she was told that she had to stop all activities. She was reluctantly forced to go into Helm Chase Maternity Home for a complete rest.

During the weeks that followed, I spent my time frantically trying to run my business which included myself operating a digger, wagon driving, organising my men as well as seeing that Mr. and Mrs. Smith got room no. 6 or Miss Jones got the single room no. 7. Fortunately I had previously devised a grid card which showed the dates and rooms one to eight so that we had the names, dates and rooms booked. Otherwise we would have been in deep trouble. At this point mention must be made of the good help provided by the part time ladies, as without their help, I would have been sunk. All the extra work proved well worth it when on the 2 August, Stephen Michael Bolton was born. We now had three fine sons and we were both very proud of them!

All went well. Wendy and Stephen came home to Glenburn and within a couple of weeks or so we were all back into our usual routines. I had men and machines working regularly for the local authorities such as the water board, the gas board, the county council and the G.P.O. to whom I hired out my tractors fitted with heavy duty winches. These were used to pull a mole plough, a piece of equipment through which telephone cables are fed underground.

In January 1974 I was involved with the demolition and removal of what might be considered something of a historic landmark - the central block of buildings on Oxenholme Railway Station. It had been decided by the rail authorities that the buildings, which were situated between the main north south line and the Windermere line, were to be replaced by something more modern. The old building provided a licenced public bar, eating facilities and rest room. It had been built at the same time as the station and was now considered out of date. The waiting room had been the scene of high drama when, in February 1965, a fugitive fleeing from Carlisle police, attempted to hide in the building. He was discovered by two policemen and, sadly, the outcome of the incident was that one policeman was shot dead and the other was badly wounded.

At the time the demolition was to take place, I had just bought a brand new Poclain wheeled three hundred and sixty degree excavator. It was the first of it's kind in the district. Because it was on wheels and not on tracks, it was considered to be more suitable for the business of travelling on the station platforms and so the main contractors, Brown's of Carlisle, hired me and the machine. Before making a start on the demolition I was taken on one side and given a lecture on safety. I was to be under the direct instructions of a man from the railway who was to have total control. When he said stop, I was to stop dead, not in a minute, but there and then regardless of what I was doing.

I was not more than an hour into the job before I realised the potential dangers and the reason for the tight safety regime. The station is on a bend and the express trains shot through at goodness knows how many miles per hour. My approach to the job was that I would cave each wall inwards starting from the northern end of the block. It was a good strategy as it turned out, but not without a few anxious moments. On more than one occasion I had the wall, which was built of large blocks of stone with huge dressed stone lintels, swaying as if deciding which way to fall. This was of some considerable concern as, if it had gone the wrong way, a lot of stone would have finished up on the track. I don't like to think of what might have happened even now!

As the job neared completion the last section to be knocked down was the public bar, which greeted travellers as they walked up the paved ramp leading onto the northern line. The licensee's name, which I can't for the life of me remember, was on a board above the door. Underneath the bar, as in most licensed premises, was a beer cellar, which of course, like all the rest of the buildings, was empty. Empty that is except for one thing - a large basket work hamper.

Purely out of curiosity I and other workers opened the basket, which was about four feet long and two feet six wide and a couple of feet deep. It was crammed full of L.M.S. (London Midland Scotland) Railway tea mugs. I took it on myself to approach the works foreman and suggested that we remove the basket. "No way, we aren't allowed to touch or remove any railway property," insisted the foreman, "just get it filled in!" With great reluctance I did as I was told. I am no railway buff, but I hate to see sheer wanton destruction, but I had no say in the matter. However there it is, if anyone wants to wait till the present building is considered past its usefulness and is knocked down, they will find some very collectable L.M.S. mugs. Perhaps some will still be in one piece.

As the guest house was kept open seven days a week, for fifty one weeks in the year, it is not surprising that occasionally we had one or two incidents, some amusing, some rather annoying and some a mixture of both. There were rarely less than four or five people in the house. The most we ever had was twenty one, which was made up of twelve separately booked guests and nine young Chinese students who arrived on the doorstep at about eleven o'clock one night. No amount of explaining to these young people that we had only two rooms left would put them off. They were pretty desperate and were not going to be deterred. Finally

Wendy and I agreed that they could take the two rooms with no extra charge. How they allocated the beds and who slept where they themselves would have to decide. The only stipulation was that they got themselves settled down and were quiet.

Considering the fact that nine people were being charged for the price of six, and that they all went away with a good breakfast inside them, you would expect them to have been pretty grateful. However our kindness was rewarded by them somehow putting feet marks up the walls and across the ceiling as well as filling the door locks up with chewing gum. We were not amused at the time, maybe I have missed the point, could this be some sort of a Chinese custom? We were a little wary of groups of young ones after that.

I would not like to leave the reader with the impression that running a guest house was a series of negative happenings and that most guests were in one way or another problematic, quite the contrary. We were privileged to meet some exceptionally nice people enjoying many pleasant conversations, usually in the evenings after our guests had been round the lakes. Despite all the positive aspects of owning and running our own guest house in such a beautiful area, I gradually became aware that both Wendy and myself were becoming bogged down with nothing but work. The children were not enjoying the freedom which they should have been getting and were always being told: "You can't do this or that, it'll disturb the visitors." I felt somehow that things would have to change.

Because of my deep rooted interest in farming, I had always read the farming columns in the local paper, the *Westmorland Gazette.* One day an advert caught my eye. It read: "Small holding of eighteen and a half acres for sale" and what's more at a figure which I knew was less than the value of Glenburn. At first I wrote the advert off as a pipe dream of mine and put it to the back of my mind, but after the advert appeared again and again for a number of weeks, curiosity got the better of me and I persuaded Wendy to at least go and have a look at the place. I would see it, satisfy my curiosity and that would be that!

THE FAMILY GO FARMING

Great Eskrigg End turned out to be all that was left of a medium sized farm after most of the land had been sold off to neighbouring holdings. It had been, at one time, a farm of eighty or so acres but was now reduced to just eighteen and a half. The farm itself was accessed by leaving the old Kendal to Kirkby Lonsdale road at the little hamlet of Middleshaw, and then making one's way up a narrow winding lane which ends up at the two farms of Great and Little Eskrigg End. It was the former that on a rather nice spring morning Wendy and I set out to view. We had little difficulty in finding the farm but, as we rounded the bend in the lane, we were faced with two groups of buildings and with no for sale boards around, we were unsure as to which property we should be looking at.

For a while we remained seated in the car, not wishing to intrude where we were not supposed to. Then I became aware of a rather farmerish looking fellow leaning over a yard gate. He had obviously seen us arrive and was now watching us. I decided to approach him.

"Could you possibly tell me which of these properties is Great Eskrigg End?" I enquired. For what must have been at least a minute I received no answer to my question, just an enquiring look as though the chap was deciding how he would reply.

"Yes I can, that's it over there," he said nodding in the direction of the buildings over to our left. "And I'm the chap who lives over there," he indicated again, this time to the right. " And if you don't like the look of me, you'd better get in your car and go back the way you came from!"

Over the years I had had many dealings with farmers. I had worked with them, for them, and had lived with some of them and so had instantly recognised the dry humour that I had just been confronted with. Somebody less familiar with this mischievous humour might have taken his words at face value and done just that, turned and and gone. My reaction was to take up what was actually a sort of challenge and came back with some reply equally as dry.

Leaving my new acquaintance, who I later learned was Robert Woodhouse, we approached what I now knew to be the front door of Great Eskrigg End. We were immediately greeted by the owner Mr. Edwin Postlethwaite who at that time had retired from farming and instead was happy to let his land to his son who shared the same name.

The house itself was quite a decent size, though by no stretch of the imagination in anyway equal to the quality of construction that we had in Glenburn. The rooms were small with low ceilings but had a very pleasing cottage feeling about them. The doorways surprised us most - not one of them allowed me at half an inch short of six feet to pass through without very slightly dipping my head.

On the first floor there were four reasonably sized bedrooms and a creaky staircase which led to a one room attic which was the full length of the building. Straight away I was struck with a strange sense of almost foreboding. I put it down to the fact that all the wooden beams and bare floorboards were so dark having been creosoted many times over the years. I suppose the farm servants would have slept in this room in the early part of the 20th century and before.

Outside, on the left hand side of the tarmac road which came to an abrupt end only yards past the buildings, was a semi-modern cow shed with tying up for twenty cows. Below was a stirk shippon built to accommodate a similar number of young stock. On the right hand side of the road stood an old and very large stone hay barn which stood around thirty feet high above the road level, and was almost sixty feet in length. Underneath this building were the original low ceilinged cow stalls and heavy horse stables, accessed by three separate doors. The floors were the original cobbled ones, worn smooth with a couple of centuries of hooves wearing away at them.

The next stage of the viewing was to walk round the land which went with the place - three fields in all. The largest one, a seven acre meadow, stretched from immediately behind the house on a fairly level plain until half way across it climbed dramatically to a two acre plateau from the top of which you could see as far as Black Coombe on the west Cumbrian coast. The other two fields made up the eighteen and a half acres. All the land seemed to be in good heart.

On the way home we discussed the positive and negative aspects of what we had just seen, and agreed that we were both rather disappointed at the rather run down state of the house and some of the buildings. Although the place was clean and tidy, little attempt had been made to bring either the house or the buildings up to date. Over the next few weeks, which were pretty hectic all round, the subject of Eskrigg End came up for deliberation on many occasions. We had come to terms with the fact that the rather run down state of the place directly reflected the seemingly low asking price. Had the place been ultra up to date, no doubt it would have been out of our reach. No, that was not the main issue. The main issue was, were we prepared to cast aside the life style of both of us, working every waking hour and our kids living in a work place, rather than a home, for a place out in the sticks. It would be a totally different way of life.

I don't remember the exact circumstances of how we came to our decision. Suffice to say that it was probably the pressures of our two businesses that must have finally got to us and made us decide that enough was enough. So much so that we made an offer, subject to the sale of our own property, for Great Eskrigg End. Within weeks we had a buyer for Glenburn - there was now no turning back!

I suppose, to be truthful, I had some doubts in my mind when we finally walked out of what had been a thriving and chaotically busy establishment and into a house at the top of a dead end lane, where the only sounds were those of cattle, sheep and the birds in the hedgerows. Anyhow we had taken the plunge, so now it was up to me. Having a wagon of my own, admittedly not the normal type of removal van, but never-the-less one capable of transporting all our belongings to our new home, (we had left most of the furnishings from the guest house for the new owners), it seemed only sense to use it. I did several trips in the day and then we finally settled down for our first night in the countryside.

Next day, after sleeping like a log, I awoke at the crack of dawn, had a quick cup of tea, and walked out of the house before any other member of the family stirred. It was a beautiful morning and as I walked across the meadow behind the house, taking in the sweet air, I was struck by the realisation that here I was walking in my field, on my beautiful earth. I had many times worked in other people's fields, but this was mine. I don't think if somebody had given me the crown jewels I could have felt any happier than I did at that time. I will never forget the moment! For the uninitiated, in this case someone who has never lived with or worked on the land, my euphoria might be hard to understand. But to somebody like myself, who had endured the extremes of the seasons and the hardships of having to keep working despite the often debilitating temperatures, one's feeling for the land heightens in a strange way.

After a few days and nights we all started to become acclimatised to our new style of living. Wendy was possibly the most affected. For my part, after the first two days, I returned to my normal routine of managing my earth moving business, which obviously involved a little more travelling, depending on where I or the men were working. Poor Wendy was, for the first time since we were married, left on her own with only baby Stephen and Cindy our labrador dog for company. Another facet of country life is of course, that there are no shops just around the corner. At first you fall into the trap of not planning far enough ahead resulting in having to make more journeys than necessary to the shops, in our case in the village of Oxenholme four miles away. Never-the-less Wendy persevered and very soon adjusted to the new life style in a way that even surprised herself.

In my previous paragraph I alluded to Cindy, our golden labrador bitch, a beautiful animal most intelligent, trustworthy and with the perfect temperament. She had been given to the family by Mrs. Jean Mackereth in gratitude for the part I played in helping to rescue her husband from the lake in January 1964. Cindy was with us for twelve years and she is still mentioned from time to time even now.

Plans to make radical changes at Eskrigg End started to take place. Our first job was to extend the living area. To do this I turned my attention to the barn which was attached to the eastern end of the house. The idea was that we would break through the end of the house into the barn and convert it into a lounge. Some lounge - when we eventually completed it, it measured 28 feet long, 18 feet wide, and 17 feet high to the apex. At the time that we did the conversion, I was fortunate in knowing a chap who was a self employed builder called Peter Noble. The arrangement was that Peter did the building and I did the labouring. The end product was a show piece lounge with exposed beams, a dramatic three tier fossilised limestone open grate fireplace, oak covered window seats, glass sliding doors giving access to the rest of the house and a view of most of our land.

The converting of the building to a lounge had been done mainly in the late afternoons, evenings and weekends so as not to interfere with our regular work, which also helped to keep the cost down. We now felt that we should turn our attention to an outside project that would hopefully bring in a bit of income. For this reason we applied for planning permission to site a static caravan. The idea was that Wendy would attempt to let the caravan for holiday visitors. This seemed an ideal way for her to occupy herself and at the same time boost the family's income.

After a couple of site meetings and a lot of deliberating, a reluctant planning officer finally gave the go-ahead for a large static caravan to be set up in the orchard behind the house. We bought a rather nice caravan, water and electricity were installed on site, and with a few well placed adverts, Wendy soon had this attractive project under way. My role was little more than keeping the grass mown round the caravan.

By the time we had been at the farm for a year, it would be fair to say that we had decided that our move had been the right one. None of us missed the hustle and bustle of the guest house, and the children and their friends had a fantastic time in the fields and woods around us. Wendy and I had between us set out a loose sort of plan for our future. I would increase the farm's stock (we had by this time a dozen ewes, ten six-month-old stirks which I had reared from being only days old, and a few hens and turkeys about the place). I would alter the big hay barn into a stock rearing building, and we would try to get planning consent for a few more caravans, all of which combined with my earth moving would hopefully provide a reasonable income and allow us to save something for the day when we could no longer work.

Were these the best laid plans of mice and men? The next project was to make something of the huge barn. It had been built originally to hold all the hay produced on the then many times larger farm. Now it was more or less obsolete as the amount of hay that could be produced on the present day farm would go in a tiny corner of the building. I was determined to find another use for it. The barn itself was still a fine building, just as square as the day it was built although the wooden floor, which was of course the ceiling of the cow shed below, was rotten and in a pretty poor state. To make full use of the building we came up with the idea of a battery hen enterprise.

A standing joke with our family, which I am sure was entirely undeserved, was that I was a much better hand at demolition than I was at construction. I believe that I had gained this notoriety, not because my finished projects were in any way sub-standard, but rather that when I started a demolition job I never went about it with timidity. Things had to fly and the barn was no exception. When I finally got started, power saws and sledge hammers were the order of the day, and within a short space of time, with all the timbers and stone boskins removed, the interior was

The fire at Morecambe Promenade's pier

transformed into one cavernous room, big enough to hold a dance in.

The stripping out completed, the next stage was the lifting of some of the cobbled floor which was in a pretty poor state. This was replaced with six metres of concrete, (about eighteen tons) which is often referred to in civil engineering terms, because of the large number of Irish workers employed, as Paddy's porridge. With the help of a very good friend of mine, Geoff Wightman, who was a partner in a local building firm, we spread the concrete right through, leaving a level floor from one end of the building to the other. Now, just to give the reader the full picture, we had a perfectly smooth and uninterrupted area of approximately fifty feet by twenty feet (a thousand square feet) and twenty one feet to the underside of the huge wooden beams above.

Some short while later, I saw an advert which offered for sale several thousands of linear feet of Keruin hardwood planking. A follow up to the advert revealed that the wood was from Morecambe Promenade's pier, which had not long since suffered a fire which had destroyed most of the middle section, leaving the end of the pier looking like an island on stilts. After being given a description of the materials on offer, I arranged that I would go and have a look at the materials myself, and accordingly, on a wet and windy day, I found myself standing on the promenade talking to the site foreman looking out to sea.

"We'll have to go out in the boat if you insist you have to see the stuff," said the chap, "but it's just the same as that bit lying there." He pointed to a few planks leaning against a porta cabin nearby. I wasn't convinced as I had experience of "it's just like that" before. I wanted to see it for myself as it might be half rotten. These guys were out to make what they could. We did go out in the 'boat', a tiny little dinghy, so low in the water that I feared we were going to sink. From the 'boat' we climbed a make-shift ladder up on to what remained of the pier where workmen had stripped at least half of the decking which was now piled up in a huge heap.

"That's it, if you want some you'd better shout out, there's plenty wanting it," he said. He was right, the condition of the planking was excellent, as sound as new. We returned to the porta cabin where it was arranged that I would buy some four thousand feet of the Keruin boards. I would collect the planks from off the promenade. For some reason or other, when the time came for me to collect my timber, my own wagon was not available. No matter, my friend Geoff Wightman's wagon, a rather nice Sedon sixteen tonner with a Mercedes engine, was. Again the day turned out to be a wet one, but everything had been arranged so we, myself and Gordon Campbell, the chap who had gone with me when I bought my first Drott and who now worked for me, set off to bring the timbers home. Imagine my annoyance when, after much planning and a lot of hassle, and absolute assurances from the agent that my load would be sitting waiting for me on the promenade, I arrived to be told that it was still on the half demolished pier.

At the time we had landed on site, it just so happened that the tide had gone out leaving only a stretch of glistening sand between the promenade and the end of the pier. It was suggested that I should drive the Sedon down the nearby ramp onto the sands and out to a point where we would be able to have the wood passed down to us. By now I was somewhat sceptical of anything that I was being told, so when the agent assured me that it was absolutely safe to drive out on the sands, I remained unconvinced. However here we were, and out there was my load. I had seen vehicles on the sands before, but never anything as heavy as a fully loaded Sedon. Anyhow it was a choice, muck or nettles, I either bit the bullet and went, or went home empty handed. Faint heart ne'r won fair maiden, I didn't need a fair maiden but I did want that load of wood. With no more ado, I drove down the ramp and out towards the end of the pier.

I was extremely relieved to find that, although the wagon caused considerable compaction in the sand, it didn't appear to want to break through the surface. This was with the wagon empty, it might be a different story coming away loaded. However with the rain still pouring down incessantly, we started to load. Strangely the pier head seemed dramatically higher from underneath looking up than it did from off the promenade. The men above us were having some difficulty to reach us even though most of the planks were around twenty feet long.

The loading seemed to take for ever, no doubt exaggerated by my anxiety, but eventually we finished with an estimated 4,000 feet of timber on board. I was unable to tell the exact weight, but knew by the way the springs were depressed that I was somewhere near the legal maximum. With the incoming tide now lapping at the wheels, I decided that rather than stay to rope the load, it was now imperative that I got the wagon and its load onto dry land. Real doubts started to enter my mind, I had been stuck in mud before, but never with twenty feet of water threatening to engulf me.

Climbing into the cab and starting the engine I knew that I must straight away attempt to pull clear otherwise there was a danger that the vibration from the big diesel engine would tend to dig us into the sands. Very slowly I eased the clutch out. I knew that I wouldn't get two chances. It was the moment of truth. Slowly the vehicle started to move forward. The water was now several inches deep around me. Holding my breath I maintained a comparatively low engine speed, too many revs and the drive wheels would spin; it only needed a couple of revolutions and down we would go.

Luck was on my side that day. It had been a miserable experience on a miserable day, but as we came up that ramp I was happy as a sand boy, pardon the pun. I had succeeded with what I had set out to do and got a lovely load of floor boards with which to make a second floor to my barn. And I wouldn't have to phone my mate to tell him his wagon was immersed in twenty feet of salt water, I really should have had more sense!

Whilst at Sherbourn House Farm in my late teens, I had gained quite a bit of knowledge of intensive farming, particularly the management of pigs and poultry. Because of the comparatively small acreage we owned, I knew that I would have to go intensive if I was to make a go of farming the holding and I had other plans for some of the land that weren't strictly agricultural anyway. I finally settled on battery hens.

Before I was able to start any intensive husbandry, I had to sort out the second level in the barn. A careful measure up and a load of 'H' section girders were ordered. We already had a sound concrete base and so, when the girders arrived, with Gordon's welding skills we soon erected a framework for a new floor, doing it in such a way that allowed for the width of the girders together with the thickness of the Keruin flooring to make two floor levels with ten feet clearance above them which would allow me to erect sufficient units to make the project viable.

I have always been aware that the subject of factory farming is a controversial issue, and that battery hens are often at the forefront. However, I maintain that in the case of battery hens, provided that they are not overcrowded, are kept clean, well fed and watered, they are better off

Stephen pictured at the farm with eggs ready to be delivered.

than the hens you see scratching round in the cold and wet outside.

Once the framework was up, the next step was to floor it out with the hard won planks. I then had to find some cages which I eventually located, surprisingly enough, only a mile away at Cliff Rhodes' hen farm. Anyone who has ever had anything to do with the assembling or dismantling of a row of battery cages will have sympathy with what came next. To say that it was harder to take battery cages to pieces and reassemble them than a thousand piece jigsaw of a flower garden will not be telling a lie. The whole thing was a nightmare of wires and clips. However, after a few weekends and evenings spent puzzling it all out, the day came when I was ready for business. I had already placed an order for a thousand point of lay pullets and they were expected to arrive not long after the installation of the unit. As could be expected, the birds which were just nineteen-weeks-old, took a couple of days to settle down but were soon cackling away quite happily. Ten days later the first egg was laid.

Perseverance paid off and gradually my poultry unit started to produce. I had now fully occupied the top half of the barn and planned to duplicate the system down below on the ground level. The project had involved a lot of spare time work, but if I got really organised, it was hoped that I would be able to justify staying at home a good bit more. Outside on the land, I had now built up my stock to include twenty mule ewes and a Suffolk tup (ram) which I was confident would produce thirty lambs or so each spring. In addition I had some fifteen yearling stirks which I had reared from calves.

Having always had a passion for horses it was not surprising that I did my best to pass this on to the boys. Whilst we were at Glenburn, I had arranged for regular riding lessons for Delmar and Simon at Miss Jagger's Riding School on the Craig Level. Now they were to have the loan for the winter of two ponies from the Mrs. Oakden's school, Wynlass Beck, Windermere. When Edwin Postlethwaite's black mare, which had been mated with a thoroughbred called Red Justice, produced a most beautiful chestnut colt, we made a deal that, when the foal was weaned he would sell it to me. When the day came that the colt was to be parted from his mother he came to Eskrigg End.

The boys called him Rusty and what a fine fellow he was. He was a beautiful pale 'rusty' brown with four white socks and a white blaze from between his ears to his nostrils. He was as nice a looking animal as you could find anywhere. Rusty settled in well and didn't seem to miss his mother too much. He was housed in a loose box with plenty of straw about to keep him warm. Just before retiring to bed I made a regular round to check on all the inside stock which of course included Rusty. One cold night I wanted to make sure that my pride and joy was safe and had sufficient hay, water and pony nuts to keep him happy and, of course, have a good talk to him, (very important to build up his confidence).

Outside the night was as black as ink as I entered the stable. The door was of the conventional type, in two halves with an upper and a lower section, Rusty took little notice of me as he was too busy chewing away at the sweet meadow hay in the hay rack. After I had been in the stable for some minutes I saw the colt suddenly look up and put his ears forward. He had heard something and, with a sudden movement, he almost jumped towards the door. Then I heard what he had heard - a clip clopping of horse's hooves which seemed to be coming down the lane and would pass between the stable and the stirk housing opposite. Strange, there shouldn't have been any horses in the vicinity.

By now Rusty was leaning hard on the closed bottom section of the door with his head sticking out into the dark night. At the same time he was whinnying in an attempt to talk to the horse which had just passed by. It took me several minutes to persuade the colt to back off from the door sufficiently so that I was able to squeeze through and out onto the lane. Despite half an hour spent checking all the closed gates, nooks and crannies, and every conceivable corner where a horse might be hiding, no horse was found that night. Neither was there any trace of a horse's hoof print or any give away found the following day. I might have imagined it, but Rusty certainly didn't! Was it the phantom horse of Eskrigg?

THE RECESSION AND HOW IT AFFECTED US

By early 1977 the country as a whole was feeling the effects of an economic slow down. At first I, like many others, didn't realise the seriousness of it all. I had enjoyed a number of years of steady business. Work in the tipper haulage and earth moving business had been there in abundance for anyone who was prepared to invest a bit of money and a lot of hard work. I was not alone in believing that this was only going to be a temporary set back. It wouldn't be long before the government stepped in and sorted the job out and we'd be back to normal.

My regular customers such as the water, gas and electricity boards started to cut back on their on going work programmes. The first which affected me being the North West Water Board who ordered all their depots to axe all but the most important new installations and to hire in outside plant (diggers) only in emergencies. Until then I had been supplying diggers and my wagon almost on a full time basis. Following close behind the water board was the gas board. They suddenly started insisting on substantial cuts in the contractors' hire rates. Gradually the hourly rate which the board was prepared to pay for a digger and operator dropped from nine pounds to as low as six pounds fifty. At the same time as these drops ware taking place, the cost of new machines, spare parts, tyres, fuel, road fund licence and insurance, public liability insurance and employer's liability insurance was rising at an alarming rate.

With the shortage of work, the various authorities tended to play one contractor against another, and to make matters worse the building industry had just about ground to a halt. Building firms who had bought their own diggers when house building was on fire were now hiring out their machines and operators to the authorities in direct competition with us contractors. All in all nobody was making a living!

Back on the farm I had managed to persuade the planners to allow me to install a second static caravan which helped by providing a little more income. The two vans were proving very popular providing our guests with a relatively cheap holiday and were at most times in the season fully booked. The battery hen project however had proved to be at worst a total disaster and at best a waste of time and effort. This wasn't because the hens performed badly, they could not be faulted. Quite simply it was my luck to pick the time when wholesalers were paying as little as thirteen pence a dozen for eggs and the price of feedstuff, when you could get it, went up daily. There was no chance of me expanding into the lower half of the barn now.

I have never had a lot of time for people who whine about everything around them being wrong and I have no wish to turn this story into one long moan about how the wicked world was treating me at this time. However I would find it quite impossible to explain the next series of events without familiarising the reader with the conditions which prevailed at the time and helped to dictate the Bolton family's fortunes for the next few years.

The first major crisis that year was the death of my father on 7 November. He had endured several months of pain and distress before having an operation which it had been hoped would have extended his life. It failed to do so and ten days later he died. To myself and my sisters our father had been everything a father should be and we all missed him very much.

Over the next two years with less and less viable work about, it became more and more difficult. All the time we were thinking that surely economic recovery was just around the corner. I had kept men and machines on in that belief, but was now advising them to look for other jobs. I perhaps unwisely hadn't the heart to just finish them. In these circumstances I found it hard not to feel that I had in some way let them down. My one consolation was that far cleverer people than me were also having difficulties.

Despite the general doom and gloom, one line of business seemed to be weathering the storm rather better than most - the tourist industry, particularly in the smaller, less expensive, accommodation department. With our two static caravans doing well, the natural progression suggested that a wise move would be to try to expand with further vans. After all there were quite a number of caravan sites in the district, but none near us.

The ingredients for an attractive site were space, scenery, access and facilities. The first two we had plenty of and the second two could be arranged, surely there shouldn't be any tenable reason why we shouldn't be allowed to proceed along those lines. I had the land, the machinery and the ability to make a first class site. As the poultry project had come to nothing, I found myself again with a huge building on my hands which was of very little immediate use. We put in an application for planning permission to convert the building into four holiday flats. This met with a refusal and so I again turned my attention to caravans.

Our first caravan occupant told us how much he and his family had enjoyed their week's stay, in particular he had found great joy in waking up with the animals in the fields nearby and the birds in the hedgerows singing. From that time I had begun to have a vision that one day I would have my own caravan site, nothing too big, nothing too crowded, perhaps a dozen or so vans. A stream which ran along the side of the big meadow could be diverted to form a tiny lake with weeping willows overhanging at one end. The vans would be set back into the hillside in such a way that they would all enjoy a view of the countryside around them and flowers and shrubs would screen one van from the other. All of this was not to be. The planning authorities had other ideas. The irony is that twenty years on the barn, no longer in my possession, was given the go ahead for conversion and another caravan was allowed yet none of the conditions prevailing at the time of my refusal have changed one tiny bit even to this day. Thanks, members of the planning board, for stealing my dreams!

The early part of 1979 promised no improvement in the construction industry and nothing had changed which might suggest a relaxation of the planning laws to allow us to progress with any of our projects. The overdraft situation which had threatened to get out of hand was marginally improved from the sale (or near give away) of redundant diggers as one by one the men left to take up employment in other fields. Inevitably with the departure of my last employee, I was now faced with the prospects of having to repay the overdraft from my earnings. It was then that I realised that I should have been a bit more ruthless and finished my men at least a year sooner. In essence I had put their considerations before the welfare of the family.

Things were bad. Nearly four years of recession had taken its toll. We now had to think the unthinkable - we would have to dispose of some of our assets, which were of course land and property. One consideration was that we could sell all the land which would settle the overdraft and pay off the small mortgage we had on the house, but this was rejected straight away. We couldn't have lived in the house and looked out on the fields which had represented our dreams and know that they were gone. No, we would rather sell up and move away.

In April 1979 we decided to put an advert in the properties for auction section of the *Westmorland Gazette* to announce the sale of the property known as Great Eskrigg End. It was to be auctioned in the Bindloss Rooms at the Town Hall, Kendal. As is usual the holding was to be sold in three lots - lot one the house, garden and the two caravan sites, lot two the meadow behind the house and the shippons thereon and lot three all the land on the western side of the lane. This was how it was going to be and there was no turning back. Whilst arrangements for the sale were taking place, Wendy started to look about for our next home. It wasn't long before she found one which was within our price range. There were plenty to choose from just at that time.

Croft House was a little stone built property standing by the roadside midway between Kendal and Endmoor in the tiny, spread out, hamlet of Barrow's Green. Built about the turn of the century, it enjoyed a large garden which had been extended when two cottages were demolished when the road was re-aligned. The land from these cottages was added to Croft House's garden making a decent sized garden. The house was accessed from road level at the front with three decent sized rooms, one being the kitchen. On the second level were four bedrooms and a bathroom. Finally at a lower level, accessed from the back of the house or an internal staircase, were two more rooms which could be used for a number of purposes.

The day of the sale arrived and Wendy and I made our way to the Town Hall where in the sale room around fifty seats had been set out in anticipation of that number of interested parties. I knew already that the sale had provoked a lot of interest, but I also knew that there would be a lot of neighbouring farmers who would be there perhaps to get a free valuation on their own holdings by comparing their's with ours. The bidding started with lot one not reaching its reserve and being withdrawn. Lot two was also withdrawn - was this a complete disaster? Lot three did the best but even then fell short of the reserve price.

The auctioneer said: "I'm sorry ladies and gentlemen, but there will be no sale. If the last bidder for lot three cares to come forward we might be able to agree a sale." It is customary for the last bidder to have the chance to offer just that little bit more in an arrangement with the auctioneer as a last ditch attempt to make a sale. In this case it was only lot three which was negotiable. The other two lots were considered too far from their reserve. The bidder came forward and a sale was agreed, a deposit paid and our holding was reduced in acreage by over half but we still owned our home, the big meadow and all the buildings. We would have to try to find a private buyer but at least we now had some breathing space.

Life went on pretty much as normal following the sale. I was working long days mostly away from the farm. I had sold all the stock in anticipation of moving and so I let the land for the summer. It gave me no pleasure to see someone else's stock on my land. The heart had gone out of it. During the months that the farm was still on the market, various prospective buyers came to view. One gentleman from somewhere down south spent a full afternoon looking round. He must have been impressed because the following day his wife came to look for herself. Unfortunately just at the moment she chose to walk across the yard, our pet cat Regan decided he would drop half a dead rat in her path. She made a quick exit and we never heard from them again!

Eventually a young chap who had a good job with the Agricultural Training Board and lived fairly nearby came forward expressing an interest in the place. After quite a few visits and much discussion he made me an offer, not quite as much as I had been hoping for, but he seemed a genuine sort of a chap and so we finally agreed on a figure and shook hands on the deal.

The owners of Croft House at Barrows Green must have been finding disposal of their property just as difficult as we had, as their place was still on the market. We had been quite taken with the place and so thought it worthy of another visit. Wendy's plan was that, because of the layout of the house, it would be possible to do a bit of bed and breakfast, not of course on the scale of Glenburn. Being by the side of a main road no doubt it would be possible to pick up passing trade. We thought that we were unlikely to find a better or more suitable property and so an offer was made which was duly accepted. Croft House was to be our next home.

We moved to Croft house on the 30 November 1979 and so we were pretty well settled in by the Christmas. Dave Hill, the buyer of Eskrigg End was by virtue of a financial arrangement not taking possession of the farm until 1 February the following year. Under normal arrangements, a seller would normally only grant entry to a buyer after completion, but as there was a two month time lapse before the completion date, and Mr.

Hill was anxious to make certain alterations which would facilitate an easier settling in for his family, I allowed him access.

On 5 February I was driving home from work near the Duke of Cumberland public house on the A6 and was making slow progress due to traffic conditions, when on the opposite side of the road, I saw a vehicle which I recognised as that of my former neighbour. As we drew alongside each other, Jack Hammond the neighbour who had obviously also spotted me, was leaning out and seemed to be going to unusual lengths to attract my attention.

"Pity about your old house." he shouted. I didn't understand what he meant. "Pity about the house," he repeated. My blank expression and lack of response must have told him that I hadn't a clue what he was talking about.

"You don't know then? Last night your old place burnt to the ground." At this point the traffic around us cleared and we were unable to pursue the conversation further. From that moment, with Jack's words ringing in my ears, I just couldn't get home fast enough and had hardly got through the door before Wendy was with me.

"Dave Hill's been trying to get hold of you all day. You'd better phone him straight away, the farm's burnt down." Wendy couldn't get the words out fast enough. A quick phone call first to my solicitor removed the niggling doubt which I had had since I first learned about the catastrophe. I wasn't sure who actually owned the property at this sad moment of time. Fortunately for me, and unfortunately for Dave Hill, he was the rightful owner. He had just completed the final stage of the transaction the day before.

Eskrigg End had stood for the best part of 300 years. A visit a few weeks later revealed a mere shell with half burned beams lying at grotesque angles. Looking up through the hole where the front door had once hung you could see the now floorless corner where we had slept and the part where the boys' room had stood. We felt sheer disbelief and sadness. It had gone so dreadfully wrong for Dave and his family. Thank God that they had not moved into the house before the fire.

CROFT HOUSE, GINGERBREAD AND THE BLUE WORKS

The next couple of years rolled by. Delmar went to Longlands School in Kendal, Simon carried on at the Old Hutton Village school and Stephen went to the little village school at Crosscrake which he hated. We had upsets just about every morning he ever went there. Wendy got going again with the bed and breakfast, and as we had hoped, there was plenty of passing trade, mainly commercial travellers and a few holiday people. Being closer to town had its benefits. Both the older boys had various interests in Kendal, one being the local judo club. It was a lot easier to slip them into town from Croft House than it had been from the farm.

Whilst on the subject of judo, through my job I had come into contact with a chap called John Rooney who had come down from West Cumberland to manage the newly built plant hire depot of B.E.C. (Border Engineering Company) on the Mintsfeet Trading Estate. John was within a couple of years the same age as myself, and was a character and a half. He was a big powerful man who, whilst having a great sense of humour, could leave the more dubious type of customer (you do get them in the construction industry) in no doubt that he would not be messed about. He was, without a doubt, the perfect man for his job. Beside being a manager, John Rooney was passionately fond of judo and was himself a fourth Dan (three grades above a black belt). I was to form a lasting friendship with John.

Kendal Judo Club was a strong club and enjoyed pre-eminence due partly to the fact that Tony MacConnal, twice British open all weights champion, resided in the area. Tony, one of the very few British fighters ever to attain the status of eighth Dan had a cottage at Lambrigg just north east of Kendal. I was introduced to him by John Rooney when he was the current British National Team Coach and used to bring the national squad, sometimes around twenty strong, to train in the area. This is where Wendy and her bed and breakfast came in!

Finding accommodation for a full squad of extremely fit and boisterous young men was somewhat of a problem. However, by splitting them into three groups it became less so. Wendy found herself on many occasions making up beds for eight or so of the team who, after training hard on the fells around us, and on the mat in the Kendal Club, would come in ravenous and eat everything put in front of them. Our house rapidly became a firm favourite amongst the lads. They always received plenty of good wholesome food and Wendy's gingerbread became a legend. The last piece of gingerbread was something worth fighting for in its own right!

Getting back to my role in the family's fortunes, decent excavation jobs were few and far between. However I had the good fortune to come across a fellow called Alan Taylor who was expanding an already established caravan site. The site had provision for about 150 vans, and he now had approval for a couple of hundred more. Putting aside the resentment that I had at the way I had been treated with my application for approval on my own minuscule venture into caravans, I jumped at the opportunity to take on the excavation side of the job, i.e. the laying of cables, water pipes and drainage to the new stands, plus drainage of surface water etc.

At the same time as Alan was developing his site, parts of Kendal were undergoing a radical restructuring of the sewage system. The main contractors were a firm called Killroy. One of the problems of the new system was that several thousand tons of earth was being displaced and had to be disposed of. Most of the earth went to Alan Taylor's Ashes Lane caravan site. Things could not have worked out better. The yet undeveloped part of the site was extremely rugged and low lying and needed lifting which required a huge volume of in-fill. Killroys were desperate to get rid of their spoil - the perfect solution! I was at Ashes Lane from the late summer of 1981 right through to the spring of 1982 during which time I established a very good working relationship. I found Alan to be a very fair employer with some great ideas. He must have had an understanding bank manager as well!

With the tourist season of '82 under way, all but essential work on the site stopped in order be out of the way of the increased number of caravanners. Besides my normal tasks, I was taking on small jobs, some of which had nothing to do with digging, just to make an honest shilling or two. One such job was very occasional relief driving of a freezer wagon for Swift's the meat wholesalers. The job came about through John Robinson, the manager, who found out I had a heavy goods driving licence. On a number of occasions he was desperate for a driver and asked me to help. Unfortunately the job required that a large freezer truck, loaded with ten tons of freshly slaughtered carcasses, had to arrive at Glasgow Meat Market before seven o'clock in the morning. This meant setting off at between two and three o'clock. On one occasion the wagon broke down right in the middle of some traffic lights on Glasgow's London Road. All the phone boxes I could find had been vandalised and so it was over an hour before I got the vehicle moved. In the rush hour traffic the chaos had to be seen to be believed.

Just about this time, we were beginning to hear about Sunday markets; things like table top sales and car boot sales hadn't yet come about, there were just the old fashioned rummage sales and established week day markets. The idea came to me one day that perhaps a Sunday market would go down well in our area. I put the idea to my friend Alan Taylor suggesting that when his site shut down for the winter, he should consider using the open area for a venue for just such an event.

My suggestion, with certain provisos, was met with considerable enthusiasm. Alan was quite prepared to allow the event to take place on a monthly basis, but only on the understanding that I organised everything and supervised the running of the market. The place had cafe facilities, toilet blocks, adequate space for market stalls and customer parking. It was a superb place out in the country where it wouldn't bother anybody. It was the perfect venue to hold a Sunday market. We set the date of our first Sunday market for 31 October 1982 and placed a number of adverts in north west newspapers and market advertising magazines. The stage was set.

What was proposed was that stall holders would pay a fee on a footage basis, and a discount would be given to pre-booked stalls. Alan and I would split any revenue from the stalls down the middle and he would be be responsible for, and keep any takings from, his cafe. The bookings rolled in and the event seemed assured of success!

In amongst the bookings and cheques however, came a letter that was not quite so welcome. It was from the clerk and chief executive's department of South Lakeland District Council, stating "It has come to the council's notice that a market is proposed to be held...." The letter went on to tell me that if the market went ahead it would be in breach of the Shops Act 1950, section 47, etc., etc. and that after a meeting on 20 October of the council's environmental health emergency sub-committee, the members resolved to do everything in their power to prevent the proposed market taking place.

"Oh really," I thought. I had no idea that such an innocent attempt to provide a service for the general public and make a few quid would cause such a threat to the environment and cause so much consternation amongst the ranks of our public spirited elders. Once again bureaucracy had stepped in to thwart my attempts to make something out of nothing!

Together with the prohibition notice came a list of things which could not be sold under section 47, fifth schedule which included aircraft parts and fodder for mules, though there were not many people rolling up at markets on mules or in aeroplanes. The outcome was that I attended a meeting with a representative of the S.L.D.C. legal department where I decided that, though in my opinion the case against me was nonsensical, it appeared that the authority would have the last word and I didn't want to get landed with the costs of a threatened legal action against me. I had little choice but to cancel the market and return all the cheques to the people who had so sportingly backed the never-to-be event. I don't hear anything about illegal Sunday car boot or table top sales these days. Perhaps all the mules have died off and there is no longer any fear of anyone wanting to buy fodder for them on a Sunday?

I think it would be true to say that despite Croft House being quite an attractive house in appearance and one that most people would be proud to own, neither Wendy nor I ever had the feeling that we would wish to live there indefinitely. One aspect was the lack of a community spirit which seemed somehow to be missing. Well aware that you only get out what you are prepared to put in to such a phenomenon, we had tried to become involved with any local events. But it was just as though we were searching for something which wasn't there, unlike at Old Hutton where we had sensed a kindred spirit right from the earliest days at the farm. One theory I had was that the two cottages which had once stood where the bottom of our garden now was, had never been replaced. In previous years one of the cottages had been a shop and its loss left the hamlet a poorer place.

The 'unease' prevailed until one day Wendy announced that she had seen a nice property on South Road in Kendal which was for sale. The current owners were a mother and daughter who had been using the place as a guest house. It was bigger than Croft House and was, she thought, worthy of a viewing. After a good look round the South Road property, Wendy seemed quite taken with the place. There were more rooms which she thought would allow her to to maintain the same level of bed and breakfast business yet give the boys a room each instead of sharing.

South Lakeland District Council

CLERK AND CHIEF EXECUTIVE'S DEPARTMENT
STRICKLANDGATE HOUSE, KENDAL, CUMBRIA, LA9 4QQ
Tel: KENDAL (0539) 24007
CLERK AND CHIEF EXECUTIVE
ALAN F. WINSTANLEY, LL.B. Solicitor

22 October 1982

M.R.M. Bolton Esq.
Croft House
Barrows Green
Sedgwick
KENDAL, Cumbria

Your Ref:

Our Ref: 0372/MEB/MMS

This matter is being dealt with by .... Miss Bailey ..... Ext: 4⁹

Dear Sir

Proposed Sunday Market - 31 October 1982
at Ashes Lane Caravan Park, Ratherheath

It has come to the Council's notice that a market is proposed to be held
on Sunday, 31 October, on land belonging to Mr A. Taylor at Ratherheath,
and of which you will be the operator.

You may not be aware that Section 47 of the Shops Act 1950 provides that
"every shop shall save as otherwise provided by this .... Act, be closed for
the serving of customers on Sunday".

Only certain goods listed in the fifth schedule to the Act can be sold on
Sundays, and I enclose a list of those goods permitted to be sold, for your
information.

It is an offence to contravene Section 47 which, by s.58, will apply to retail
trading elsewhere than in shops, e.g. market stalls.

At a meeting of the Council's Environmental Health Emergency Sub-Committee held
on 20 October, the members resolved that they would do everything in their
power to prevent the proposed Sunday Market taking place for sales other than
those permitted under the Act, including seeking an injunction to restrain it
taking place, if necessary.

I write, therefore, to let you know that unless I have your written undertaking
that no goods other than those permitted by the fifth schedule to the Act will
be sold at the market on 31 October or thereafter on this land, by 10 a.m. on
Monday, 25 October 1982, then I shall proceed to seek an injunction for which I
shall also claim the Council's legal costs.

If you should decide not to hold the market at all on that date or subsequently,
I should be obliged if you would also let me know.

I have also written to Mr Alan Taylor, the owner of the above land, along
similar lines.

Yours faithfully

Alan F Winstanley

Section 47

FIFTH SCHEDULE

TRANSACTIONS FOR THE PURPOSES OF WHICH A SHOP MAY BE OPEN IN ENGLAND AND WALES FOR THE SERVING OF CUSTOMERS ON SUNDAY

1. The sale of—

(a) intoxicating liquors;

(b) meals or refreshments whether or not for consumption at the shop at which they are sold, but not including the sale of fried fish and chips at a fried fish and chip shop;

(c) newly cooked provisions and cooked or partly cooked tripe;

(d) table waters, sweets, chocolates, sugar confectionery and ice-cream (including wafers and edible containers);

(e) flowers, fruit and vegetables (including mushrooms) other than tinned or bottled fruit or vegetables;

(f) milk and cream, not including tinned or dried milk or cream, but including clotted cream whether sold in tins or otherwise;

(g) medicines and medical and surgical appliances—

(i) at any premises registered under section twelve of the Pharmacy and Poisons Act, 1933; or

(ii) by any person who has entered into a contract with an Executive Council for the supply of drugs and appliances;

(h) aircraft, motor, or cycle supplies or accessories;

(i) tobacco and smokers' requisites;

(j) newspapers, periodicals and magazines;

(k) books and stationery from the bookstalls of such terminal and main line railway or omnibus stations, or at such aerodromes as may be approved by the Secretary of State;

(l) guide books, postcards, photographs, reproductions, photographic films and plates, and souvenirs—

(i) at any gallery, museum, garden, park or ancient monument under the control of a public authority or university; or

(ii) at any other gallery or museum, or any place of natural beauty or historic interest, or any zoological, botanical or horticultural gardens, or aquarium, if and to the extent that the local authority certify that such sale is desirable in the interests of the public; or

(iii) in any passenger vessel within the meaning of Part II of the Finance (1909–1910) Act, 1910, while engaged in carrying passengers;

(m) photographs for passports;

(n) requisites for any game or sport at any premises or place where that game or sport is played or carried on;

(o) fodder for horses, mules, ponies and donkeys at any farm, stables, hotel or inn.

2. The transaction of—

(a) post office business;

(b) the business carried on by a funeral undertaker.

They were growing up and needed more space. To cut a long story short, we made a provisional offer for the house and it was accepted and Croft House was put on the market.

With mortgage rates high, property sales were rather sticking, so when a couple came up with an offer very close to the asking price on our home, we accepted. One condition of the offer was that we gave the buyers an early completion date. The Boxalls were expecting an addition to their family and it was not long before the due date. They wanted to be in the house nicely before then. Understanding their concerns and not seeing this proviso as a problem, we accepted the arrangement, agreed on a date and started to prepare ourselves for the forthcoming move.

It was three or four weeks after we had made the deal that things started to go wrong. The owners of the property which we had agreed to buy suddenly announced that they were no longer prepared to sell. They said it was something to do with the daughter's marital affairs. We were now in a dilemma and had to decide whether we broke our contract, which no doubt would cause stress for the heavily pregnant lady, or agreed to carry on in the hope that we would find a suitable alternative property. It was a truly undesirable situation! Again putting other's interests before our own, we chose the latter option, trusting that all would work out for the best in the end.

In the next few weeks, with removal day getting nearer and nearer, we spent a great deal of time looking around for a house. We felt that the inconvenience of possibly having to find temporary accommodation would be offset by the fact that we would have nothing to sell. This would be a bargaining ploy when we did see the right place. Well that was the theory, the facts turned out to be rather different.

A tiny cottage in the village of Endmoor turned out to be our place of refuge. We went through with the sale of Croft House, put our furniture into store and moved into the next to the end, of a terraced row of local stone built cottages known as Woodside. The place had been adequately furnished and was being let as a holiday cottage. We thought this would do us until we found our ideal home.

One day I was travelling back from Windermere to Kendal with my now considerably aged digger (a J.C.B. all but in name) when I heard a rather disconcerting cracking, creaking, noise which appeared to be coming from around the big driving wheels. It didn't take long to determine that the wheel was in fact starting to collapse. Cracks in the welding were causing the central hub to start to break away from the rest of the wheel; so much so that the wheel was in danger of collapsing completely. A couple of years previously the situation would have been seen as no more than an annoying inconvenience but, at that time and on that day, I was feeling particularly, yet uncharacteristically, very down at heart. I had been reflecting on the gradual slide in fortunes we had endured, perhaps some of which was due to bad judgement on my part. I had, up till then, believed that hard work and dedication was the sole key to success. I was now realising that far more components are necessary, not least of which is luck, in the struggle for success. I didn't seem to have had too much of the latter for quite a while!

I decided to risk driving the rest of the journey. I would drive to the plant hire yard of my friend John Rooney where I knew that he would do what he could to help me. I drove on listening to the creaking which seemed to get worse by the minute, this I thought was the time when I would have to consider just where my future lay. With my one remaining machine virtually falling to pieces underneath me was I going to borrow money and buy a new one? A new J.C.B. would cost in excess of £20,000. Should I struggle on with the old one? At that moment I felt that everything was against me.

John was in his office as I drove into the yard but, on seeing my arrival, characteristically came to see if he could help. "No problem," he announced, "I'll stop behind tonight and we'll fix it between us." Between us was a rather an overstatement. I wasn't a bad hand at rudimentary mechanics, but I was useless at welding. It would be mainly as a result of John's efforts if I was to get sorted out that day.

Around six o'clock John had finished with his normal duties and, true to his word, he set about sorting my problem out. The wheel was set up in its correct alignment and my friend set about the tedious task of reinforcing all the mounting points. Half way through he glanced at me and said with his usual mischievous grin: "This is going to cost you!" I knew John better than that, underneath that hard exterior, for any genuinely needy person, he was an unstinting giver with a heart of gold. At that moment in time I think I was ready for a little help. It was well into early evening before the job was done. The wheel was repaired and so was my spirit. Those few hours chatting to my friend had done me the world of good. With kindness like that I no longer felt that I was fighting the system on my own.

The charge for time and effort made by John Rooney was one square yard of ginger bread. John was well aware of the popularity of Wendy's cooking and baking amongst the judo lads in particular and, typical of his sense of humour, asked for settlement of his account in the same! I guess John got paid in full eventually, even if it was in installments of four square inches at a time on the occasions when he called at our home!

We had been in Woodside Cottage since the May 1982 and it would soon be August. The availability of suitable properties had dried up, in fact houses of any description were just not coming on the market. Estate agents were opening on Sundays because of people desperately looking for houses. In the space of three or four months the availability had gone from a surplus to a famine. To add to our problems, our landlord announced that we would have to vacate the cottage for at least two weeks as he had a booking which had been made prior to us renting the place. We spent those two weeks in a borrowed caravan.

With no improvement in the excavation business, and my old digger now becoming unsuitable for hire work, I had to come to a decision as to whether I was going to invest in a new machine (mostly with borrowed money) or hang on to what money was available and find myself a job

Mike with digger and wagon working on Windermere Park, formerly part of Lickbarrow Farm.

working for someone else. To take the last of the two options would damage my pride, but I could live with that, to embark on further borrowing with the industry still in recession would be nothing short of irresponsible. Yes, I resolved, I would find myself a job!

At the foot of Windermere where the sole outlet, the river Leven starts its short journey into Morecambe Bay, lies the little village of Backbarrow. At this time the huge building known as the Blue Works was just starting to be completely restructured. The place had been owned for many years by Reckitts, the 'dolly blue' company. Their blue dye was famous the world over and was used for a number of purposes, the best known being its ability to make washing whiter.

The name of the construction company who had bought up the old building and the immediately surrounding land was Douglas Construction. They were to convert the place into a luxury hotel and time share complex. The hotel was to be known as the White Water Hotel, appropriately named because of the torrent of water usually to be seen rushing past at all but the driest times.

My friend John Rooney, to whom I have alluded in earlier paragraphs, was supplying items of plant such as air compressors, dumpers and smaller pieces of equipment to the construction company. Through his connections with the company I came into contact with the site manager, a chap called Eddie Kennedy. Eddie was trying to recruit site workers locally and John was able to put in a good word for me. I met Eddie on site and was taken on as machine driver - for the first time in sixteen years I was no longer self employed. I was once more working for somebody else and stupid as it may sound, it hurt!

The first stage of the project was the ripping out of all the floors in the old blue works. They were to be replaced with new ones at different levels. I found myself driving J.C.B's, rough terrain fork trucks and concrete breakers, sometimes outside the building and sometimes inside. As the building had been used for somewhere in the region of a 100 years for the production of dolly blue, it was no surprise to find that every nook and cranny in the walls, the floor boards and every conceivable space imaginable, was full of blue powdery dust. A permanent blue haze literally covered everything and everybody around. All this brought back the memory of Wendy telling me that when she was an apprentice hair dresser at Alex Walker's shop in Ulverston, they used to be able to tell without asking which of their customers worked at the Blue Works by the faint blue line on the customer's neck after a hair cut. No matter how meticulous a customer was, it was impossible for them to avoid the stain on their skin. I and my follow workers were now similarly affected, perhaps more so. Each night I would have a bath, run the water away and then have another before I was acceptably 'de-blued'.

I continued to work for Douglas Construction over Christmas 1982 and through till the following spring when I moved to BOA Construction of Sandside, near Milnthorpe. BOA were a civil engineering company who undertook various building and pipe laying contracts mainly within the county. One job I was involved in was the re-building of the storm damaged stone pier at Arnside. It was the first time I had been involved on a job very much affected by tidal water. All the the work had to be programmed to fit in with the movements of the tide. More than once I had to drive my big Massey excavator into the water to lift out an air compressor or some piece of equipment or other. All this time we had been living in the cottage at Endmoor. I wouldn't say that we hated the place, but because we knew that it was only a temporary home, we couldn't help feeling a bit like nomads. This was very soon to change.

In July I returned home one day to find Wendy very excited; she believed she had found a suitable house. As it turned out, she had indeed found one on Aynam Road - one of a block of three fine houses overlooking the River Kent in the direction of the Parish Church and Abbot Hall. After satisfying ourselves that this was the house for us, and having no chain of house buyers or sellers affecting us, we were able to make an offer which was accepted. On 29 September 1983, after what seemed like a decade but was only sixteen months, we moved into the house which, though we didn't know it at the time, was to be our home to the present day.

My Own Boss Again, Minerals and Sausage Skins

With the family now settled into No. 39 Aynam Road, we began to think that perhaps now we had turned the corner, and that just maybe things would start to come right again. I had never really given up on the belief that one day I would find a fresh challenge which would allow me to again be master of my own destiny, at least as far as it's possible. We have already been into the realms of how much fate and good luck play in one's fortunes. I did feel that I had done my stint of sliding backwards for the last seven years or so.

I didn't have too long to wait for this vision of a challenge. It came by way of an advert in a farming paper which I occasionally bought. The advert had been placed by a Northamptonshire animal feed supplement company. They needed a field salesman to cover the central and southern part of the county. I had often looked at adverts of this type and thought I could do that, but had never felt the need to prove it to myself. Now perhaps there was a reason to give the subject a good bit more attention. What, I asked myself, were the necessary criteria to be a salesman? Being a good talker, well yes, but you have to know what you're talking about. I did have a pretty good knowledge of farming and I was always well received in the good old days when I was on the coaches. I brooded over the possibilities for several days.

Not long after we had moved to No. 39, Wendy had seen a job advert for a hair dresser at the Ivy Leek hair dressing salon in Kendal. She had followed it up and had been taken on straight away. If I applied for this job and got it, we would both be changing direction. The more I thought about the representative's job, the more I fancied it. Farmers were a different cup of tea to coach travellers, but I felt sure that I could adapt to the job.

Grasping the bull by the horrns so to speak, I wrote off an application and was subsequently granted an interview on the 16 July 1984 at the Tillington Hotel, Stafford. I was to be interviewed by a Mr. Richard Nevett who was the owner and managing director of a company called Starlyne Feeds. I later learned the company employed some 30 salesmen who covered, between them, most of the British Isles. The company's head office was in Finedon near Northampton. Also present at the interview was a chap called Ken Graham who was based at Carlisle. He was the north west of England and southern Scotland area manager and had his sales territory immediately north of the one for which I was applying.

It was explained that the successful applicant would be answerable to him.

In the first part of the interview the aims of the company and its product range were explained. The second part was taken up with their appraisal of my potential, with all sorts of questions about my knowledge of agriculture, particularly that of the area in which I lived. Early into the interview I explained that my only previous experience of selling was as a wholesale fruit salesman with W. B. Andersons, and that it had only been a brief affair. This fact didn't seem to bother my interviewers as I thought it might have done.

I must have said something right, because at the end of the interview I was offered the job. On 23 March I started work for the company. It was arranged that Ken Graham would accompany me round a few local farms where he would demonstrate the technique of selling for the first day. The next day I was to do the selling and the third day I was on my own. At the interview when I had accepted the job, I had been given a book full of literature on company products. I had been studying them and had more or less absorbed the contents, so much so that felt I had a reasonable grasp of the detail. I soon found out that farmers don't often ask the expected questions, but resolved that I would be honest and tell them the truth. If I didn't know an answer I wouldn't make one up, a policy that some sales people don't always adopt. It is my belief that if you fabricate an answer, it will always catch up with you in the end and cost you!

Pretty soon things started to come together. I began to understand the more complex technicalities of animal nutrition, mainly by studying books and papers on the subject. It is one thing understanding the basics of a subject like animal nutrition, but it is another thing applying one's knowledge. In a nutshell the skill is to recognise a nutritional deficiency or the possibility of one, and then prescribe a preventative or a cure. In a lot of cases animals often show signs which indicate an oncoming problem and I got quite good at picking up on them. It is one thing forecasting a potential problem, but often it is equally difficult to get a farmer to act upon the advice. This is where the trust angle comes in. Some might say that a salesman was simply trying to fabricate a problem in order to make a sale. The regrettable thing is that if a problem doesn't occur after preventative treatment, there is no proof that it would have happened. All clever stuff!

Pride always comes before a fall. Just before Christmas a paragraph written by Richard Nevett, the managing director, in the company's monthly report which was circulated to all sales staff stated that: "Mike Bolton, our south Cumbria representative has in the few months with the company opened up over one hundred new accounts. If he can do this, you can all do it." The remarks gave me a boost and enhanced the belief that I had made a good move. I loved the job and was really starting to feel quite comfortable with it.

Not long after my mention in the company's newsletter, I had occasion to call on a farm in the Barrow-in-Furness area. I had never been on this particular farm before and didn't know the owner. On driving into the farm yard I immediately spotted a man in a corner bending over a large piece of machinery which he appeared to be trying to mend.

"Good morning," I said in the most cheerful voice that I could muster.

"How do," was the immediate reply. It wasn't unusual for some farmers to delay their responses. They are watching to see if you show any signs of discomfort, all part of a little game of wits and their type of humour, But this chap responded straight away and things looked promising!

"Would you be the farmer here?" I asked.

"Yep," he said. I was beginning to get just a slight feeling that, although the chap had been polite, he hadn't even looked up to see who I was. The signs were there that this wasn't going to be an easy interview.

"Do you mind me asking you, do you currently use any type of supplement for your stock?" I asked.

"Nope," was the reply. I plodded on, this wasn't easy. I had to find out whose supplements he was using.

"Would I be right in assuming that you use Tythbarn's or Minsup's?" These were the names of the two companies which had proved to be my main opposition .

"Yep!" still no signs of a conversation forthcoming. At last I thought I had something to go at which would prize a few words of conversation from the chap. I knew we had passed the point where I had undergone the mandatory dry humour test. This was selling down to the wood.

"Well if you're using either of those two companies' products you are rather paying for the privilege," I knew as soon as I had said it that I had said the wrong thing. He had done what I believe he had set out to do, he had unnerved me to a point where I said the wrong thing.

"If you are going to talk like that, good day to you," he stood up turned on his heel and walked away leaving me feeling about two feet high. Regardless of his lack of respect for me, I had in fact insulted the chap's intelligence. I had suggested that he hadn't previously known what he was doing. The message that I had been trying to get across was that I could offer him products which would do the same job, only mine were less expensive. As I drove out of the yard I felt thoroughly deflated. How could I have been so stupid? I never made the same mistake again. Incidentally, I learned afterwards that this chap made a regular habit of winding salesmen up. Those who knew him did their best to avoid having to go to his place. I learned to use much more subtle ways of expounding the virtues of my products.

During my travels as a Starlyne representative I came across a number of companies who were selling products of a similar type to mine. Competition, particularly on price, was pretty fierce. However one small firm which covered roughly the same area as myself seemed to have established a special customer loyalty with some of the farmers whereby year after year its mineral supplements were bought, regardless of pressure to buy from the other companies.

Enquiries I made revealed that this small firm was in fact a one man business which was run from a large building in the village of Bowston which is situated about two miles north west of Kendal. The owner of this business was a gentleman named Harry Hill. His business was registered as Kendal Agricultural Supplies, or KAS. When on farms in the area, I had often seen bags of minerals with the name KAS, and had been intrigued so much so that I resolved to find out as much as I could about the firm, if only to try to find a way of pinching one or more of its customers.

One afternoon I was in the Bowston area and was about to pass the building where I understood the manufacturing of KAS products took place. Fortuitously the large barn-like doors were open. Outside stood an old dark blue Ford transit van with the large letters KAS on the side. At first I hesitated, but then decided that this was too good a chance to miss if I was to ever meet my competitor. Nosily I peered in through the doors where inside the building, which I later learned had at one time been an engine shed for a steam engine used by Croppers the paper manufacturing people, were rows of hessian, paper and plastic sacks of all sizes, stacked high on wooden pallets around the cavernous room. A pleasant aniseedy scent hung in the air. At one side of the room, underneath an elevated floor was a huge steel drum-like apparatus with large cog wheels on one end. Straight away I recognised this as some sort of a mixing drum. An elderly, stockily built man emerged from an office room at the back of the building and smilingly approached me.

I got the first words in: " I don't want to be a nuisance but I thought that, as I am in the neighbourhood I would pop in and meet you. My name is Mike Bolton and I travel for a firm called Starlyne." The man continued to smile. He said: "Yes I have heard of you from one or two customers." I wondered whether he had or whether he was just trying to put me at ease.

"I take it that you're Harry Hill the owner of this." I indicated that I was referring to the tidy set-up which surrounded us. "Yes that's right." The ice was broken. From the moment I showed that I was interested Harry set about explaining how he manufactured his products and the basics of how he formulated the mixes. I had been selling similar products for over six months but until then had no knowledge of what was entailed in their manufacture. Before I left Harry told me he had started the business 25 years previously with an old cement mixer to mix his ingredients. Things had sure changed since those days. I shook his hand, thanked him for his kindness and left with an invitation to call in again any time I saw the place open.

One product which Starlyne had for sale which didn't come in a bag was a product known as a liquid feed, which was a by-product from the whisky distilleries. The feed was called pot ale syrup and it was a brown, thick, syrupy substance. Cattle and sheep were very fond of it, so much so that steps had to be taken to ensure that the animals didn't gorge themselves which in extreme cases could cause death. From the human angle, pot ale has a most pleasant smell but is extremely bitter to the taste. A tiny touch on the tongue with a finger dipped in the stuff is sufficient to test its potency.

On my travels round the farms I would always have at hand a few samples of the various products in the Starlyne range. Pot ale was one of them. I carried this in a small screw-top bottle which I kept in my pocket. One day I called on a farm which I shall simply describe as being in the south lakes area. Just before I arrived on the farm, so had an articulated wagon loaded with twenty tons of beet pulp nuts. These nuts are another by-product feed and had not been ordered through me. The farmer and his man had started to carry the heavy bags from the wagon to a storage shed nearby.

In later years, with more experience, if I had found my prospective customer already engaged in the laborious task of unloading a twenty ton wagon, I would simply apologise for intruding when he was busy, and promise to call back at a more convenient time. As I was relatively inexperienced at that time, I pressed on.

"I haven't time to talk to you today," said the chap as he trotted past me with a sack of beet nuts on his back. I didn't recognise the futility of the situation and pressed on. It is a recognised fact amongst travellers that quite a lot of farmers tended to see their time as more important than yours.

"I'd just like to quickly tell you about a liquid feed we have available at a very advantageous price," I said. He again shot past me heading for the store.

"I have a sample here, I'd just like you to take a sniff at this," I said holding out my little sample bottle. With no warning the fellow snatched the sample from my hand, unscrewed the top and, to my horror, took a huge gulp of the brown syrup. I have already explained the potency of the product and so nobody could be surprised at the outcome. The poor chap dropped the bottle, clutched at his throat with both hands and emitted a terrible choking noise. This went on for half a minute until he suddenly made a dash for the house, presumably to take on water.

It was some while later that the farmer emerged from his house, his eyes still watering and clearing his throat. He was not a happy chappy and remonstrated with me: "You reps are a bloody nuisance !" I apologised for what had happened and realised that he had interpreted my saying take a sniff as "take a swig." No Brownie points for me that time. I was left without an order and he with a bad taste in his mouth, (sorry couldn't resist that). I never did sell him anything!

The second time I called at the mill, Harry was busy mixing a batch of his minerals. He made no attempt to avoid my seeing exactly what he was doing, but instead went out of his way to explain the procedure. Some twenty or so carefully measured separate ingredients went in. Some were measured in hundreds of kilos and some, such as vitamins, were measured in grammes. All went into one of the two huge mixers as the giant cog wheels revolved with a deep rumble. The end product was finally bagged off from a spout underneath the machine, carefully weighed into 25kg plastic sacks and then heat sealed, leaving exactly 40 bags or one tonne of minerals.

I was truly fascinated with the whole process. I was already aware of all the minerals, trace elements and vitamins and their functions within the realms of animal nutrition, but that was the first time I had had anything to do with their formulation and the manufacture of a finished product. A few days later I got a phone call from Harry asking if I would care to call and see him one evening at his home. I was a little surprised but agreed straight away to go. Here was a man who knew his stuff and any chance to talk with him had to be a bonus. I could learn a lot about my own job through him.

My visit to the Hill household had been arranged for seven o'clock and I made a point of being on the doorstep bang on time. I figured that Harry was of the old school and would expect punctuality. The building was a dorma-type bungalow which I later learned had been more-or-less built by Harry himself. I was straight away ushered into the lounge to meet Harry's wife Rose who had laid on a pot of tea. It wasn't long before we were chatting about various things we had in common. Eventually the conversation drifted round to the subject of Harry's business. He said: "You know I'm coming up to 65 and I will be retiring from the manufacturing business." It suddenly dawned on me why I had been asked round to the house.

"Now a younger chap like yourself, with a bit of knowledge and a bit of drive could do far worse than take over a business like mine. I've been watching you and I think you could be just the man to do it. We're not talking about it costing you a fortune, but I'll guarantee that you would get back what you would invest in twelve months."

Harry spent the rest of the evening explaining what he had in mind and the figure he had put on his business. "You give this proposition a lot of thought," he said as I finally bid good night to them both. I certainly had plenty to think about, my head was spinning with all that I had heard. Over the next few weeks I tried to take stock of the situation. Was buying Harry Hill's business a sensible thing to do? He had shown me some trading figures which on the face of things appeared to show excellent profits, and had promised that I could show them to my accountant and bank manager. Was the business a sound investment or was Harry just a first class salesman attempting to make his biggest sale yet?

I suppose the fact that I had never really accepted having to give up the role of being my own boss had a lot to do with my pattern of thinking, but was I experienced enough to guarantee the same turnover of business let alone expand on it, which I would surely have to do? Harry had no mortgage or young family to keep as I had, and yet was this an opportunity of a life-time and too good to miss? All of these thoughts were running round my head.

A talk to my bank manager confirmed that, subject to seeing the Kendal Agricultural Supplies accounts and them showing the turnover and profits discussed, there was no problem with help for the finance. The one big stumbling block if I was to go ahead would be premises. Harry was really wanting to sell the mill. I would take over all the equipment but there was no way I could afford to buy the building. A solution to the problem was that I could have the building rent free for three or four months, after which, if I hadn't found alternative premises to rent, I would then rent the existing mill.

I had spent a number of weeks dillying and dallying about. It had now come to decision time. Harry had schooled his customers such that practically all of them paid on delivery and so I would have immediate cash flow. The business was there waiting for me. With Wendy's blessing, I finally made the decision. I would once more make the leap into the abyss of self employment. I agreed to take over KAS, now I only had to tell my present employers the news that I was in effect going, in my own small way, in opposition to them. It wasn't something which I was looking forward to. I was very conscious of the fact that it was they who had got me started. To a degree I felt somewhat guilty that I had let them down, but then consoled myself by rationalising that Richard Nevett had not got to his position in life without a bit of manoeuvring about. I would hand in my notice forthwith.

The big day came and, after a final haggle over the settlement figure, on the 13 April 1985 the business was signed over to me. I was now responsible for the manufacturing, including the quality control (which was subject to strict government control), sales, distribution and last, but not least, the financing of the business. Harry had had the advantage that he had started from nothing, and had gradually eased his way into business. I was doing it the hard way by jumping in at the deep end, but as it turned out, Harry was as good as his word and helped me through the initial period with both advice and hands on assistance.

For the first few months I continued to operate from the mill at Bowston, but it was obvious that with the place up for sale, someone might come along at any time and want to buy the place which might mean me having to move. It was imperative that I find premises of my own and pretty soon. As things turned out, this time lady luck was on my side. After viewing several buildings, mostly totally unsuitable, I was able to secure a warehouse on the Mealbank Industrial Estate which lies a couple of miles north east of Kendal, roughly about as far away from where we were living as the Bowston Mill.

The new premises were very similar in construction to those at Bowston with a tremendously high ceiling, about a thousand square feet in all. Fortunately the building had electricity available which I would need to drive the big mixer. It did occur to me that it was a pity that we no longer owned the big barn at Eskrigg End which would have made a superb warehouse, if planning consent had been given, but then that had gone.

For a few days I had to abandon all my farm calling and concentrate on setting up the new mill at Mealbank. I was fortunate in being able to borrow a 30cwt. pick-up truck from my friend Geoff Wightman whose business was also on the estate. He was also kind enough to allow me to use a fork lift truck which meant that I had my own fork lift, inherited with all Harry's other equipment at the Bowston end to load on to the pick-up, and Geoff's at the Mealbank end to unload - some of the machinery was pretty heavy. Within days I was up and running. I made my first tonne mix at the new premises and was out on the road within the week.

When visiting farms, you always have to be prepared to encounter a wide variety of situations, some amusing and some less so. On the small farms, often run by only a husband and wife team, it is very hard to land in the yard to find them both busily engaged in unloading a wagon load of hay or straw and stand there talking to them while they throw heavy bales about. The temptation is to join in and half an hour later finishing up wet through with sweat and muck. On one occasion a farmer and his wife were shoveling rolled barley into large hessian sacks. I chivalrously took the job of holding the empty bags open whilst the farmer filled them up. By the end I was covered from head to toe in barley dust which has an oily content making it impossible to brush off completely. I swear he was making more dust than was necessary and I had to go home and change.

Another incident was when I was in the Kirkby Lonsdale area. I was travelling along a country road when I saw in a corner of a field, what appeared to be a farmer struggling with a cow that was attempting to give birth. I stopped the car and approached the chap who was on the ground behind the animal pulling on a cow band (the usual tool used for that purpose) attempting to pull the calf free. He didn't appear to be making much progress. I could see from the calf's drooping head and lolling tongue that the cow had been struggling for some while and it was now imperative that the birth was to be completed quickly if the calf was to remain alive. With no more ado I took off my jacket and joined the chap on the ground. With a steady strain and both of us pulling, the calf slid out into the wide world. A brisk rub with a handful of straw and it was breathing well.

All this time not one word had been spoken, both of us concentrating on the job in hand. What followed left me flabbergasted - without so much as a thank you, the chap picked up the cow band and bits and pieces, climbed into his Land Rover and drove off. To this day I don't know who the man was. Perhaps he thought I was going to ask him for some business.

Now fully operational I decided to widen the range of products which I would offer. My thinking was that when I landed in a farm yard the more different products I had to offer, the more chance of a sale there was. One of the first new lines was that of liquid feed such as I had been selling for Starlyne. The difference was that whereas with Starlyne I simply took the order and handed it on to head office and they did the rest, now I intended to install a large tank buy in bulk and deliver it out myself. I bought a 2000 gallon bulk tank and a 1000 litre delivery tank which fit in the back of the transit, together with a petrol driven pump. I was then able to offer an early delivery liquid feed service which immediately started to do well.

The next product on offer was a dog feed. I devised a large square box affair with a wide sliding trap door on the front. Into this box I would put layers of various ingredients such as flaked maize, cooked wheat, vitamins, cod liver oil and my 'secret ingredient.' The trap door was then opened and the self mixing ingredients were bagged off into 25kg paper bags.

In Middlesbrough there was a family run company who traded under the the name of W. Wescenfelder and Son. Wescenfelder's main business was making sausage skins from the treated intestines of mainly pigs, although I was led to believe that other animals' innards were also suitable. The process involved washing the intestines then the best and most suitable were processed and finally packaged ready for distribution to butchers to be filled with sausage meat. The unused intestines were then heated to a high temperature, the fat was spun off them in a machine rather like a giant spin drier, and the now crumbly residue, rich in protein, was sold off for dog feed. There were a number of companies selling dried meat from the knacker's yards but, as far as I knew, none offering such a potent product as this one.

This was my secret ingredient which, together with the other fine ingredients, helped establish mine as the best working dog feed around. One customer who was recognised as a top authority on dogs, used to ring up and ask for half a dozen bags of rocket fuel! He told me that since starting to use my feed, his dogs could go all day without tiring.

In the spring of 1987 I met Barry Clarke, a chap who like myself ran a one man business. He was based near Chorley in Lancashire. Barry told me about a company called Balanced Feeds of Chelford near Macclesfield. Balanced Feeds was owned by a qualified nutritionist called Mike Mortimer who had come up with a bright idea. He would buy up as many of the waste products from selected food processing plants and factories as he could, and blend them into a high protein feed for cattle.

Being a highly trained animal nutritionist, he was able to assure the correct and best ingredients went into the appropriate mixes. Amongst the waste products used were sweets, chocolates, Mars Bars, Wagon Wheels, toffee cigarettes, all types of confectionery, bread and cooked cereals. All the products were perfectly wholesome but had failed to meet quality control or were end of runs at the food processing plants. By law the waste had to be disposed of within so many hours. When these ingredients were mixed with conventional animal feeds such as maize, wheat and barley, the result was a very desirable and potent animal feed.

Barry Clarke had taken on the agency in the north for sweetmix as the feed was called. Having nobody in Cumbria, he offered me the sub-agency which, after travelling down to Chelford to see the feed mill, I accepted. Pretty soon I was working flat out doing most of my manufacturing in the evenings and at weekends, travelling around the farms during the week always in my transit van both delivering and looking for new business. With a far wider range of products than ever, KAS was running well and making money!

The sweetmix sales were within a very short time proving to be a runaway success. The product was delivered in wagons capable of carrying 24 tonnes at a time. Every wagon had the body divided into four sections, each section capable of carrying six tons. The feed was blown with a turbine along sectional flexible pipes and into feed bins on the farms. Very soon with three or four wagons a week being delivered into my area, the commission from sweetmix sales was proving to be a very useful addition to the business's coffers.

Hauling cattle feed around the district brought back memories of the old days when I was in my early twenties driving for Whittakers. The loads were only half the size, but in the old days I had to carry every single ounce of the stuff in sacks on my back. Now I would just stand and watch the wagon blow the feed into a hopper - how the industry had changed!

One incident I remember makes me smile when I think back. I had been to Liverpool to the Sefton Mill and collected a ten ton load of freshly made cow cake, the pungent smell from the warm molasses used in the process made you feel that that you could open a bag and eat the stuff. Just before leaving, the mill manager had approached me and asked if I would do a slight detour on my way back to Windermere. He had a parcel which he wanted delivering to a farm in the Melling area. I was fully loaded with the wagon nicely sheeted and roped, but no problem, the parcel would sit comfortably in the passenger side of the cab. I set off, travelling as far as Lancaster and then taking the road by Melling to deliver my parcel. It would then carry on by Kirkby Lonsdale and Kendal to home. It would be a pleasant change of route.

All went well and I could see the farm at the top of hill which was accessed by a steep tarmac road with fields on either side. The weather was poor, cold wet and windy, not that that was a problem. Then a battered Land Rover appeared coming towards me at a fast speed. The problems started - one of us was going to have to give way - logically an empty Land Rover with four wheel drive, descending a hill should give way to a heavily loaded and climbing wagon.

At the very last moment, with the other vehicle still holding his line, I wrenched the steering wheel to my right, the side where the ground looked firmer. I was wrong. The Land Rover driver was seemingly oblivious to the problem he had caused and disappeared down the road. I was still moving forward but sank deep into the rain softened ground. On stopping the engine and opening the driver's side door and with the wagon leaning at an angle, I practically fell out into the field. Fortunately the load was well roped and sheeted and was still intact but its sheer weight was adding to the severe angle at which the wagon was now leaning .

The outcome was that, despite the farmer's reluctance to allow me to use his phone and at the same time denying that any Land Rover had been near the place that day, I contacted John Key, my immediate boss and he collected me, leaving the problem of the wagon to be sorted out the next day. That was not the end of the saga. When we arrived together with a heavy break down truck to pull the wagon out the next day, the vehicle was surrounded by about 40 fat bullocks who were getting even fatter eating a number of burst bags of feed which were lying about the field. The bullocks had got the scent of the molasses in the feed and had literally chewed their way into the load, damaging the tarpaulin sheet and destroying several bags. Something which has always puzzled me is the fact that there wasn't an animal to be seen in the field when I was there the day before. It makes you wonder!

Easter 1987 saw me set up a sales cabin on the Kendal Auction Mart's vehicle park. I had answered an advert which offered an 18 feet by 10 feet wooden garage for sale. Unfortunately the garage was in Preston but again I was able to borrow a pick-up from my friend Geoff. Delmar and Simon came with me to collect the garage and were amused that it looked like a British Airways Air Bus perched on top of the pick-up. I was lucky not to get booked for excessive overhang, but the garage was successfully bought, collected and finally erected on the designated site.

Sales directly from the cabin naturally came a little slow at first, but very soon both regular and new customers came to expect to see me every Monday and Wednesday, the main sale days. I found myself having to literally stack the thing to the ceiling with bags of minerals, dog food and sweetmix which I was by then offering in 25kg. bags just to get people interested enough to buy in bulk. The amount of goods left only a narrow gap to a make shift desk.

Much as my little cabin at the market proved to be a valuable asset to my business, I had a recurring problem of break ins. Over the years that I kept the cabin on site I had no fewer than six. Strangely enough the only things taken, bar once when a paraffin stove went missing, were bags of dog feed. I suppose everything else was of no use unless, of course, the thief had a cow in their back yard. Nobody was ever caught or charged with the thefts, but I always suspected the lurcher brigade. There were always a number of these people wandering around the countryside with their dogs, having no regard for private land or ownership and recognising no boundaries. Oh well, at least it was the dogs that got fed and not their owners.

THE OLD FIRM AND DAD'S BIKE

Since the mid 1980s the viability of farming had quietly started to decline. It was nothing dramatic at first, just one or two happenings, both natural and man-made. Possibly the first set-back was that of milk quotas whereby farmers were limited to the amount of milk that they were allowed to produce. The quotas were based on a percentage of how much they had produced in a specified period previously. Following the introduction of this measure, male calves from dairy cows became worthless as they were obviously at least half dairy-bred as opposed to beef-bred. They were of little or no value and many were simply destroyed.

Next came sheep quotas which meant that most farmers and flock masters had to reduce the headage of sheep in their flocks. These manmade measures helped to de-value and destabilise the farming industry. Man made restrictive laws are one thing, but nature, aided by man, also has a say in the fortunes of the farming industry. The first 'natural' phenomenon to strike was that of B.S.E. (bovine spongiform encepalopathy, more commonly known as Mad Cow Disease) which was first diagnosed in Britain in November 1986. Scientists later made a connection between B.S.E. and the human condition of C.J.D. All these regulations and maladies took their toll on British farming. The situation was not helped when just as one problem seemed to be dying down, those in positions of trust who should have been trying to keep the situation calm and controlled, seemed to delight in trotting out unfounded and alarming forecasts of animal borne pestilences which would sweep through the country affecting every other person.

The media were no better, the same footage with a supposedly B.S.E. infected black and white cow sliding about on a sloping cobbled yard has shamefully been shown on our television screens for well over ten years. Such excessive coverage is totally unnecessary and destructive to the reputation of the British farmer.

By 1990 the effects of the decline and the loss of confidence in British agriculture was beginning to affect my business. The cost of the raw materials which I used in making my minerals was going up and up, mainly, they told me, due to increased haulage costs. I was buying in relatively small quantities therefore I was paying a premium, putting me at a disadvantage to my competitors. I was experiencing rising costs in all departments - rent, rates, delivery costs - all of which I was not able to pass on because the farmers were in a no better position themselves. Regrettably and I might say unwisely, minerals are one of the first things which are cut back on in a monetary crisis. With my overheads threatening to overwhelm me, I had to find a way round the problem. I couldn't possibly work any harder!

Again fate decided to move in and play a hand. It came to my notice that my old firm Starlyne were looking for a new salesman for the south lakes. Since I had left them in 1984 they had had a succession of salesmen, four in all, and were now looking for their fifth. It was not that these chaps had been no good at their job, it was more that the range of products was limited, more so than mine anyway. Plus the nature of the district dictates that most of the farms are comparatively small. Where you have bigger farms you naturally have bigger orders.

After the usual period of deliberation, I decided to write to Richard Nevett suggesting that there were grounds on which we could perhaps come to some sort of arrangement whereby I could represent his company on a free agency basis. No doubt Richard was surprised to receive my letter, but he straight away phoned me suggesting that we meet and discuss the matter. He would be at the Blue Bell at Heversham on a certain day, could I be there?

Just as in 1974 at the Tillington Hotel in Stafford, both Richard Nevett and Ken Graham were there to greet me. This time though it was a much more enlightened and experienced potential representative that they were talking to. I now had a sound understanding of the subject of animal nutrition and the manufacture of and distribution of nutritional products. It wouldn't be often that they interviewed people with quite as wide an understanding of the subject.

Both Richard and Ken seemed genuinely pleased to see me. After a few pleasantries we got straight down to the real reason for us being there. In anticipation of Richard's business-like approach, I had taken with me evidence of the levels of business which I had generated over the years since leaving his company. I guess he must have been suitably impressed because we went on to do a deal whereby I, instead of manufacturing my own minerals, was to sell his on a commission basis. My thinking behind it being that I would wind up the mill, dispose of all my equipment thereby leaving me a lot more time to find extra sales. It was also agreed that I would be free to continue acting as agent for any company providing that such a company was not in direct competition to Starlyne. I now had the backing of a first class larger company who could cope far better than me with the down turn in the economy, and I had more than halved my expenditure.

At first I had some doubts as to whether I had done the right thing, but these were soon dispelled when I thought back to the days when I had continued on with men and machines during the earlier part of the recession, when I should have cut my losses. I was not going to make the same mistake again. It was a pity that the manufacturing side had to go, but that was how it was.

The next few years went by and my relationship with Starlyne went well. Balanced Feeds extended their range of sweetmix products and I took agencies with two other firms, one selling fertiliser made from seaweed and the other a dairy cow feed based on bi-products from the whisky distilling industry. Kendal Agricultural Supplies had changed from a manufacturing business to a supply one, with all income derived from commission with one exception - I continued to manufacture a

The KAS trade stand at the Westmorland County Show, pictured left to right: the author, Geoff Wightman, Robin Holliday of Barker Knott Farm, Winster, and a friend of Mr. Holliday.

Dad.s re-built Brough Superior SS80 bike at Wimpole Hall, Cambridgeshire, after winning the Ike Webb trophy for best SS80 at the 1995 B.S. Club Rally.

sheep drench which can be best described as a sheep medicine. Animals which failed to thrive could often show dramatic improvement after a dose of my drench. It was made from a mixture of several minerals and trace minerals suspended in water. It was reasonably easy to manufacture, very effective and very much appreciated by regular users.

In March 1994 my eldest son Delmar married a lovely girl called Lisa Webster. To add to the excitement, they chose to get married in Cyprus in the old part of Paphos. Both sets of parents, Wendy's parents and a number of friends travelled to be at the ceremony which took place in the Town Hall and was performed by the Mayor of Paphos. After the ceremony a reception was held at the magnificent Venus Beach Hotel, which stands on the bay of the same name and looks out over the Mediterranean Sea. With swimming pools and wide marble staircases, the place seemed to be like something out of an American movie. The best photograph turned out to be the bridegroom standing in the blue waters of the Mediterranean, trousers rolled up to his knees with his bride in his arms, her gown flowing into the water. The locals thought we were mad! The rest of our stay on the island was spent touring in a hired car with visits to beautiful villages, churches and beaches. Wendy's parents although both nearly 80, enjoyed every minute of the holiday.

The next happening in the family was a sad one. On 2 February 1995 I lost my dear mother. She had been living in Sutton Coldfield in the West Midlands since not long after my father's death in order to be near my twin sister Margaret. My parents had been the most devoted couple and had created a perfect family environment, my three sisters and I would be for ever in their debt. Mother had missed my father terribly since he had died seventeen years earlier, now she was with him again. We must be happy for them both.

On the evening of 13 June I got a phone call from a rather excited friend of my father-in-law, a retired farmer called Arthur Slee. "Have you seen the *Evening Mail?*" he enquired, "Your Dad was called Harry and he was an RAC man wasn't he?"

"Yes," I was somewhat perplexed at his line of questioning.

"Well it's in the paper, all about your Dad's Brough motor bike!" he went on: "There's a chap trying to find out about a motor bike. He's looking for anyone who knows anything about it." From the rest of Arthur's conversation I learned enough to prompt me into going out the following day and buying a copy of the previous night's *Evening Mail*, a Barrow based paper. From it I was able to get the telephone number of a Mr. Gordon Button who had persuaded the paper to run practically a whole page article on the story of how he had bought a Brough Superior motor bike of 1938 vintage in 1992, virtually as a box of bits, and after restoring it to its original condition, was now trying to trace the family of its original owner.

Using the information in the article I contacted Mr. Button who was delighted that his enquiries had borne fruit. I was able to tell him that the photograph of my Dad on the Brough which had been used in the article was taken outside the Kirkstone Inn at the top of the Kirkstone Pass. My one regret was that my Dad was not alive to enjoy his beloved Brough's phoenix-like rise from the ashes. I have since corresponded with Gordon on a number of occasions and was delighted to learn that through the Brough Owner's Club, of which he was a long standing member, he had entered the bike in several top competitions and had won the prize for the best Brough Superior S.S. 80 in the country. Dad would have been proud.

BACK TO NATURE AND A SAD, SAD DAY

I continued to travel the district during 1997, calling on my regulars and following up any leads which might result in any new business, but farming was far from the buoyant industry of only ten or fifteen years earlier. It seemed that it was just one crisis after another with no respite in between, all of which, despite my enjoyment of a certain amount of customer loyalty, made my job of securing and maintaining satisfactory levels of business all the harder. Trade diminished as farmers began to lose confidence due to depressed prices at the markets. Beef on the hoof was being sold at less than the cost of producing it, milk prices were the same, male calves out of the dairy herds which previously would have fetched over a hundred pounds were literally worthless and, at the same time, the sheep people were faring no better - all reasons not to buy anything but the bare essentials.

Travelling as I had done since 1984, I had come to love the job and could never understand when some farmers would make remarks to me like: "I wouldn't have your job for a gold clock." I could only assume that they meant that they wouldn't like to have to deal with people of like temperament to themselves. Some were admittedly more difficult to deal with than others! However, there were days when I myself had my doubts whether it was all worth it, particularly with the industry in such a free fall. There were times when I began to see the situation as a replay of the decline of my previous business and there didn't seem to be much I could do about it.

It was times like this, that I really appreciated the kindness of some of the salt of the earth folk like the Hodgsons of Stybeck, Thirlspot - Joey and his wife Jean, and their two sons Chris and Michael and Gordon and Marjorie Tyson of Troutbeck Park and their grown up children Thomas, Jean and Zena. I never in the many years of calling on them went away without a kind word and the offer of a drink, regardless of whether or not they required anything from me. To these people and a few others I will be eternally grateful.

By April 1998 with business at an all time low, I happened to meet up whilst on my travels with a chap who I knew as brother to Ada Wightman, Wendy's best friend. Eddie Todd was by trade a dry stone waller, building walls without using cement. Eddie knew quite a bit about my background, particularly relevant was the fact that I had done quite a bit of stone walling myself.

At the time of our meeting, Eddie explained that he was having to work on his own because of the illness of his partner of 22 years. He went on to ask me if I thought there was any possibility that I could give him a few days. We parted company with me saying that I would consider the matter and get back to him. For a few years the government had been operating a scheme whereby farmers and landowners in certain mainly upland areas, who met with certain criteria were able to claim a grant which went a long way towards the cost of rebuilding of the dry stone walls on their holdings.

It was work covered by this grant scheme that Eddie Todd was engaged in. He had a programme of work before him which had to be completed within certain specified times in order for his customers to claim this financial help. Knowing that I was coming to what would be normally be the quietest time of the year, grass time when farmers would be amongst their silage, I decided to take Eddie up on his offer of work. I had always from my first days of handling stones and re-building fallen down walls at Helsfell as a boy, had a love of the skill and had been involved on many occasions since. Here was another opportunity to practice the art and be paid for it.

It began with me working two days a week, for which my friend was genuinely grateful. This left me with plenty of time to deal with the diminished trade I was doing, some due to the seasonal down turn, but regrettably most due to the reasons already explained. Eddie asked me: "You couldn't give me another day? We're catching up but not fast enough." Seemingly he had been in touch with his regular partner Tommy Westbury, and the news was not good, there was little chance of him returning for at least the foreseeable future.

For several weeks this arrangement continued. Eddie working full time and myself sometimes two, sometimes three days in the week, depending on my other commitments. At first I had found the continuous bending and lifting had my back aching by the end of the day, but by the time I had a couple of months under my belt, I was a stone lighter and could go all day without so much as a twinge. Just as a point of interest, and to give some sort of perspective to what is involved in re-building a typical fell wall of about five feet six in height, each yard will contain approximately one ton of stone (can't get my head round metric measurements) therefore a six yard stretch, which represents an average day's work, pulled down , sorted into appropriate heaps then rebuilt, logically would mean the handling of six tons of stone twice by two people, or six tons each in the day.

One morning during a coffee break, Eddie broke the news that his regular work mate would not be coming back. Tommy was already of retiring age and his doctor had advised him to do just that. This left Eddie in a difficult position. "I know you have other business interests Mike, but what do you think about working with me full time?" It wouldn't be right to say that I was totally surprised at Eddie's straight out approach. The thought had crossed my mind that this situation might arise, but now it was a reality, should I straight away dismiss the idea as ridiculous? After all I was 62-years-old. I told Eddie that I would give the matter some thought and we agreed to leave it at that for the moment.

Obviously the proposition which I had received began to take over my thoughts more and more and I found myself once again deliberating over my future. I had always planned to work until I was 65 on a full time basis. It was so important to me that, in later years, I would be able to say that I had done fifty years of solid work, and that I had done my bit towards the country's prosperity. I had several more knock backs involving farmers. For the first time in years, farmers had decided to go ahead with their silage making without the use of an additive, a product which helps the fermentation of the grass. The commission on this product represented a large slice of my income at that particular time of the year. The balance of whether or not to abandon my now devastated business started to tip in favour of walling.

Finally the truth dawned. I was looking for an excuse to make to myself for winding up my business. The long period of sustained pressure from all the problems that had arisen in the industry had taken their toll. In truth I was burned out and a job which I had loved had turned sour on me and was now nothing more than a chore. I was now travelling up into the hills two or three days a week, and spending the day without a care in the world. In front of us were dilapidated heaps of stone, behind us we were leaving beautiful stretches of new walls. The satisfaction was indescribable, during those days I couldn't have been happier.

It wasn't without a little touch of sadness that after confirming with Eddie that I was to work with him full time, I contacted Richard Nevett to inform him of my intentions. Although he seemed genuinely sorry to see me leave his team, he understood and thanked me for the way I had conducted myself whilst representing his company. I thanked him for his kindness and the professionalism with which his company had dealt with the business I had passed on to them. I left them on the best of terms.

Very soon I was fully into the swing of things. We had a valuation done of the stone walling equipment, the main items being a rather long in the tooth Land Rover, a few picks and shovels and a couple of chain saws (we were to spend the worst of the winter hedge laying, more about that later) axes, heavy hammers etc. A figure was agreed, no great expense and I gave Eddie a cheque for half - we were now equal partners which simplified matters.

Most of the farms we worked on were under SSSI (Sites of Special Scientific Interest) status and were allocated from between fifty yards and a hundred yards of wall per annum to be re-built. Depending on the size and location of the holding, this would mean that we would expect to spend between two to four weeks on each farm. The weather that summer wasn't too kind to us but we persevered and more or less caught up with the scheduled work. These farms included the Handleys' Cockin Farm at Whinfell, Frank Potter's Lambrigg Park, Desmond Holmes' Bradley Field Farm near Kendal and Richard Gardner's Barrowfield at Brigsteer.

The last walling job of the season was to be undertaken for Bill Sharp at Russmicle in the Lythe Valley. It would soon be October and the hedging season was almost upon us, so regardless of the bad weather at that time, we decided to push ahead. The wall which we were to build was rather a more substantial one than the usual farm wall, mainly because of the fact that it was to be built in a steep sided hollow where there had been no wall previously. By the time we arrived on the site, Bill's son Edward had already tipped 40 tons or so of stone in readiness for us starting.

"Look at these!" said Eddie giving one of the larger pieces a kick, "they wouldn't go amiss in a bloody rockery. How the hell are we going to shift these?" He was quite right, a few of the stones would have tipped the scales at around half a ton and there were many more at several hundredweight. "That's easy, we borrow Bill Sharp's digger." I knew Edward had loaded the stone from the scree beds of Whitbarrow, the fell which adjoined their farm, the landowners of Lythe are able to take stone from the screes by ancient charter. As it turned out, Bill was only too happy to lend us the machine, and so with myself using it to place the bigger rocks into position for the foundations, the job went well reminding me of my digging days.

During the first two weeks in October the weather became atrocious. The ground was water logged and the stones were more difficult to handle. A wet muddy stone can easily slip from your grasp, as I have found out to my cost on more than one occasion, but still we pressed on. Eddie had already had telephone calls from his regular hedging customers asking when we would be with them.

The next part of my story is so traumatic in content that I find it almost impossible to relate it with the dignity that it deserves, but I'll try as it must be told. We were within a two days of finishing the job. The weather was no better than it had been since starting. At around ten o'clock on 26 October 1998 we stopped for a drink from our flasks and a sandwich as normal. "We want to be about a couple of inches higher in that gate hole," said Eddie. "I'm not so sure about that, those top stones are pretty big ones. We don't want to get too high to match the other side," I replied. We often discussed such details in order to arrive at the best results. "Let's have a cuppa and think on it," I suggested and we made our way to the Land Rover.

We had not been in the vehicle long, only long enough for me to pour myself a cup of hot water onto a tea bag as I couldn't stand stewed tea from a flask, a relic of my early days in the woods with old George Carlton. Eddie always brought with him a large flask of coffee. I had already noticed that Eddie was unusually quiet but put it down to us both being pretty fed up with the atrocious conditions in which we had been working.

Suddenly I got the strangest feeling that something was not quite right. Eddie was never quiet for this long. He always had something to say about one thing or another. Looking across I saw that Eddie was sitting staring forward and he hadn't yet poured himself a drink.

"What's bothering you Eddie?" I asked. There was no reply just the same stare ahead. Something was drastically wrong. I reached across and pushed his shoulder, "Eddie what's wrong, what's wrong?" Within seconds the realisation that my mate was in some sort of a coma hit me. A further shaking produced no reaction at all and here we were sitting in the old Land Rover in the middle of a field. I had to get help right away.

Quickly I started up the engine and, with my left arm supporting Eddie to prevent him from falling forward, I drove through the churned up muddy gateway and onto the lane leading to the farm house where I hoped desperately I would find the Sharps at home. Fortunately both Bill and his wife were in their kitchen. No doubt they were as shocked as I was when, without knocking I simply burst in, but they both responded magnificently. Mrs Sharp took on the job of phoning the emergency services and Bill dashed outside and immediately began an attempt to resuscitate Eddie.

I do not know how long it took for the ambulance to arrive, it couldn't have been long. The crew spent the best part of an hour working with the equipment which they had at their disposal but to no avail. Despite everybody's attempts to save him, a doctor who had arrived examined poor Eddie and pronounced him dead. There is nothing I can now say about my friend Eddie which would lessen the impact which his passing has had on his family, except to say that during the six months I had worked with him, usually with only a half built wall between us, I learned a lot about the man. Eddie was a kindly outgoing character with a zest for life which had gained him countless friends. This was obvious at his funeral in the tiny spread out village of New Hutton. The church was packed solid with nearly as many people left outside.

A few days after the funeral, I returned to the unfinished wall. This time I was on my own. The point where the height had been under discussion was still unfinished. I placed the last stones on the wall thinking that if Eddie's spirit was watching me, I hoped that he would find the finished wall to his satisfaction. The wall remains as do the miles of walls which he helped build over the years, a monument to Thomas Edward Todd's life on Earth.

THE FULL CIRCLE

Over the next week or so, I realised that I was now on my own and in the same position as Eddie had been when he approached me. I was going to have to try to find someone else to work with me - remarkably the problem was solved by someone very close at hand. Simon my middle son, had just completed a degree course in modem languages - Spanish and Italian which involved, amongst other things, a year teaching English in a Spanish school. Simon had been under immense pressure in his last year of studies and exams before finishing his BE Honours degree, and on hearing me discussing the issue of looking for a work mate, suggested that he was thinking of taking time out. "What about me Dad?" were his exact words, "I'll give you a hand at least until you find someone else."

I had not really thought of Simon as a waller but there was absolutely no reason why he shouldn't join me, albeit that the arrangement would be temporary. There are the puritans who believe that dry stone walling is a skill that takes a life time to learn, but I am not one of them, believing as I do that provided a person is instructed in the correct procedure and is prepared to listen and act accordingly, there is no reason why any reasonably strong and able person shouldn't build a wall. Simon was no exception.

So Simon joined me and was very soon showing a first class aptitude, so much so that a number of very discerning farmers were happy to have us undertake their work. The fact that we returned to the same farms endorsed their confidence. We wouldn't have been asked back if they had been in any way dissatisfied.

One of our regular customers was a farmer called Thomas Knowles, or Tommy as we knew him. Tommy was and still is considered a top authority on the breeding of cattle and sheep as well as being a well known teacher and exponent of the art of dry stone walling. In his younger days he won countless prizes and competitions for walling. Simon and I did a lot of work for Tommy, as had Eddie and I previously. Thinking back to one particular day when both Eddie and myself were working at Tommy Knowles' Hollow Gate farm, Tommy had been passing by the job and had stopped for a minute or two. The subject of correct techniques had cropped up and was being discussed. "You've got to keep your belly full, it's important that you keep your belly full," stated Tommy most adamant;y.

"Oh I always keep my belly full. I always eat plenty when I'm working," said Eddie.

"Not your belly you daft bugger, the wall, the belly of the wall!" replied Tommy. We all fell about laughing. I don't know to this day whether Eddie had fallen for the observation, or whether he was just trying to wind Tommy up, either way we all had a good laugh. The belly of a wall is of course the middle and it is important to keep packing it tightly with stones, otherwise it will soon fall down, just one of the important musts.

The back end of 1999 saw us hedge laying on a number of farms, but one was very special as far as I was concerned. As a boy of fifteen working for the Stanleys, I had been set to in a field thinning turnips. I had crawled on my hands and knees up the stitches with sacks tied round my knees. Now fifty years later, I was back in the same field. Elm Tree Farm was now being farmed by Mr. Harry Robinson and his son Arthur. The Stanleys had long gone. In my capacity as an agricultural sales person, I had done quite a lot of business with the Robinsons, now I and my son were working again in that very same field.

In March 1999 I lost Harvey Leigh my old friend and ex-employer from my coach driving days with whom I had kept up a friendship for nearly 40 years. He had reached the age of 98 and had been living in a nursing home in Kendal for the previous two years. I had visited him at least twice a week and when the weather and his health permitted, taken him out for short trips around the surrounding countryside.

Harvey and I had always enjoyed a rather special understanding of each other. I had always been amused by his wicked sense of humour which seemed to be more in evidence the older he grew, and which he retained practically until the time of his death. At times he would deliberately contrive to cause embarrassment, and then sit back to watch how the situation was resolved. The lady who ran the nursing home eventually tumbled to his ploy and enjoyed the humour that ensued.

Harking back to 1966 when Harvey and Teddy had disposed of their business and Harvey had bought himself a brand new Jaguar car, with just over one hundred miles on the clock, he had, knowing my love for nice cars, insisted that I take Wendy off for the day using his new acquisition. I had expressed reservations. What if I were to scratch the car or even worse? Harvey would hear nothing of my 'what ifs', after all I had done around 100,000 miles in six different new coaches without doing any damage. As far as Harvey was concerned I could walk on water. I took him up on his offer and travelled with Wendy and my mother to to see my grandmother Bolton at Leyland. Up to that day I had never driven such a splendid car. I enjoyed every yard of the journey and vowed to myself that one day I would drive a Jaguar of my own. I got that Jaguar 34 years later in July 2000, not a brand new one, but as good as.

I got three surprises in the second half of that year. The first was the Jaguar, I had not intended to buy one until after February 2001 when I would be 65, but a friend who was sales manager for the local Jaguar agency had found a particularly clean low mileage car. Once I had seen it, sat in it, and driven it, I was hooked and bought it.

The second surprise was the most exciting news I could have wished for. My youngest son Stephen and his partner Claire presented Wendy and I with the most beautiful granddaughter Jessica Abigail Bolton; our world was complete!

Some time in August of that year, Wendy made an observation that I was showing a slight tendency to drag some of my words. I rather rubbished the idea. A few weeks later when I started to find that I was experiencing sore throats and a slight difficulty in swallowing that I decided to seek medical advice.

"It could well be acidity getting back from your stomach that's causing your problem," suggested my doctor. To cut a long story short, I was sent to see a Mr. Whitfield, ear, nose and throat specialist at Barrow-in-Furness Hospital, who under a general anaesthetic, and with the use of a gastroscope examined my throat and found nothing amiss. However, unknown to me, whilst anaesthetised he had noticed some unusual muscle spasms on my arms and shoulders. Following these observations I was handed over to a Dr. Keeting who also examined me.

On my return home, I was straight away back to work re-building walls. On the whole I felt fine and put the sore throats down to working too hard, after all I was 64 and had been working as though I was 44. I would be 65 in a matter of months and then maybe I would start to wind down a bit. I had set my heart on at least completing 50 years work. Two weeks had passed and it was time for me to visit my G.P. He would by now have received the specialist's report and so I had better make an appointment and see him. I was not too concerned, after all I was throwing rocks around all day for a living and was still as strong as a horse.

"I have a letter here from Dr. Keeting, would you like me to read it out?" asked Dr. Mitchel my G.P. who was sitting opposite me behind his desk. "Do please!" I said.

He was not long into the letter when suddenly I heard the words Motor Neurone Disease. My heart stopped for a few seconds and momentarily a feeling of panic hit me. The doctor hesitated, "Do you know anything about Motor Neurone Disease?" he asked. "Enough to know that it is one of the most progressively debilitating diseases known to man," I replied, my head spinning. The doctor went on to explain that they wanted me to go to Preston Acute Hospital to have further tests. Motor Neurone was a difficult disease to diagnose, but according to Dr. Keeting I had all the classic symptoms. Only specialised tests would confirm beyond any doubt whether I had the illness.

This was the third surprise that back end. Two had given me great happiness, and one left me devastated. All through my working life I had met with all sorts of challenges, I had manoeuvred, adapted, and taken all sorts of measures and finally overcome all sorts of adversities. This was one situation that I wasn't going to get out of. I now had to go home and break the news to my family.

It had been my intention at this point to call it a day as far as telling my story. I had managed to work out the basics on the computer which Wendy had bought me for Christmas to laboriously, and with two fingers, get it into print. I had rather apprehensively given this story to two friends to read and both said: "It's not finished. You haven't really mentioned what the family's reaction was or how you reacted to your bad news."

This is where I tell everybody: "Well it was a bit of a shock to us all, but we soon got over that, we soon got back to normal." But that wouldn't be the truth. From the moment one hears those three words Motor Neurone Disease everything changes, not just for the affected but for everyone around him or her.

In my case as I have already stated, I was at that time busy working full time in a particularly energy demanding occupation. I believed the symptoms which had provided the 99 per cent sure diagnosis were, until that moment, only the result of working too hard and would easily be put right by easing up in my imminent retirement. The reality was I now knew that there was no cure for my problem. After walking the mile home, I found Wendy busy as usual. She was preparing food in the kitchen where I broke the news.

I will never know the full extent of the shock my news had on either Wendy or the boys. Wendy from that very moment became a pillar of strength, the boys were told in turn at what seemed the appropriate moment, if indeed there is such a thing. They, without exception, reacted in a manner which straight away told me that their only concerns were for me, not allowing themselves any indulgence in self pity. I was immediately surrounded by a wall of protection. I know their private feelings of sadness at their Dad's predicament came later.

It is now June 2002, some eighteen months on since my positive diagnosis. What has happened since then? Well firstly I have changed from an ultra fit 64-year-old capable of doing a full day's hard graft alongside chaps less than half my age, to a scrawny staggering old bloke who has difficulty swallowing, drinks a cup of tea with a table spoon, can't walk more than a few yards without having to sit down and speaks a mumbled lingo that only his wife and sons can decipher.

Wait a minute though, before anyone jumps to conclusions and proclaims: "Poor chap, such a shame, lost his marbles," assuming that my brain's working at the same speed as my legs and speech. They would be wrong as I'm thinking as sharp as I ever did. I'll excuse anyone who knows me having a little titter at that statement!

Joking apart, I'm as happy as I have ever been. Knowing the statistics for survival of anyone affected by MND perhaps I shouldn't feel so, and perhaps this will give way to a different state of mind as my illness progresses. I really don't know, this is new ground to me. I would be a liar if I didn't confess to some doubts. Anyhow I'm stuck with it so it's no good making a fuss, it would just have the effect of getting everyone around me upset!

There are some amusing aspects - one of the symptoms of MND is that one's balance is affected which, combined with loss of mobility of the limbs, gives the appearance of somebody under the influence of alcohol. To make matters worse in cases such as mine the speech is reduced to an indecipherable slur. The result is that I get the most curious reactions ranging from amusement to looks of disapproval. This seemed to stop when I was finally forced to use an extra long stick in order to keep my balance.

Another symptom is that one tends to yawn a lot. The other day I was sitting in the supermarket and effected a rather exaggerated yawn resulting in a large amiable elderly gentleman asking: "Are you tired mi lad?" Unfortunately I couldn't excuse myself, had I attempted to do so I would in all probability have been classified as someone under the influence.

Of course it's not all amusing. There is a great deal of frustration. I have always enjoyed being the handyman fixing all the little things that went wrong about the home. I also had plans to pave our back yard and so on but that's all gone out of the window. It's as much as I can do to grip a pen let alone pick up a pick axe or use it. Enough now of my woes. I'm 66-years-old now and have had a great life. The secret in my opinion, for what it's worth, has been that I have always looked on my work, varied as it has been, as more a way of life than just a job.

There, that's my story told. I hope you have enjoyed reading it. I wish you all the best and hope that all goes well for you and that you live a long and happy life. Meanwhile I will continue to love my wonderful extended family and my friends. I have a darling little granddaughter who's nearly three to lavish my affections on. I hope that she will in turn grow to recognise and value the true love that exists in a close family. I am a truly lucky man!

MORE BOOKS FROM HAYLOFT

Odd Corners in Appleby, Gareth Hayes, (£8.50, ISBN 1 9045240 0 1)

The Building of Carlisle, The Life and Times of Percy Dalton, City Engineer and Surveyor, 1926-1949, Marie K. Dickens, (£8, ISBN 0 9540711 9 0)

The Herdwick Country Cook Book, Hugh and Therese Southgate (Hardback, £19.95, 0 9540711 8 2) (Paperback, £14.95, 0 9540711 7 4)

A History of Kaber, Helen McDonald and Christine Dowson, (£8, ISBN 0 9540711 6 6)

The Gifkin Gofkins, Irene Brenan, (Paperback, £2.50, 190 452 401X)

A Dream Come True, the Life and Times of a Lake District National Park Ranger, David Birkett (£5.50, ISBN 0 9540711 5 8)

Gone to Blazes, Life as a Cumbrian Fireman, David Stubbings (£9.95, ISBN 0 9540711 4 X)

Changing Times, The Millennium Story of Bolton, Barbara Cotton (£12.50, ISBN 0 9540711 3 1)

Better by Far a Cumberland Hussar, A History of the Westmorland and Cumberland Yeomanry, Colin Bardgett (Hardback, £26.95, ISBN 0 9540711 2 3) (Paperback, £16.95, ISBN 0 9540711 1 5)

Northern Warrior, the Story of Sir Andreas de Harcla, Adrian Rogan (£8.95, ISBN 0 9523282 8 3)

A Riot of Thorn & Leaf, Dulcie Matthews (£7.95, ISBN 0 9540711 0 7)

A Country Doctor, Dr. Isaac Bainbridge, Dawn Robertson (£2.25, ISBN 0 9523282 32)

Military Mountaineering, A History of Services Expeditions, 1945-2000, Retd. SAS Major Bronco Lane (Hardback, £25.95, ISBN 0 9523282 1 6) (Paperback, £17.95, ISBN 0 9523282 6 7)

Yows & Cows, A Bit of Westmorland Wit, Mike Sanderson
(£7.95, ISBN 0 9523282 0 8)

Riding the Stang, Dawn Robertson (£9.99, ISBN 0 9523282 2 4)

Secrets and Legends of Old Westmorland, Peter Koronka and Dawn
Robertson (Hardback, £17.95, ISBN 0 9523282 4 0)
(Paperback, £11.95, ISBN 0 9523282 9 1)

The Irish Influence, Migrant Workers in Northern England, Harold Slight
(£4.95, 0 9523282 5 9)

Soldiers and Sherpas, A Taste for Adventure, Brummie Stokes.
(£19.95, 0 9541551 0 6)

North Country Tapestry, Sylvia Mary McCosh (£10, 0 9518690 0 0)

Between Two Gardens, The Diary of two Border Gardens,
Sylvia Mary McCosh (£5.95, 0 9008111 7 X)

Dacre Castle, A short history of the Castle and the Dacre Family,
E. H. A. Stretton (£5.50, 0 9518690 1 9)

*Antarctia Unveiled, Scott's First Expedition and the Quest for the Unknown
Continent,* David E. Yelverton (£25.99, 087 081 5822)

You can order any of our books by writing to:
Hayloft Publishing, Great Skerrygill,
South Stainmore, Kirkby Stephen,
Cumbria, CA17 4EU, UK.
Please enclose a cheque plus £2 for UK postage and packing.
Tel: +44 (0)17683) 42300
For more information see: www.hayloft.org.uk